"A fine feast is set by this book. Andrew Purves not only gives us a compelling intro-duction to three important Scottish theologians, he also puts them in conversation with each other on the central affirmations of the Christian faith. Even more, he makes vividly clear the urgency and gift of theology for the sake of the church. Readers will encounter in this book a vision of deep faithfulness to the gospel. A fine feast, indeed."
Leanne Van Dyk, president, Columbia Theological Seminary

"In this fine study, Andrew Purves draws upon his long experience of teaching and reflection to expound the work of three illustrious Scottish theologians—John McLeod Campbell, H. R. Mackintosh and T. F. Torrance. Each stressed the deep connection between the person and work of Christ, both as a corrective to some distortions within the Reformed tradition and also as a recovery of key scriptural and ecumenical insights. Standing foursquare in this tradition, Purves provides an admirable exposition of their work for a contemporary audience."
David Fergusson, professor of divinity and principal of New College, University of Edinburgh

"In this groundbreaking book Andrew Purves offers a powerful, engaging and care-fully constructed theology of atonement in its connection with Christology, the doctrine of justification and the doctrine of the Trinity that shows exactly how and why pastoral or practical theology is intrinsically connected with systematic the-ology. Purves expertly traces the positive teaching embedded in the thinking of three influential Scottish theologians, with particular emphasis on the theology of T. F. Torrance. He demonstrates how important it was and continues to be for theo-logians and pastors to allow the strength and power of their presentation of the truth of the Christian faith to be shaped by the living Christ in his true humanity and true divinity as the crucified, risen, ascended and advent Lord who mediates between sinful humanity and God the Father in the Spirit. This is a mediation of God's love that is best understood in filial rather than legal terms since it involves our union with Christ and thus union with the Father in and through the incarnate Son in his unique eternal relation with the Father into which we are drawn by the Holy Spirit. This book will be indispensable for theologians interested in the thinking of John McLeod Campbell, Hugh Ross Mackintosh and Thomas Forsyth Torrance. Torrance scholars in particular will benefit greatly from the insightful connections made among these three important figures."
Paul D. Molnar, professor of systematic theology, St. John's University, Queens, New York

"The greatest value of Andrew Purves's new book, *Exploring Christology and Atonement*, lies not in the manner in which he places these two essential doctrines of Christianity back on our front burner, and does so with such eloquence, although the value of this contribution is without question. The greatest value of this book rests in bringing together in a single essay the contributions of three extraordinary theologians. Arguably no other theologians have provided more profound insights into the life and work of Christ and the nature of the atonement than have John McLeod Campbell, H. R. Mackintosh and Thomas F. Torrance. This book reminds the church and theologians of this fact at the same time that it contributes Purves's own distinctive voice to historical and constructive theological conversation in these vital areas."

Michael Jinkins, president and professor of theology, Louisville Presbyterian Theological Seminary

EXPLORING

CHRISTOLOGY

& ATONEMENT

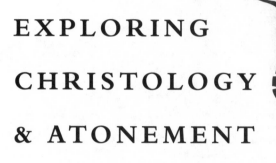

Conversations with

JOHN MCLEOD CAMPBELL

H. R. MACKINTOSH

T. F. TORRANCE

ANDREW PURVES

IVP Academic

An imprint of InterVarsity Press
Downers Grove, Illinois

InterVarsity Press
P. O. Box 1400, Downers Grove, IL 60515-1426
ivpress.com
email@ivpress.com

InterVarsity Press® is the book-publishing division of InterVarsity Christian Fellowship/USA®, a movement of students and faculty active on campus at hundreds of universities, colleges and schools of nursing in the United States of America, and a member movement of the International Fellowship of Evangelical Students. For information about local and regional activities, visit intervarsity.org.

Scripture quotations, unless otherwise noted, are from the New Revised Standard Version of the Bible, copyright 1989 by the Division of Christian Education of the National Council of the Churches of Christ in the USA. Used by permission. All rights reserved.

Cover design: Cindy Kiple
Interior design: Beth McGill
Images: crucifixion: © yurumy/iStockphoto
grunge paper background: © asimetric/iStockphoto

ISBN 978-0-8308-4077-9 (print)
ISBN 978-0-8308-9873-2 (digital)

Printed in the United States of America ♾

Library of Congress Cataloging-in-Publication Data

Purves, Andrew, 1946-
  Exploring christology and atonement : conversations with John Mcleod Campbell, H.R. Mackintosh and T.F. Torrance / andrew Purves.
     pages cm
  Includes bibliographical references and index.
  ISBN 978-0-8308-4077-9 (pbk. : alk. paper)
  1. Atonement. 2. Campbell, John McLeod, 1800-1872. 3. Mackintosh, H. R. (Hugh Ross), 1870-1936. 4. Torrance, Thomas F. (Thomas Forsyth), 1913-2007. I. Title.
  BT265.3.P87 2015
  232'.3--dc23

                                                                                    2015018833

P 23 22 21 20 19 18 17 16 15 14 13 12 11 10 9 8 7 6 5 4 3 2 1

Y 34 33 32 31 30 29 28 27 26 25 24 23 22 21 20 19 18 17 16 15

In grateful memory of Rev. Alasdair I. C. Heron, ThD (1942–2014).

With thankfulness for the three Scottish doctors of the church who have for long been my theological companions:

John McLeod Campbell
Hugh Ross Mackintosh
Thomas Forsyth Torrance.

To my students who were exposed to this manuscript fresh from its writing: thank you for your affection, trust and interest.

David A. Bindewald, James R. Downey, PhD, Robert (Deacon) Dressing, Travis L. Fernald, Steven D. Gallego, Lance R. Hershberger, Charissa A. Howe, Matthew A. Jones, Randy T. Maki, Craig T. Meek, Rachel R. Riggle, Mary Louise Russell, MD, Benjamin R. Schneider, Jean A. Smith, Matthew C. Williams (who helped with the editing and footnote checking), Christopher Garrett Yates.

And, as always, a huge "thank you" to Cathy for her love and support.

CONTENTS

PREFACE

Christology and Atonement

THIS BOOK OFFERS AN ACCOUNT of the relations between Jesus Christ, who is the incarnate Son, and the Father, the result of which is the atonement, for in the incarnate Son the relation between God and humankind is savingly established. We cannot reflect on who Christ is, on his person, without having to reflect on his purpose and work. To cite the notable words of the German Reformer Philipp Melanchthon, "This is to know Christ, to know his benefits." To reflect on Christology or atonement as separate categories would be to deal with abstraction. Thus the topic is Christology and atonement, the doctrine of Jesus Christ and, its consequence, the work of salvation. The consideration of who Jesus was and what he did must in every way be held together, for the one can be understood only in view of the other. That is to say, the hypostatic or personal union of God and humankind as the man Jesus of Nazareth and the atonement that he effects as the meaning and purpose of the incarnation belong together. Christ's being and action are one reality.[1]

Clearly, too, this account of Christology and atonement must cast light on the doctrine of God as Father, Son and Holy Spirit, for as the man Jesus, God, from the Father and by the Spirit, became incarnate for us and for our salvation. This undoubtedly is the great and central mystery of Christian faith, as it is also the central message of Christian proclamation.

---

[1]Right at the beginning it is appropriate to point out that the word *humankind* is difficult to define. Throughout I have tried to suggest that Christ assumed our human nature, and mostly that is what is intended when the words *humanity* or *humankind* are used. But to what does human nature refer? Karl Barth, for example, preferred the German word *Wesen*, which is translated "essence," but which is perhaps even more abstract than the English "human nature" (see, e.g., *Church Dogmatics* 4.2, trans. G. W. Bromiley, ed. G. W. Bromiley and T. F. Torrance [Edinburgh: T & T Clark, 1958], p. 44.) The reference behind these words is to intrinsic being or nature.

Theology, however, exists not for its own sake. Certainly, one trusts, theology is offered to God as the voice of faith thinking about what faith confesses. But as a work of the church, theology also has a responsibility to lay forth its claims for the sake of ministry. For this reason, the conclusion of what we explore in the following pages addresses the relation between Christology, atonement and pastoral care. This is offered in view of the great need today for pastoral ministry to be fully informed at every point by theology and especially, it seems obvious to say, by the central doctrines of Christian faith. There is a sense, then, in which this is a work of pastoral theology, even of practical theology, for there is no knowledge of a nonacting God, and there is no God other than the God who acts for us in Jesus Christ. Reflection on Christology and atonement is reflection on the God who acts; this is the first and primary meaning of practical theology.

The exploration of Christology and atonement is done here by way of a presentation of the relationship between the Father and the incarnate Son as I am guided by the theologies of John McLeod Campbell, Hugh Ross Mackintosh and Thomas Forsyth Torrance. These three Scottish Presbyterian theologians, beginning with the induction of Campbell to the parish of Rhu in Dumbartonshire in 1825 and concluding with the death of Torrance on the first Sunday of Advent in 2007, represent a trajectory in Scottish Reformed theology that was both ecumenical and pastoral, drawing insight as much from the Greek church fathers as from the principal Reformers while also seeking to speak to the ministry of the church in Scotland. In due course, all three, especially Torrance, have become known beyond their native borders. All three were committed churchmen, with a heart for ministry and an evident, passionate piety.

McLeod Campbell, Mackintosh and Torrance worked with a critically realist view of the incarnation in which the pattern and nature of God in Christ were allowed to shape their thinking. Indeed, obedience demanded it. In, through and as Jesus Christ, God had in fact taken on human flesh, becoming as we are, to do from the side of God and from the side of humanity, in the unity of his incarnate personhood, that which was necessary for us to have a new life with God. Thus the atonement was worked out in such a way that it was entirely of God and entirely as human being, in that God as the man Jesus was wholly God and wholly human while remaining one person. That surely is the great mystery at the heart of the gospel that was grasped so clearly by the theologians with whom we will be in conversation. Rejected was any sense that the atonement was an instrumental or external act of God, the results of which are imputed to us; affirmed was the utter seriousness of the becoming flesh of God as the man Jesus so that the atonement was worked out within his incarnate life in history, atoning from the inside, as it were. In this way, these theologians cast Christology and atonement in historical and ontological terms rather than external or instrumental terms.

Central to the common perspective of these three theologians, each in his own voice, was the doctrine of the vicarious humanity of Christ. That is, they saw Christ's humanity not merely as exemplary but rather as through and through substitutionary, in which the covenant between God and humankind was entirely completed in and by him for us. God's coming as the man Jesus was the act from the side of God and from the side of humankind that forged a new relationship in which everything that God requires of us is given by God and to God on our behalf by Jesus Christ. In this way, these theologians stood in the lineage of Athanasius of Alexandria, who taught that Jesus ministers the things of God to us and the things of humankind to God, all in the unity of his divine-human person. At the heart of this bidirectional ministry of Christ is the filial relationship between the Father and the Son wherein Jesus offers the Father in our stead the human life of obedience, trust and love that gladdens the Father's heart. In this way, especially through Christ's active obedience, the atonement is presented as a kinetic, relational and personal event entirely worked out through the relationship between the Father and the incarnate Son. This relationship is not something worked "above our heads," as it were, but is stubbornly a divine act within history that establishes our relationship with God and acts upon us in such a way that we become changed persons. McLeod Campbell and Mackintosh especially, as we will see, repeatedly pull their readers back to what Mackintosh called an "experimental" faith, as by the Holy Spirit's mediation of Christ we, with the apostle Paul, must speak of God in Christ for us, and we in Christ for God.[2] Theology and piety belong together; theology and ministry belong together.

McLeod Campbell, Mackintosh and Torrance, arguably, are linked as a trajectory in Scottish theology that is more at home with the Scots Con-

---

[2]H. R. Mackintosh, *The Christian Experience of Forgiveness* (New York: Harper & Brothers, 1927), p. 226.

fession of 1560 than with the Westminster Confession of 1647. That is, the three theologians placed emphasis on Christology, with attention to the doctrines of the person, life and work of Jesus Christ, rather than on covenant theology construed in theistic rather than christological terms. Their arguments were conducted a posteriori and inductively rather than deductively and rationalistically. However, I do not think they constitute a theological "school" in the tight sense that word suggests. Each clearly remains himself. Nevertheless, Mackintosh was familiar with and somewhat critical of McLeod Campbell, and Torrance sat in Mackintosh's classroom in Edinburgh in the early 1930s and writes affectionately of the influence his teacher had upon him. Torrance too remained deeply and critically appreciative of McLeod Campbell. (Full disclosure: I in turn sat in Torrance's classroom in Edinburgh.)

My manner of approach here is to take up a number of themes that bear upon Christology and atonement as they arise in the writings of McLeod Campbell, Mackintosh and Torrance and engage in reflective discussion with them. The intended result, then, will be more than a monograph on three Scottish theologians. The goal is that by way of this process a case will be made for the relation between Christology and atonement that can guide the church today in preaching, teaching and pastoral care. In view is a contemporary presentation of Christology and atonement as that arises out of the discussions as they proceed.

So-called atonement theory is a wide-ranging and multifaceted inquiry. Whether we consider the shape of soteriology or typologies of atonement theories,[3] the fact is that the ecumenical church (excepting particular denominations) never canonized any single theory in a manner similar to the doctrine of Christ or the trinitarian doctrine of God. Yet even given the accepted christological and trinitarian creedal formulations of the ecumenical church, much remains unexplained, as if the language used by the church fathers is intended to protect the central mysteries of God and Christ rather than explain them. With the atonement, certainly, we confront the great saving mystery of God's saving grace in Jesus Christ. If we think we

---

[3]See John McIntyre, *The Shape of Soteriology: Studies in the Doctrine of the Death of Christ* (Edinburgh: T & T Clark, 1992), where a catena of twelve models of soteriology are identified and discussed; see also Leanne Van Dyk, *The Desire of Divine Love: John McLeod Campbell's Doctrine of the Atonement*, Studies in Church History 4 (New York: Peter Lang, 1995), chap. 3 especially, where Van Dyk lists a number of typologies analysts use to characterize atonement theories.

have explicated it, we haven't! It is surely a mystery to be adored and received rather than a theological problem to be picked apart, analyzed and solved. Nevertheless, I wish in what follows to suggest one way, arising from engagements with the authors named, in which Christology and soteriology can be helpfully and hopefully construed. While offering this way, I recognize that no attempt at understanding can cover, much less explain, the mystery of our salvation in Christ.

There is a significant mass of material to draw from, especially in the case of Torrance, who produced a very substantial and often difficult body of published work. What follows draws mainly from principal publications in which the themes with which I deal are already apparent in the book titles. My working texts are John McLeod Campbell, *The Nature of the Atonement* (1856); H. R. Mackintosh, *The Doctrine of the Person of Jesus Christ* (1912) and *The Christian Experience of Forgiveness* (1927); and T. F. Torrance, *Incarnation: The Person and Life of Christ* (2008) and *Atonement: The Person and Work of Christ* (2009), both edited by Robert T. Walker and published posthumously. I will draw upon other work as required, and en route will note secondary sources, but with the intent to keep that at a minimum.

Allow me to offer a personal note. I have cast what follows as critical theological engagements. I do not mean that lightly. All thinking, whatever the subject, surely involves a conversation with received tradition. At the most elementary level, to use language is to be situated in a received context; otherwise we would not be able to communicate, and I doubt that we could think. Theology is a traditioned discipline, and necessarily so, because Jesus Christ is a historical event, and the church is a historical community of worship, discourse and service of God. To do theology is to be plunged into history. By selecting these three theologians as my conversation partners, I am owning my lineage and receiving it thankfully. Yet I am also seeking to understand it more fully while engaging it critically. But more, I believe that John McLeod Campbell, Hugh Ross Mackintosh and Thomas Forsyth Torrance were doctors of the church. They were theologians—men who knew God in Jesus Christ. To read them is to be spiritually and not just intellectually and theologically elevated. In their company one is drawn into their love for Jesus Christ, shaped by the intensity and quality of their theological grappling with the God who encountered them, and invited to stand and look with them for a while. We, in turn, under their instruction, may also catch a glimpse of the beauty and glory of God given in the face of Jesus Christ.

A BRIEF THEOLOGICAL REFLECTION ON COLOSSIANS 1:15-20

Many biblical references could be brought to bear to set the ground for the journey ahead. I will allow a passage from Colossians to do duty for them all. Here we have a very early confession of the church's faith; it also incorporates many of the major subjects of theology, treating especially the relation between Christology and the atonement.

Jesus Christ is "the image of the invisible God." Reference is made here to the incomprehensibility of God and to Jesus Christ as both God himself and the revelation of God. Notice: we start with Jesus Christ, not with speculative metaphysical or epistemological questions. *An Deus sit?* (Does God exist?) is not the opening question. The opening question is, "Who are you, Lord?" (Acts 9:5), as we will see in due course. There is no independent reference, no extrinsic epistemological authority or ground in the common currency of human discourse to which appeal is made a priori. God either has or has not come among us as the man Jesus. Faith trusts that this is true on the singular ground that God has met us in revelation, and that all subsequent faith, knowledge and life is post hoc, after that fact.

He is "the firstborn of all creation." The reference is to Christ in the flesh affirmed as Lord. God for us is an actual event in history as the man Jesus.

"In him all things in heaven and earth were created, things visible and invisible." The reference is made to Christ's role in creation; he is the creator Word. Note also the reference to "all things," and to the fact that in creation there is more than meets the eye. Not just in revelation, but even in creation itself, not all is clear and immediate to inspection and human control. We are confronted even in revelation with God's veiling, with things invisible.

"All things have been created through him and for him." The reference is now made to Christ as both the source and the goal of creation; he is Alpha and Omega, the first and the last, the beginning and the end. Again we note the reference to "all things."

"He himself is before all things, and in him all things hold together." The reference is made here to Christ's ontological priority. He is Lord, and without him all things—again, twice—fall apart. He is the Pantocrator, the

Lord of the cosmos. By now the sheer size of the Christology is overwhelming. (For a parallel thought, see Eph 1:10 for God's plan to sum up or gather up [*anakephalaiōsasthai*, "to gather up together under a head"] all things in heaven and on earth in Christ.)[4]

"He is the head of the body, the church." The text now moves from reference to God, through Christ's role in creation and lordship over all, to the church, of which Christ is the head, the place wherein he continues to work in his continuing visible body.

"He is the beginning, the firstborn from the dead, so that he might come to have first place in everything." The text now affirms Christ's resurrection. He who was before all things were created is declared to be the firstborn of the dead. Thus again Christ's ontological priority is stressed.

"For through him all the fullness of God was pleased to dwell." In a circling move, the text declares the doctrine of the incarnation. Jesus Christ, bodily, is the fullness of God, whole God. There is no God behind the back of Jesus. Who we see God to be in, through and as Jesus Christ is who God is.

"And through him God was pleased to reconcile all things, whether on earth or in heaven, by making peace through the blood of his cross." And now, of course, reference is made to atonement, and again all things are brought within the sweep of his salvation. Reconciliation (*apokatallassō*, an intensive compound) here indicates restoration of peace and love that had been destroyed. The relation between redemption and creation is fully established, reaching out to include all things. God, as always, is the acting subject, through Christ. Now all things are in complete unity in Christ in a vast cosmic peace.[5] (Parallel reference may be made to Eph 2:13-16, where the *phragmos*, the hedge or wall that divides, is broken down, thus making peace.) This peace is through the blood of Christ, by which God has satisfied the will of his love in taking our judgment on himself and bearing it in our stead. God in Christ enters into our separation from God, which is caused by our perversity, and God's separation from us because of his holiness and therefore God's judgment on our sin. The consequence is that God in Christ assumes us, as well as all things, into fellowship or, better, into communion with himself.

---

[4]Thomas F. Torrance, *Atonement: The Person and Work of Christ*, ed. Robert T. Walker (Downers Grove, IL: IVP Academic, 2009), p. 132n93.

[5]Ibid., p. 144.

Note how Paul moves from Christ, Lord, to God, to creation, to church, to resurrection, to incarnation and atonement. Note again the sweep: all things. The movement of this passage will be reflected in our journey as we move from Christology to atonement. At each point our plumb line will be Jesus Christ, "the image of the invisible God," in whom "all the fullness of God was pleased to dwell" and "through whom God was pleased to reconcile all things."

INTRODUCTION

Locating Theology

WHAT IS THEOLOGY? What kind of activities does it involve? What is the scope of the discipline? This chapter serves as an introduction to a way of doing theology that is indebted to the work of Thomas F. Torrance. Although Torrance is often cited in the pages that follow, and therefore he serves as guide and teacher, the intent is to give my own account of theology rather than a detailed account of theological method in Torrance's theology. Two major themes are discussed: the relation between theology and baptism, and realism and fallibility in Christology and soteriology. A number of subdivisions will mark the discussion as it proceeds. This introduction should serve as a methodological signpost to aid the journey ahead as it unfolds.

THEOLOGY AND THE COMMUNITY OF THE BAPTIZED

The chapel at Pittsburgh Theological Seminary, where I teach, has recently been reformed. The old pews, bolted to a slate floor in a series of rigid rows that allowed napes to be piously considered, were unbolted and disposed of. The immovable pulpit was moved (a crane was seen one day!), consigned to some other use. Fresh paint, with color, was applied. And new, expressly designed chairs, font, table and pulpit were moved into (movable) place. Now, students, administrators and faculty who gather to worship must enter this beautiful, flexible space negotiating the baptismal font, which is placed, awkwardly but with intent, right in the middle of the entrance to the chapel. In order to worship we must enter through baptism. This is a wonderful metaphor for a theological seminary.

We do theology because we are baptized. Theology is a work of the communion of saints, a work of faith in which we try to understand the God who in Jesus Christ has claimed us and bound us to himself, and thereby made us the church. Theology is an expression of our baptismal identity in and of our belonging to God. It is a work not just of the theologian but also of the church as a historical theological community. Theology does not seek to know about God in an abstract, speculative manner (how, in any case, could the living God be known in such a manner?), but seeks to know God more fully as the God who in and as Jesus Christ has joined us to himself and made us the community of the baptized, the community bound to Jesus Christ.

The relation between baptism and theology is reciprocal in this way. Baptism leads to theology in order to understand as faithfully as we can who it is in whom we live and move and have our being (Acts 17:28), while theology is more or less pointless without baptism, a mere chasing after God-thoughts fitfully flitting around in our brains (Calvin).[1] Theology reminds us that baptism is not an empty ritual devoid of content. One goal of baptism surely is living in Christ Jesus, rooted and built up in him and established in the faith, just as we were taught (Col 2:6-7). In this case, one goal of theology is *pietas*. Baptism reminds us that theology is a holy work of the people of God, part of the vowed life of discipled people whose lives are transformed by the renewing of our minds (Rom 12:2). Julie Canlis has pointedly summed up this perspective: we attempt to do theology in terms of "the belief that we are neither isolated Christians nor objective scientists, but rather within a church and stream of tradition."[2] We are after what John Webster once called "theological theology," by which he meant theology that dares to think God, relationally and experientially, as it were, rather than think about God, as at some kind of distance, remotely and neutrally.[3]

As baptism is a public act of the church, likewise theology is a public work of the church, for the glory of God, one hopes, but also for the sake of the church, for testing proclamation and teaching, for guiding ministry, and for nurturing and maturing intelligent and well-informed faith and life. In this

---

[1]John Calvin, *Institutes of the Christian Religion*, ed. John T. McNeill, trans. Ford Lewis Battles, 2 vols. (Philadelphia: Westminster, 1960), 1.13.2.

[2]Julie Canlis, *Calvin's Ladder: A Spiritual Theology of Ascent and Ascension* (Grand Rapids: Eerdmans, 2010), p. 23.

[3]John Webster, *Confessing God: Essays in Christian Dogmatics II* (London: T & T Clark, 2005), chap. 1.

sense, theology is for the sake of the baptized, with particular concern for the sanctification of mind leading to well-instructed faith, well-informed worship and well-guided ministry. Theology has little obvious purpose otherwise. However, far too often it seems that this bond between theology and baptism as they intersect in and for the faith, worship and ministry of the church is much unloosed. Theology can be arcane, obscure and downright technical, a discipline for experts with terminal degrees, having little apparent contribution to make to the situational demands of congregational and personal life. Unmoored from baptism, theology easily becomes lord over its own life, a discipline of the academic guild rather than the church. But, there is nothing wrong with expertise when it is put to the right use, and when it is offered with humility in view of the enormity of its task and mindful of its subject of study. Theology is in service to the church.

Clearly, when the connections between theology and the community of the baptized become unloosed, both suffer. Theology without baptism has lost its anchor and its purpose, becoming a discipline listlessly wandering the corridors of the academy, whimpering for a seat at the table. Baptism without theology never matures into Christians having the mind of Christ. The meager fruit can be cliché-ridden piety or a drift toward narcissistic experience-centered authoritarianism. Both a theology that is no longer accountable to baptism and an unthinking faith, surely, are offensive to the gospel. If these are caricatures, perhaps enough of truth abides to make a valid point.

Theology can be learned. A discipled life takes discipline. Both living the life of a thoughtful Christian and doing theology can be hard work. They involve skill sets to be learned, just as we need education to do physics or plant a garden or raise children. Gathering information and the thoughtful interpretation of experience interact in all knowing. Further, knowledge draws upon received wisdom. A theologian works in gratitude for a tradition handed down, not to be followed uncritically of course, but received with respect and delight. And this is done within communities of discourse that at some point express faith through common worship and shared ministry. Thus the relation between baptism and theology is caught up in a multilayered series of connections and responsibilities. If baptism is the empirical point of entrance to the Christian life, theology is part of God's provision for the purpose of growth and maturity in that life. Theology is for the building up of the church. The goal of both baptism and theology is Christian identity and formation so that the Christian lives and thinks "in Christ."

Hugh Ross Mackintosh (d. 1936) once noted, "Theology is simply a persistent and systematic attempt to clarify the convictions by which Christians live."[4] We cannot do theology in neutral terms. This is borne out when we place a central Christian conviction before us for consideration: God was in Christ reconciling the world to himself (2 Cor 5:19). We cannot know God without being reconciled to God, for there is no God to know except the God who has come among us savingly as the man Jesus. The *logos tou theou* (2 Cor 2:17), the word of God, cannot in Christian terms be other than the *logos tou staurou* (1 Cor 1:18), the message about the cross. Christian faith claims knowledge of an acting and saving God. Jürgen Moltmann notes, "It is he, the crucified Jesus himself, who is the driving force, the joy and the suffering of all theology which is Christian."[5] Our task as theologians is to make faithful witness to this God who encounters us in, through and as the man Jesus Christ, as he is attested by Scripture and as we are led by the Holy Spirit together as the body of Christ to share in the communion of love between the Father and the Son. The subject matter is God whom we know in Jesus Christ to be Savior and Lord. The theologian tries to make some sense of this in spite of the fact that God is not reducible to our sentences. Our task in theology, then, as T. F. Torrance notes, is to yield the obedience of our minds to what is given, which is God's self-revelation in its objective reality, Jesus Christ.[6] Our approach "can only be from the standpoint of sinners whose sins have been forgiven, and for whom Christ is the Son of the living God become flesh in order to reconcile the world to God."[7] Theology is a confessional discipline, obedient to and humble before the mystery of Christ (e.g., Col 2:25-27; Eph 3:4), seeking to learn what is to be known of God from that mystery as he declares himself to us.

This is exactly what we find in a famous sentence from Philipp Melanchthon at the beginning of his *Loci Communes* (1521): *Hoc est Christum cognoscere,*

---

[4]H. R. Mackintosh, *The Christian Experience of Forgiveness* (New York: Harper & Brothers, 1927), p. 4.
[5]Jürgen Moltmann, *The Crucified God: The Cross of Christ at the Foundation and Criticism of Christian Theology*, trans. R. A. Wilson and John Bowden (New York: Harper & Row, 1974), p. 87.
[6]Thomas F. Torrance, *Incarnation: The Person and Life of Christ*, ed. Robert T. Walker (Downers Grove, IL: IVP Academic, 2008), p. 1 (slightly adapted).
[7]Ibid., p. 11.

beneficia eius cognoscere; "This is to know Christ, to know his benefits."[8] We know Jesus Christ insofar as we know him to be Lord over us, to be Savior for us and as such know him as God who encounters us. To cite Torrance again: "The knowledge of Christ arises in the knowledge of his salvation. *How* we know Christ and *what* we know of him belong inseparably together."[9] What is important here, and what was central for Melanchthon, is that it is not because Christ brings us benefits that he is Lord for us, but that he reveals God to us, and as such we know ourselves to be sheltered and healed in him.[10]

The danger in our task is that in seeking to bring knowledge of God to faithful expression we strip God of his glory. After all, theologians most likely are *masters* of divinity and *doctors* of philosophy. How easy it is to forget that here we speak of holy things, we who are not holy. How easy it is to forget that there is no humanly rational explanation for incarnation and atonement, or for the resurrection and ascension of Jesus, or for knowledge of God—Father, Son and Holy Spirit. Rather, in theological knowledge, and in order to know God in a Godly manner, our minds must undergo a profound *metanoia*, a change of mind that involves radical alteration in our thinking (see Rom 12:2). Explanation assumes some kind of continuity between God and us, and that exactly is what we do not have. Thus the gospel is foolishness, unreason, to "the Greeks" (1 Cor 1:22-25).[11] Only in God's light do we see light (see Ps 36:9; 119:105). Or to put that christologically, only in the light of Christ, and thinking out from a center in him, can we come to know God rightly, coming to know the Father as Jesus the Son reveals him to us (see Mt 11:27). Knowledge of God can happen only according to the way that Christ himself provided for our understanding. Not only with respect to discipleship, but also in theology, we must learn to follow Christ. By God's grace and in the communion of the Holy Spirit theological knowledge is the fruit of sharing in Christ's life.

We approach our task with humility, drawing near to the throne of grace only because we are summoned, having access through Christ in

---

[8]Wilhelm Pauck, ed., *Melanchthon and Bucer*, Library of Christian Classics 19 (Philadelphia: Westminster, 1969), pp. 20-21. See Torrance, *Incarnation*, pp. 33-36.

[9]Torrance, *Incarnation*, p. 33.

[10]See Alister E. McGrath, *T. F. Torrance: An Intellectual Biography* (Edinburgh: T & T Clark, 1999), p. 93.

[11]Thomas F. Torrance, *Atonement: The Person and Work of Christ*, ed. Robert T. Walker (Downers Grove, IL: IVP Academic, 2009), p. 4.

one Spirit to the Father (Eph 2:18). We neither storm the gates of heaven nor gather theological arguments like arrows in a quiver to use as weapons to advance our theological cause. We approach our work with an attitude of worship, with the deepest respect for the task before us, and perhaps with a sense of amazement that we are here to be about this duty in the first place. Let gratitude be the mark of our endeavor, that Almighty God has called us to bring his gospel to expression as we fulfill the work of theology.

God chooses to be known by us. Christian faith itself and the church's work of explication, interpretation and proclamation of God's revelation arise singularly from God's gracious willingness to reveal himself as savior and draw us into a knowing communion with himself. Jesus Christ is both the crucifixion of all theology that is not Christian and the resurrection, and therefore the possibility, of all theology that is Christian. That statement may seem overly harsh, but I see no alternative to it if Jesus is who the New Testament says he is.

That is to say, Jesus Christ is not an addendum to the doctrine of God or some important but outer ring some way from the supposed theistic center. Jesus Christ is at once both the center of and the entryway into the doctrine of God. "No one knows the Son except the Father, and no one knows the Father except the Son and anyone to whom the Son chooses to reveal him" (Mt 11:27). Here, as elsewhere throughout the New Testament, we find the ontological relation between the Father and the Son in being and act to be the sole ground of revelation and salvation. In the final analysis, this is the singular content of preaching and teaching. Thus theology, and in particular the doctrine of God, is a knowledge of the Father, through the Son, and in the unity of the Holy Spirit. Such theology is at all points thoroughly trinitarian, for knowledge of God is mediated through Jesus Christ, and therefore God is known through encounter, for God is Spirit.

Our task is more rather than less faithful knowledge of God who encounters us, with the end of a right relationship with God and the faithful living of the Christian life. In a recent book Matthew Myer Boulton noted, "For Calvin, Christian doctrine is properly conceived and articulated in the first place for the sake of Christian formation"; the goal of theology is "practical life in God."[12] When we get God wrong, we get living in the world wrong. Theology is education in godly piety and to that end is paideutic; it is "grateful love and reverence for God induced by relational, pragmatic knowledge of divine benefits."[13] In a similar vein John Webster argues,

> The end of theology is practical knowledge of God, that is, knowledge which aims at the furtherance of the life of the Christian community, the salvation of humankind, and godly discipline. Theology is thus more a process of moral and spiritual training and an exercise in the promotion of common life than it is a scholarly discipline. "Skills" are kept firmly tied to their end; in and of itself, the cultivation of learning is profitless because, unless directed to holiness, it is not only unattached but vicious.[14]

REALISM AND FALLIBILITY IN CHRISTOLOGY AND SOTERIOLOGY: ALL THEOLOGY IS EN ROUTE

On August 17, 1560, the Scottish Parliament adopted a document that was four days in its writing as "doctrine founded upon the infallible Word of God." The confession is a setting forth of the faith of the Scottish Reformers. But, as the preface to the confession notes, it is open to amendment and correction should it be found to be contrary to God's word.

> If any man will note in our Confession any chapter or sentence contrary to God's Holy Word, that it would please him of his gentleness and for Christian charity's sake to inform us of it in writing; and we, upon our honour, do promise him that by God's grace we shall give him satisfaction from the mouth of God, that is, from Holy Scriptures, or else we shall alter whatever he can prove to be wrong.[15]

As is common within Reformed traditions, confessions are understood as subordinate or provisional standards, not as static and timeless declarations. In keeping with the notes by which the true church is determined, the confession of Christ Jesus rather than the confession of the Scots Confession is

---

[12] Matthew Myer Boulton, *Life in God: John Calvin, Practical Formation, and the Future of Protestant Theology* (Grand Rapids: Eerdmans, 2011), p. 4.

[13] Ibid., p. 5.

[14] John Webster, *Holy Scripture: A Dogmatic Sketch*, Current Issues in Theology 1 (Cambridge: Cambridge University Press, 2003), p. 116.

[15] *The Scots Confession of 1560: A Modern Translation by James Bulloch*, Documents of the Church of Scotland (Edinburgh: Saint Andrew Press, 1960), preface.

avowed, and this in local congregations rather than in some abstraction called the universal church.[16]

This historical reference illustrates how theology is an "open" discipline—open, that is, to correction as Christ continues to shape the mind of the church and as the church is consequentially repentant of its theology (see Rom 3:4). There is no eternal theology; all theology is en route, hopefully to a deeper faithfulness. Theology is never in itself the truth, for that truth lies in Christ, to whom theology bears witness. As human statements, theology suffers from all manner of problems, not the least of which is the theologian's sin. Likewise, there is no eternal Christology and soteriology. Even the most sublime references to Jesus Christ and what he does for us do not contain the whole truth in them, but remain wracked by sin in some way or another. That is to say, Christology and soteriology as written by theologians and even as attested in official creeds of the church are fallible. Torrance has noted, "The very beliefs which we profess and formulate as obediently and carefully as we can in fidelity to God's self-revelation in Jesus Christ are themselves called into question by that revelation, *for they have their truth not in themselves but in him to whom they refer.*"[17] God, in other words, is not a sentence, and certainly is not containable within our sentences. At best we try to be more rather than less faithful in our references to Christ. But God is not reducible to sentences and arguments, for God is personal being, uncontainable within our ideas.

The fallibility of Christology and soteriology is the predicate of the nature of God, of God's incomprehensibility, holiness and majesty, yet too of our humanity with all of its frailty and misknowing. But note these words from Karl Barth: "As ministers we ought to speak of God. We are human, however, and so cannot speak of God. We ought therefore to recognize both our obligation and our inability, and by that very recognition give God the glory."[18] We are called thus to do what we cannot do except as God enables us by a mighty act of grace in giving himself to be known.

All theology is en route. Barth's question, "What as Christians do we really

---

[16]Ibid., article 18.

[17]Thomas F. Torrance, *Reality and Evangelical Theology* (Philadelphia: Westminster, 1982), pp. 18-19 (italics added).

[18]Karl Barth, *The Word of God and the Word of Man*, trans. Douglas Horton, Harper Torchbooks 13 (1928; repr., New York: Harper & Row, 1957), p. 186.

have to say?"[19] leads to an observation: all theology not only comes out of encounter with Spirit and Word, as transmitted through a tradition, and not only comes from a theologian or church, but also comes in a form that it is written or spoken for today. Barth's question, from his *Dogmatics in Outline*, was posed in 1946 amid the bombed-out ruins of Bonn University. One imagines him waving his arms at the devastation as he asks his question. We may crave certainty, but what we have is theology that is circumstantial.[20] Nevertheless, what do we have to say? We may attempt to write something magisterial and definitive; nevertheless, such good intentions cannot erase provisionality or fallibility. Even with our best theological sentences we see as in a mirror dimly. Creeds and theologies arise out of geographical and, indeed, political placement, and they give guidance for the church at a particular time. Theology is always en route, always open for correction and revision, always trying to become more faithful.

John Knox of Edinburgh burned his sermons after they were preached in the High Kirk of St. Giles. They were for this congregation, on this day. Likewise, theology is written for today, not for the future and certainly not for eternity. The cry "Back to Nicaea!" or "Back to Westminster!" fails to understand the provisional nature of theology. Theology is not the worse for that, for the occasional character is the nature of the case. All theology, like all science, is both kinetic and open-ended, and faithfulness must be worked out in terms of these given processes rather than in propositions and deductions that are static and closed. Theology, alas, is provisional and messy.

In knowing God in Christ we are up against a fundamental mystery that is not explicable in terms of our abilities or deducible a priori, from first principles. Rather, from the side of God in the flesh of our humanity, Jesus Christ, in the presence of the Spirit, confronts and encounters us, and he does so on his own terms. We know God by faith. As theologians our task is to clarify that knowledge by bringing it to faithful expression. But we can do so only in terms of the nature of this mystery, and not by transmuting it into something that we can grasp on our own terms or in terms of predetermined criteria for knowledge. We must learn to be real in our thinking by

---

[19]Karl Barth, *Dogmatics in Outline*, trans. G. T. Thompson (New York: Harper & Row, 1959), p. 11.
[20]See also William J. Abraham, *Crossing the Threshold of Divine Revelation* (Grand Rapids: Eerdmans, 2006), pp. 108-9.

thinking in a manner appropriate to that which we seek to know. At the end of the day, the teaching of Evagrius of Pontus from the fourth century marks the bounds of theology: "If you are a theologian, you will pray truly. If you pray truly, you are a theologian."[21]

Realism in theology: some illustrations and observations. An illustration may be helpful here. After around seventy pages clearing the ground for his presentation on the nature of the atonement, John McLeod Campbell offers a programmatic statement on method: "It is in the way of studying the atonement *by its own light*, and of meditation on what it is revealed to have been, that I propose to proceed in seeking positive conclusions as to its nature, its expiatory virtue, and its adequacy to all the ends contemplated."[22] McLeod Campbell has no interest in asking an abstract question after the fashion of "What is an atonement for sin?" Rather, the thing itself is to be studied on its own terms, in its own light. The intent is absence of speculation; the method is a posteriori. The procedure has the character of "What do we have here?" What we have here is Jesus Christ and an atonement accomplished by him.

The theologian who stands head and shoulders above everyone else in modern times, and who tried to write his theology according to the proper form of theological reason, was Karl Barth. However, the theologian who brought theological reason or theological rationality to its fullest expression in terms of meaning and method, and notably was in dialogue with both Barth and the philosophy of science of his day, was Thomas F. Torrance. Turning now to reflect on the nature of reason in theology, we will be guided by Torrance along the way.

A basic point is to distinguish between reason/rationality and rationalism. Rationalism is reason abstracted from its object, operating solely out of itself without attention to what is given. It is thinking dictated by reason alone, severed from objects of knowledge as they are given to be known. Rationalism is ordered by first principles and formed by logically deducted propositions. An example of rationalist theology is found in the so-called ontological proof for the existence of God that goes back to St. Anselm in the eleventh century.

---

[21]Evagrius Ponticus, *The Praktikos: Chapters on Prayer*, trans. John Eudes Bamberger, Cistercian Studies Series 4 (Spencer, MA: Cistercian Publications, 1970), p. 65.

[22]John McLeod Campbell, *The Nature of the Atonement* (1856; repr., Grand Rapids: Eerdmans, 1996), p. 108 (italics added).

He states that the concept of God is "a being than which no greater can be conceived." Since existence is possible, and to exist is greater than not to exist, then God must exist (if God did not exist, then a greater being could be conceived, but that is self defeating—you can't have something greater than that which no greater can be conceived!). Therefore, God must exist. Later Descartes did much the same thing, starting from the idea of a perfect being. Thus we have an a priori argument where existence is a predicate of definition. But this argument is seen by many thinkers to have been destroyed by David Hume (who argued that there is no being whose nonbeing implies contradiction) and then Immanuel Kant (who argued that existence is not a predicate).[23]

Rationality, on the other hand, refers not to something that lies within reason itself, but rather to our ability to relate thought and action to objective intelligible realities.[24] The Scottish philosopher John Macmurray (d. 1976) observed, "The rationality of thought does not lie in the thought itself, as a quality of it, but depends upon reference to the external world as known in immediate experience"; and again, "Reason is the capacity to behave consciously in terms of what is not ourselves. We can express this briefly by saying that reason is the capacity to behave in terms of the nature of the object, that is to say, to behave objectively. Reason is thus our capacity for objectivity."[25]

We distinguish between thinking that is characterized by deductive logical processes, thinking that is independent of experience, a priori thinking, and thinking that seeks to know what is present to experience, a posteriori thinking. New knowledge cannot be raised in abstraction, but only concretely—not a priori, but a posteriori. In theology we are concerned with positive thinking, thinking that is obedient to what is given, empirical thinking.

Knowledge of Jesus Christ is sought a posteriori (known from experience), not a priori (deduced from first principles). We begin not by asking, "Can we know God or Christ?" but rather, "God and Christ are known; who, then, is God?" It is in this way that Paul's question in Acts 9:5, "Who are you, Lord?" is the controlling christological question, as we will see in the next chapter. With this manner of reasoning we reach conclusions on the basis

---

[23]For a survey, see Alasdair I. C. Heron, *A Century of Protestant Theology* (Philadelphia: Westminster, 1980), pp. 14-15.
[24]Thomas F. Torrance, *Theological Science* (London: Oxford University Press, 1969), p. 11.
[25]Cited in ibid., pp. 11-12.

of what has earlier been observed or experienced. The conclusions arrived
at, however, are never absolutely certain. They are suggested in varying degrees of strength, or, in the language of the analytic philosophers, with
greater or lesser robustness. A classic example is the conviction that tomorrow the sun will rise. This conviction is grounded on the observation
that every day in the history of noticing these things, the sun has always
risen. But there can be no absolute certainty that just because the sun rose
every day in the past, it will rise again tomorrow morning. The conclusion
is very strongly suggested, of course, and really it entails a practical necessity,
or we would never get out of bed. But it remains unproven in any absolute
sense. In spite of common assumptions to the contrary, indicated by the use
of the philosophically vague word *fact*, empirical science also works in this
way, with its "faith" in the likes of probability and conclusions drawn from
experience rather than in ironclad "laws" such as causality or assertions
about absolute time and space.

A concrete biblical illustration may be helpful at this point: the disciples'
experience of the risen Christ. While the disciples had no experience of the
resurrection of Jesus as an event, their experience of the risen Jesus seemed
reasonably to entail such an event. Assuming lack of pathology, delusion, utter
confusion or lying, one would hardly experience and attest someone to be
alive in some way whom one knew to be dead. If we accept the disciples' accounts of encountering Jesus to be testimony in good faith—and why would
we do otherwise?—their witness is worthy of attention. Add to that our own
sense of being encountered through the Holy Spirit by Jesus as a living Lord,
and the case gets stronger by the minute. The conclusion that the resurrected
Jesus lives is not absolutely provable, but then no conclusion derived from
experience ever is—as is also the case with empirical science.

Methodologically, then, we do not start with the resurrection and draw
conclusions deductively from it. Rather, we start with the experience of faith
and with the disciples' testimony that they were encountered by the resurrected Jesus. The New Testament has no interest in inquiring into the possibility of this encounter in a prior way: can such a thing as a resurrection
happen? Nor at this point are we asking an epistemological question: how
do we know? We cannot determine in advance what would verify the truth
of the experience of being encountered by someone who was dead but is

now raised from the dead. The encounters are "given." In theology, therefore, we go on to ask who is this Jesus who encountered the disciples (again, the centrality of Acts 9:5 for Christology) and who today encounters us through their witness and our life together as the church by means of the gift of the Holy Spirit. In knowing God in Christ we are up against a fundamental mystery that is not explicable in terms of our abilities or deducible a priori, from first principles.

Calvin on realism in theology. What, then, is the nature of theological rationality? The following is largely taken from Torrance, *Theological Science*, a monumental work on the philosophy of theology written in dialogue with mid-twentieth-century philosophy of science. Although his conversation partner is now a bit dated, the thrust of the argument seems to hold.

A place to begin is with what today we call "antifoundationalism," though it is not a term that Torrance used. Given God's incomprehensibility, we can know and understand God only out of God's own rationality and under the determination of the divine being—that is, in active obedience to the demands of God's reality and self-giving. As such, modern theology in its distinctive Protestant form began with Calvin.

In his *Institutes of the Christian Religion*, Calvin reversed the order of questioning and knowing that had obtained throughout the medieval period, and in doing so he put theology onto a new footing. First, Calvin reversed the order of scientific questions. Rather than ask first of all, "What sort of thing? Can that exist? What sort of existence is it?" Calvin made primary the question, "What is it?" Colloquially put, he began by asking, "What have we here?" In doing so he changed the nature of science, asking genuinely interrogative questions that were not governed by previous abstractions and metaphysical assumptions. This is the theological ground for modern empirical science. The question led to new knowledge. Calvin wanted to begin with actuality: What is it that we have here? In theology specifically this became the "Who?" question. Thus, for example, Acts 9:5 ("Who are you, Lord?") is the primary christological question.

Second, Calvin insisted that in theology knowledge of God and knowledge of ourselves are bound together in mutuality. We cannot know God apart from the fact that *we* know God; theology cannot be cut off from the fact that God has addressed *us*. Thus there is a human pole in all proper knowing, even of God, and subject-object relations are integral to how we know. Knowing God is a personal knowing of which a relationship with God is a vital part.

Third, within these actual relations our knowledge of God must be put to the test. The principle here is called the *analogia fidei*, in which we test the fidelity of our knowledge by tracing it back to its ground in the reality known. Perhaps a problem with so much theology today is that the second point got out of hand. When personal knowledge is not tested by critical thinking that directs us back to the object of knowledge, it leads to personalism and subjectivism in which ostensible statements about God become statements about ourselves. We look into the theological well and see only our own reflection looking back at us.

Calvin brought theology back to its own ground in God—God who is person not concept, God who is known on God's terms and not according to prior and previously determined criteria; thus we speak now of antifoundationalism in theology. This is in opposition to Kantian foundationalism, which is so dominant still today: "Hitherto it has been assumed that all our knowledge must conform to objects. . . . [We must ask] whether we may not have more success in the tasks of metaphysics if we suppose that objects must conform to our knowledge."[26] Theology as Calvin intended rejects the attempt to fit knowledge of God into a previously given foundation for knowledge. For him, that would be idolatry. Instead, he tried to operate with a radical openness toward God, demanded by the very nature and mystery of God. In Torrance's mind this means that again and again we must reconstruct the constructs that we use to speak of God and by which we seek to refer truthfully to God.

Critical realism in theology. Generally, realism involves knowing things in a manner appropriate to them, and within subject-object relations of knower and something known. In perception and knowledge, as far as we are able, meaning is displaced away from ourselves and the sign that signifies, to rest upon what is indicated.[27] Thus, I look at you, I see you through the lens of my glasses, I speak of you with my words, but what I refer to is not

---

[26]Cited in Torrance, *Theological Science*, p. 88.
[27]Thomas F. Torrance, "Theological Realism," in *The Philosophical Frontiers of Christian Theology: Essays Presented to D. M. MacKinnon*, ed. Brian Hebblethwaite and Stewart Sutherland (Cambridge: Cambridge University Press, 1982), pp. 169-96.

myself, my glasses or my words. I refer to *you*, although it is I who looks and speaks. I can have an idea of you, but in order to know you more faithfully I must bring my idea of you, and the words I use to express that idea, to honest testing. As you disclose yourself to me, I should come to a deeper knowledge of you. And the words and sentences that express that deeper knowledge will themselves be subject to correction and revision. My knowledge of you is never complete.

In all knowing there is a contrast between idea and reality, between sign and thing signified, as we move back and forth, as it were, from one pole to the other in the semantic relation—between reality and our words about it. Knowledge depends on the actual bearing of the signs or symbols (words or numbers) upon the realities to which they refer. If I try to describe you and say, "Pink banana," a break has occurred between sign (pink banana) and reality (you), communication has failed, and there is no knowledge. But neither can sign image reality completely, which would be an ultrarealist position whereby we mistake sign for reality. That sort of mirroring relation between words and reality is the root of biblical fundamentalism and is, ironically, a form of epistemological positivism, which in philosophical clothes rejects what cannot be empirically verified. (On that basis quantum physics must go out of business!) Signs, rather, must have a certain detachment from that which is signified. The Word of God is Jesus Christ, and while the Bible bears witness to that Word, it is not itself the exact mirror of the Word; there is a distance between the Word of God, the incarnate Son, and biblical words about him. But neither can the sign be an artificial construct so as to be completely detached from the object of knowledge. The Bible is given by God as an appropriately detached sign, but also as a unique and Spirit-inspired sign. That is the tension within which we must work in theology.

We use the term *realism* to describe the orientation of thought in science, philosophy and theology in which we try to make a connection between our thinking/speaking and "something out there." Alister McGrath has provided the following helpful definitions:

Naïve realism: Reality impacts directly upon the human mind, without any reflection on the part of the human knower. The resulting knowledge is directly determined by an objective reality within the world. [This means that there can be perception without interpretation, which is nonsense.]

Critical realism: Reality is apprehended by the human mind, which attempts to express and accommodate that reality as best it can with the tools at its disposal—such as mathematical formulae or mental models. [This is the mature position. All knowing is in process, it intends something "out there" but never completely encompasses it by thought, number or word. It allows for subject-object relations to be taken seriously. In such a scheme a fact is really a metaphysical myth. Critical realism calls for knowing that is kinetic, full of onward movement, and always open to correction and change.]

Postmodern anti-realism: The human mind freely constructs its ideas without reference to an alleged external world.[28]

Let me try to bring this into clear focus for theology and theological rationality. On the table thus far: (1) God gives himself to be known: *revelation*; (2) *faith* is a profoundly personal sense of trust and hope in God and is integrally related to knowledge of God; (3) *Scripture* is the testimony or witness to that revelation, the putting of it into words, most often in narrative form. And all of this frames the common life of the church and the individual lives of believers. Revelation, faith and Scripture: How are they related, and where does theology fit in? God gives himself to be known. There is something or someone "out there" that has grasped us. The prime christological question is, "Who are you, Lord?" (Acts 9:5). The Bible is the Spirit-given testimony to this God who encounters us. Faith is the Spirit-given gift of being in relation with this God and thus knowing God. Theology is the attempt to sort this out as best we can. We know that our words never entirely encompass the reality of God, yet we know that some words do better than others. Thus we find ourselves in the position of critical realists. There is a God who gives himself to be known in faith, but there remains always a degree of detachment between God and our words concerning God, while we seek always to bring our words into a deeper faithfulness with respect to God's self-givenness. Even so, there remains an ineffable but wondrous sense that in theology, as in love, we know more than we say. An apophatic gap remains between what we say and the God who encounters us as the man Jesus Christ.

---

[28] Alister McGrath, *The Science of God: An Introduction to Scientific Theology* (Grand Rapids: Eerdmans, 2004), p. 141.

Actual knowledge of God. In trying to give, briefly, the compass of theological rationality I have discussed antifoundationalism and critical realism. I turn now very briefly to another aspect of theological rationality that Torrance has advanced: knowledge according to the nature of the object of study, or what William J. Abraham calls "proper epistemic fit."[29] Christian theology arises out of the actual knowledge of God given in time and space. It is knowledge of God who meets us and gives himself to be known in, through and as Jesus Christ. It is positive, concrete knowledge. Our thinking, then, is profoundly limited by the actual way in which God has given himself to be known. There is posited here an objective ontological reality, but one of a kind, sui generis, with no corresponding analogy in human experience. We can know, in such a case, only from a center in God—theo-logic. God, as it were, objectifies himself for us. Thus we must keep before us the absolute primacy of God, who is the Lord over all our knowing of him. We have knowledge of God only as grace, as forgiven sinners, and as personal knowledge—both knowledge of God as personal being and of ourselves as persons knowing. Given this, the possibility of theological knowledge of God cannot be discussed outside of God's own reality as the God who is in gracious interaction with the creaturely world by which God redemptively presents himself to us and for us.

In science as well as theology a general rule obtains: we know something only in accordance with its nature—*kata physin*. And we develop our knowledge as we allow its nature to prescribe the mode of rationality appropriate to it. In order to know God we must enter into a mode of rationality appropriate to the nature of God. Or to put it otherwise, in order to get theological answers we must ask theological questions appropriate to the nature of God. And again, in order to know God we have to interrogate God in a manner appropriate to God. It is on the mark to say that given its subject matter, theology is a pious discipline.

I set out to reflect on theological rationality and now find myself coming back to baptismal identity. Theological rationality has its home within the experience of being Christian, of being encountered by the living God, and being a person of faith, worship and Christian life, a participant within the

---

[29]Abraham, *Crossing the Threshold*, chap. 3.

community of the baptized. Theological rationality is thinking "in Christ," and it is always part of the experience of living "in Christ," which is the meaning of being baptized in the name of the Father and of the Son and of the Holy Spirit. And with this we have come full circle, having arrived at the place where we began.

CHRISTOLOGY

Who Is the Incarnate Savior of the World?

A PREFACE TO THE NEXT THREE CHAPTERS

John McLeod Campbell's axiom marks out the parameters for our consideration: "The faith of atonement presupposes the faith of the incarnation."[1] That is to say, the atonement is to be seen in the light of the incarnation and the fulfillment of God's purpose for humankind that the incarnation intends. The meaning of the incarnation unfolds as the atonement insofar as we look at the atonement as the revealing of God's goal for humankind. On the one hand, the atonement makes it necessary that we should have a Christology, while on the other hand, Christology seeks to bear witness to the ontological ground for the atonement in Jesus Christ himself. St. Anselm's question, "Why did God become human?" is answered in reference to the light that the person of Jesus Christ shines upon it, for he is the *hilasmos*, the atoning exchange or atoning sacrifice (1 Jn 2:2; 4:10). Atonement is not so much a work of Christ apart from who he is, but rather Christ himself in his work.[2] The nature of the atonement is Jesus Christ himself working out our reconciliation with God, not just in his body, but, as Calvin says, also in his soul.[3]

It is immediately striking that this proposition—the atonement is the meaning of the incarnation, and the reference is to the person of Jesus Christ himself—implies that forgiveness must be more than the application of God's will to forgive. If forgiveness, the covering of sin, involved the personal cost

---

[1] John McLeod Campbell, *The Nature of the Atonement*, 2nd ed. (1867; repr., Eugene, OR: Wipf & Stock, 1999), p. 19.

[2] Ibid., p. 154.

[3] John Calvin, *Institutes of the Christian Religion*, ed. John T. McNeill, trans. Ford Lewis Battles, 2 vols. (Philadelphia: Westminster, 1960), 2.16.10.

to God that we find in the life and death of Jesus, then two points arise. First, we must suppose something in God that required the venture of the Son into the far country of our human condition; second, we must suppose something in our human condition, at least in its state in relation to God, that required such remedial action as incarnation and atonement. To take incarnation and atonement seriously immediately points us to the mystery of God's love and holiness, such that we at least catch a glimpse, however dimly, of a gracious purpose within the divine incomprehensibility, as well as the depth of human need and awfulness in our broken communion with God that must bring us to a point of near terror when we contemplate our situation otherwise.[4] Says McLeod Campbell, "It is that God is contemplated as manifesting clemency and goodness at great cost, and not by a simple act of will that costs nothing, that gives the atonement its great power over the heart of man."[5]

The path to be taken in our inquiry, therefore, is determined by who God is for us in Jesus Christ, and what it is that God wills that we should be,[6] in contradistinction to what we are. That is, we understand the need addressed by the incarnation and the atonement in terms of what it is that God has done for us in Christ, and not by any sense of our own need.[7] We learn from the atonement why it was needed.[8] This is the way of realism in theology, by which we come to some degree of understanding regarding God and us, when incarnation and atonement are seen in their own light, to borrow McLeod Campbell's phrase. "Less than our being alive in that eternal life which is sonship, could not satisfy the Father of our spirits; nor as orphan spirits, as in our alienation from God we are, would less than the gift of that life have met our need."[9] "The fact of sin," McLeod Campbell insists, "is a discovery to the awakened sinner."[10]

Our starting point, then, must be the incarnation, and the approach will be

---

[4]With respect to Calvin on this theme, see Julie Canlis, *Calvin's Ladder: A Spiritual Theology of Ascent and Ascension* (Grand Rapids: Eerdmans, 2010), chap. 2, and especially pp. 83-87.

[5]McLeod Campbell, *Nature of the Atonement*, pp. 48-49. B. A. Gerrish observes, "What moves the sinner to faith is not love simply forgiving, but love forgiving at a cost to itself" (*Tradition and the Modern World: Reformed Theology in the Nineteenth Century*, Zenos Lectures 1977 [Chicago: University of Chicago Press, 1978], p. 82).

[6]McLeod Campbell, *Nature of the Atonement*, p. 20.

[7]Ibid., p. 21.

[8]Ibid., p. 173.

[9]Ibid., p. 96.

[10]Ibid., p. 40.

to reflect on the Savior as person. Our exploration will be with an eye constantly fixed upon what it is that God wills for us in him: in McLeod Campbell's terms, that through Christ we know God as the Father of our spirits, who asks for a filial response from us.[11] This approach, I believe, will allow us in due course to look in wonder upon the extent of the atonement—that is, whether it is a limited or a universal atonement—and to come to an answer when the question is seen in the light of the incarnation. We will not drive back, as it were, into the secret councils of God to find an answer to the question of God's intention. We will, rather, attend to Jesus Christ and seek out the requested answer from the one who is himself the atonement. The plain statement of intent, then, that we will not try to peek behind the back of Christ to a God not known in Christ, but rather will look unto him at all points, seems self-evidently legitimate for a Christian perspective on redemption.

This approach is to be contrasted with the approach that is determined by the work of Christ *when that work is seen instrumentally*—that is, as something external to his person. Such a view need not but will likely tend toward a perspective on the atonement in which God needs to be propitiated in order to be gracious toward us. In such a view the love and forgiveness of God may be seen as the effects of the atonement. Further, an instrumental perspective on the atonement as an external work of Christ, as something that he does rather than having its ground in who he is, implies a corresponding view of our relation to Christ that is developed in terms of an external arrangement. In the scholastic Protestant tradition this is conventionally developed in terms of an imputed righteousness, in which, while we are and remain sinners, God, for Christ's sake, regards us otherwise, lending the doctrine an air of legal fiction, to use McLeod Campbell's arresting image. Starting there, says McLeod Campbell, amounts to an "axiomatic deficit" that undercuts the light that shines from the life of Christ.[12]

On the other hand, it is precisely the union of the incarnation and the atonement that excludes the view that the atonement is reducible to (though it may include) a forensic transaction as the fulfilling of a legal contract,[13] or to

---

[11]Ibid., p. 28.

[12]Ibid., p. 68. This point is brought out helpfully by Leanne Van Dyk, *The Desire of Divine Love: John McLeod Campbell's Doctrine of the Atonement*, Studies in Church History 4 (New York: Peter Lang, 1995), pp. 48, 102.

[13]Thomas F. Torrance, *Atonement: The Person and Work of Christ*, ed. Robert T. Walker (Downers

Christ propitiatingly bearing the cost construed as divinely meted punishment upon Jesus in view of our failing to keep to our human side of the divine-human arrangement. That is, an ontological rather than an instrumental connection must be made between the Christ who makes the atonement and the atonement that he makes. Or, in a different set of images, we look for an organic and personal rather than a mechanical and legal connection between Christ and his atonement and ourselves. According to McLeod Campbell, "by *himself He purged our sins—by the virtue that is in what He is.*"[14] The ontic and noetic aspects of Christology and atonement that we are reaching for here may be put in this way: Christ does who he is. In which case, the problem with the human condition before God, it would appear, is more than our breaking of the divine law, and the atoning work of Christ is more than the amelioration of the consequences. The atonement, it is suggested, must be worked out in terms of our being in an internal relation with Christ, to share in his life and thus to receive adoption as sons (Gal 4:5: *tēn huiothesian apolabōmen*; not, as the NRSV translates, "that we might receive adoption as children," thereby missing the play on words). In this way, the atonement drives in an eschatological direction. We share in the Father-Son relationship, bearing witness to what McLeod Campbell called the "all-including necessity that is revealed to us by the atonement," as expressed in John 14:6, "No one comes to the Father except through me."[15]

The approach we will take perceives that God is not the object of the atonement. God, rather, is the subject who performs the act of forgiveness or atonement.[16] "But if God provides the atonement," argues McLeod Campbell in a stunning insight, "then forgiveness must precede atonement; and the atonement must be the form of the manifestation of the forgiving love of God, not the cause."[17] We find a similar understanding in H. R. Mackintosh: "All that went to the death of Christ, constituting it the definitive self-expression of God towards the sinful, not merely *reveals* God's antecedent forgiving love; it actually *conveys* forgiveness and renders it effective."[18] Understanding the

---

Grove, IL: IVP Academic, 2009), p. 182.

[14]McLeod Campbell, *Nature of the Atonement*, p. 122.

[15]Ibid., p. 150.

[16]Ibid., p. 19.

[17]Ibid., p. 45.

[18]H. R. Mackintosh, *The Christian Experience of Forgiveness* (New York: Harper & Brothers, 1927), p. 214.

nature of the atonement, what it is in itself as the person and life of the Savior as the God who forgives us, as that is unfolded through the filial relationship of the Son to the Father, into which we are incorporated by adoption, leads to an understanding of the universality of the atonement.[19]

Over the next three chapters we will reflect on the relation between Christology and atonement mainly from the perspective of Christology. We will proceed by way of discussions with John McLeod Campbell, H. R. Mackintosh and T. F. Torrance. Our process will lead to a number of interlocking circles that allow for some degree of overlap. The remainder of this chapter will consider aspects of the doctrine of the person of Jesus Christ by asking the question, "Who is the incarnate Savior of the world?" The issue before us is the person of the Son. We will move on from there in the following chapter to reflect on the mystery of Jesus Christ through examination of the relation of the Father and the Son, and the hypostatic union, in which in the unity of his person Jesus was wholly God and fully human. This reflection will point us forward to see that understanding the atonement, from an incarnationalist christological perspective, requires a trinitarian doctrine of God.[20] The third chapter will consider substitution and union under the headings of the doctrines of the magnificent exchange and of our union with Christ. We will see that we must allow the objective orientation of Christology and atonement to call forth an exploration of the relation between Christ and us if we would move successfully beyond McLeod Campbell's critique of too much atonement theory being a "legal fiction."

WHO IS THE INCARNATE SAVIOR OF THE WORLD?

Consideration of the relation between Christology and the atonement means first of all that we begin with the incarnation, with who was born of Mary, and not with discussion of so-called eternal decrees of God, with the divine reign or covenant of law,[21] or with a predetermined set of assumptions concerning God's holiness and righteousness, for example. The question "Who is the incarnate Savior of the world?" immediately and rapidly takes us away from consideration

---

[19]McLeod Campbell, *Nature of the Atonement*, p. 35.
[20]As Calvin says, apart from this only the bare and empty name of God flits about in our brains (*Institutes* 1.13.2).
[21]Thomas F. Torrance, *Scottish Theology: From John Knox to John McLeod Campbell* (Edinburgh: T & T Clark, 1996), p. 297.

of any form of abstract philosophical theism, as well as from a speculative account of human nature as a kind of "something" that the Son adopted as his own. This operating question opens up the doctrine of God in view of Jesus Christ in a manner that allows light to shine on the understanding of the atonement, and it also invites us into critical reflection on the doctrine of the two natures of Christ in traditional doctrine. In other words, the primary concern for our understanding of the atonement is the doctrine of God that arises out of the incarnation, out of God's actual saving event that gives content to who God is as the God who saves in, through and as the man Jesus of Nazareth.

The priority of the "Who?" question in Christology. The basic *fact* of Christian theology is the person of Jesus Christ, God with us, the incarnate, crucified and risen Lord who in his ascension reigns over all things and who will come again. According to Luther, "To this man thou shalt point and say, Here is God."[22] And again, "I have no God, whether in heaven or in earth, and I know of none outside the flesh that lies in the bosom of the Virgin Mary. For elsewhere God is utterly incomprehensible, but comprehensible in the flesh of Christ alone."[23] And from Calvin: "God is comprehended in Christ alone."[24] Or again, more directly relating to the atonement, "If, then, we would be assured that God is pleased with and kindly disposed toward us, we must fix our eyes and minds on Christ alone."[25] And from Barth: "We start out from the fact that through His Word God is actually known and will be known again."[26] And again, "Christology . . . is the touchstone of all knowledge of God, in the Christian sense, the touchstone of all theology."[27]

In Christian faith everything depends on knowing who Jesus Christ is, on what it means that he is confessed as Lord and Savior. If we go astray right here at the beginning by asking the wrong question, we will never grasp the radical heart and significance of the gospel. Christianity's central doctrine— Jesus is Lord!—is given as the answer to the question "Who is the incarnate

---

[22]Cited in Dietrich Bonhoeffer, *The Cost of Discipleship*, trans. R. H. Fuller (London: SCM Press, 1959), p. 223.

[23]Cited in H. R. Mackintosh, *The Doctrine of the Person of Jesus Christ* (1913; repr., Edinburgh: T & T Clark, 1951), p. 231.

[24]Calvin, *Institutes* 2.6.4.

[25]Calvin, *Institutes* 2.16.3.

[26]Karl Barth, *Church Dogmatics* 2.1, trans. G. W. Bromiley, ed. G. W. Bromiley and T. F. Torrance (Edinburgh: T & T Clark, 1957), p. 4.

[27]Karl Barth, *Dogmatics in Outline*, trans. G. T. Thompson (New York: Harper & Row, 1959), p. 66.

Savior of the world?" Biblically, this question comes in a number of forms. John the Baptizer asks, "Are you the one who is to come?" To this Matthew has Jesus immediately reply, "Go and tell John what you hear and see" (Mt 11:3-4). This question is set in terms of the inauguration of the reign of God in and as Jesus. Then there is Jesus' question "Who do you say that I am?" (Mt 16:15), in which the messianic categories are transformed. Finally, Saul of Tarsus asks, "Who are you, Lord?" (Acts 9:5). The struggle behind these questions is the birthing of the movement from Jesus who preached to Jesus who is preached. Here is the origin of Christology.[28]

Brunner and Bonhoeffer on the "Who?" question. The priority of the "Who?" question in Christology is set forth in the work of two twentieth-century theologians, Emil Brunner and Dietrich Bonhoeffer. In his landmark book *The Mediator*, published in English in 1927, Brunner put the issue in this way:

> The question, "*Who* is He?" means the same as the other question: "What has God to say to us in Him?" The one cannot be answered without the other. The first answer to the question: "Who is He?" was this: "He is the Divine Word." Rightly understood, this reply contained the whole truth. . . . When you know who He is, you know who God is. . . . Christ, Who is He? The doctrine of the Church replies: "He is true God and true Man, and for this reason He is the Mediator."[29]

Brunner goes on to note that the church has largely set aside the "Who?" question and replaced it with another: "How does He come to be what He is?" "Thus the question of the being of Christ is replaced by one which concerns His appearance in history.[30] This means that we have quitted the plane of revelation for that of phenomena within history, both moral and religious," comments Brunner.[31] The danger for Christology in asking the wrong questions is that a speculative agenda is imposed. Is the eternal God in Jesus Christ? This question may move us in a Docetic direction, suggesting a divinity that cannot bear flesh. Or, can this man really be God? This question may move us in an Ebionite direction, suggesting that the human person Jesus cannot be God.

---

[28]Jürgen Moltmann, *The Crucified God: The Cross of Christ at the Foundation and Criticism of Christian Theology*, trans. R. A. Wilson and John Bowden (New York: Harper & Row, 1974), p. 115.

[29]Emil Brunner, *The Mediator: A Study of the Central Doctrine of the Christian Faith*, trans. Olive Wyon (Philadelphia: Westminster, 1947), pp. 234-35.

[30]And which, I would add, drifts in a metaphysical direction.

[31]Brunner, *The Mediator*, p. 236.

"Who is the incarnate Savior of the world?" In setting out the priority of the "Who?" question we are instructed even more fully on this point by Dietrich Bonhoeffer. In *Christ the Center* Bonhoeffer opens up for us in a remarkably insightful way the core methodological issues that we deal with in Christology. Because the method of inquiry in theology must be appropriate to its subject, Bonhoeffer's starting point is the required beginning for what today we call a "nonfoundationalist" Christology. That is to say, the Enlightenment philosophers do not set the boundaries for Christian reflections on the identity of Jesus Christ. They do not allocate for us what is allowed to be known or not. Bonhoeffer puts it very clearly: when the word that is other than the human word—the "counter-word," he calls it—"appears in history, no longer as an idea, but as 'Word' become flesh, there is no longer any possibility of assimilating him into the existing order of the human logos. The only real question which now remains is: 'Who are you? Speak for yourself!'"[32] It is this question, "Who are you, Lord?" that Christology is concerned to answer, and that sets our inquiry on its own proper ground—that is, on the ground of Jesus Christ himself. Thus to ask, "How are you possible?"—a question posed on some human ground, a ground other than Jesus Christ—is not adequate, for a question about immanence, says Bonhoeffer, cannot address a reality concerning transcendence. To ask, "How are you possible?" is, we might say, an unscientific question, a question that does not arise out of our knowledge of the subject of study, but one rather that we impose upon it in our attempt to control it. We do not begin Christology with a question about the capacity of history to receive transcendence; rather, we begin with the fact that it did and go on from there, a posteriori. When we ask, "Who are you?" of the incarnate Savior of the world, the answer cannot be given in terms set by the boundaries of human experience or in terms of a prior notion of divinity. The answer can be given only on the ground that the Lord Jesus himself gives, as best we can understand it, as he is attested in the New Testament.

It is only after the fact that Jesus Christ has revealed himself and confronted us, and by his Spirit drawn us into a relationship with himself, that we ask aright, "Who are you, Lord?" The inquiry is conducted a posteriori, on his terms, on the terms by which *he* has established us in relationship to himself.

---

[32]Dietrich Bonhoeffer, *Christ the Center*, trans. Edwin Robertson, Harper's Ministers Paperback Library (SanFrancisco: Harper & Row, 1978), p. 30.

An inquiry conducted on our epistemological terms, terms derived independently of him, is destined to fail. There is no ground for knowing Jesus outside of Jesus himself, and what it means that by his Spirit he has brought us into union with himself, thereby to share in his life. There can be no independent reason for Jesus Christ that might have authority to ratify him as the truth of God.[33] He is self-attesting, in other words. Thus a basic principle in theology is set forth: it is only through God and on God's terms that God can be known. With Jesus Christ, autonomous human reason has reached its limits. Apart from who he is in his own identity and being, and as he gives himself to be known through the proclamation of the church by the agency of the Holy Spirit, Christology as the study of Jesus Christ has no possibility. So it is that the "Who?" question that we put to Christ is a question concerned to discover more fully the identity and meaning of a risen and ascended Lord who has already encountered us, addressed us, and claimed us as his own and, in doing so, is attested by the church as Lord. Thus theology pursues its questions a posteriori rather than a priori. We pursue our christological inquiries after the fact of Christ, and not according to a previously determined metaphysical or epistemological necessity established independently of Jesus Christ, and to which standard of knowing he must be accommodated.

What happens when we are confronted by the risen Word? Says Bonhoeffer, "There are only two ways possible of encountering Jesus: man must die or he must put Jesus to death."[34] For Bonhoeffer, the answer to the "Who?" question means that it is not we who have dealt with Jesus, but rather Jesus who has dealt with us. When the christological question is the question of the human logos, it remains imprisoned in the ambiguity of the question "How?" But when it is given voice in the act of faith, there is real possibility of posing the question "Who?" both of Jesus and of ourselves. Thus the anthropological question "Who am I?" is understood as a derivative question, for in asking "Who?" of Jesus I accept that I have already been encountered from beyond myself by the one who is the truth, and I must now either understand myself in terms of that encounter and surrender to it in faith or else try to force it to be what it is not, which is to live in untruth. In losing Christ I also lose myself.

---

[33]Ibid., p. 32.
[34]Ibid., p. 35.

One final brief and subtle point from Bonhoeffer is important to notice: Christology is not soteriology.[35] We do not know Christ by reading off his identity from his works, as it were. The reason is that he did what he did in the incognito of the incarnation. Argue, on the one hand, that Jesus was a man, and the argument back from his works to his person is ambiguous. Argue, on the other hand, that Jesus was God, and the argument back from history to God is impossible.[36] Thus is set the priority of the christological question over soteriology, of "Who?" over "What?" When we know who Christ is, we will know what it is that he does and what that means. The person and work of Christ are not separated, of course, but they are established in theological method in this way.

The "Who?" question and the incarnation. Who is the incarnate Savior of the world? This, then, is not a quizzical question, speculative in origin. His personhood is not a neutral datum of experience that we can manipulate at will. Rather, in this question we are trying more faithfully to understand who God is who has revealed himself to us, encountered us, and brought us into relationship with himself precisely in, through and as this man, Jesus of Nazareth. It is a question put by faith, not by unfaith. It is a question put *en Christō*, in Christ, and not apart from Christ. It is a heuristic question that arises out of the person of Jesus in his being as the incarnate Savior of the world, already whom we know as Lord. Or to put it differently, in asking "Who is the incarnate Savior of the world?" we affirm that in some measure we already know the answer to what we ask. In the question we seek now to enter more deeply into the reality to which we have already testified in asking the question in the first place, and to test our knowledge in the light of our continuing and deepening inquiry into God in his action toward us in, through and as Jesus Christ. Is what we preach and teach actually faithful to who Jesus is and what he did? It is inasmuch as Jesus Christ has revealed himself to us as the incarnate Savior, and therefore as the answer to our questions, that we pose our questions in order to enter more deeply into knowledge of the one whom we know to be our Savior. Thomas F. Torrance has expressed what we are about here in this way: "In scientific theology we begin with actual knowledge of God, and seek to test and clarify this

---

[35]Ibid., p. 37.
[36]Ibid., p. 39.

knowledge by inquiring carefully into the relation between our knowing God and God Himself in His being and nature."[37]

Clearly, to ask, "Who is the incarnate Savior of the world?" is immediately to enter into the great mystery that is central to Christian faith, the incarnation itself. The church and Christian faith stand or fall on the reality and truth of the incarnation. The human baby of Bethlehem is God. The incarnation is the event in which faith associates the eternal God with a contingent fact of history and attributes a saving significance to it. There seems to be no way around the observation that this central mystery of faith is a miracle. As such, we are forced to free our understanding of God from the vise-like grip of predetermined metaphysical and epistemological categories of thought and allow the subject of our christological inquiry to create his own ground and categories for understanding in our minds. We can know Jesus, and therefore God, on no other basis.

The question "Who are you, Lord?" can be answered only by revelation: "I am Jesus," to which answer the church confesses that Jesus is Lord (2 Cor 4:5). The revelation is his person in historical and ontological union, in empirical and theological union, in hypostatic union. This is Torrance's major opening point in the posthumously published Christology lectures *Incarnation: The Person and Life of Jesus*. Arguably this is the basic christological question, just as the answer is the basic Christian confession. Everything in theology that is Christian follows that form, flowing from the force of the "Who?" question, a question directed to a living Lord who encounters us on his own terms. This is in agreement with Calvin's famous dictum: "God works in his elect in two ways: within through his Spirit; without through his Word."[38] Were we to begin anywhere else than with a Lord who encounters us as the one who through the Spirit is proclaimed in sermon and celebrated in sacrament and, as such, brings us into communion with himself, would not a semideistic axiom already control our thinking? We would be reflecting on a god who does not act in the world, who did not become incarnate, a god who has not and does not bring us into relationship with himself and, as such, a god who, in the nature of the case, remains unknowable. The obverse, however, is the recognition that by asking the "Who?" question arising from being encountered by the living Lord

---

[37]Thomas F. Torrance, *Theological Science* (London: Oxford University Press, 1969), p. 9.
[38]Calvin, *Institutes* 2.5.5.

in the proclamation of the church, a question that includes confession within it, we acknowledge already a personal relatedness, union with Christ as the gift of the Holy Spirit. Being encountered by Jesus Christ is not a neutral datum of experience. Rather, our christological inquiries are put within the framework of faith and confession. The rigorously analytic Scottish theologian John Mc-Intyre insists that in our christological reflections "we are dealing with a person towards whom the proper attitude is not one of scientific curiosity, or detached inquisitiveness, but ultimately one of worship and adoration, trust and obedience."[39] In this case, our inquiries, while critically realistic (in an epistemological sense) and lively—not speculative, theoretical and abstract—are also worshipful and appropriate to Jesus Christ.

The person of Jesus Christ. Let us now hear from two of the Scottish theologians already identified, H. R. Mackintosh and T. F. Torrance, as they lead us to a deeper reflection on the person of Jesus Christ.

H. R. Mackintosh. H. R. Mackintosh's contribution at this point, though somewhat brief, is suggestive of possible development. At the beginning of his preface to the devotional book *The Person of Jesus Christ*, Mackintosh states that the question "Who was Jesus Christ?" is the most urgent question of our time.[40] For the Christian person, the question still stands a century after Mackintosh wrote these words because of what the Christian in faith confesses. According to Mackintosh, we cannot say what the Christian doctrine of God is except as we include Christ in that statement;[41] neither can we, approaching any aspiration to orthodox confession, say who Jesus Christ is except as we include reference to his divinity. In which case, we cannot make any Christian statement concerning God or Jesus Christ that does not now include at every turn reference also to the humanity of Jesus Christ. The real force of the "Who?" question in Christology, however, is not just how we put all this together into a coherent package, but how we understand who he is who comes to us as Savior and Lord. Thus we see the continuing urgency and necessity of christological inquiry for the person of Christian faith. Is Jesus who the New Testament and the church say he is? And given who he is, can I rightly and

---

[39]John McIntyre, *The Shape of Christology* (London: SCM Press, 1966), p. 45.

[40]H. R. Mackintosh, *The Person of Jesus Christ*, ed. T. F. Torrance (1912; repr., Edinburgh: T & T Clark, 2000), p. 3.

[41]H. R. Mackintosh, *The Doctrine of the Person of Jesus Christ*, 2nd ed. (Edinburgh: T & T Clark, 1913), p. 292.

safely give over my life and death to him? The inquiry into the person of Jesus Christ immediately becomes the inquiry into what it means that he is Savior and Lord, not in neutral terms but rather in terms that affect *me*. It is this personal and existential dimension of Christology, perhaps, that Mackintosh has latched on to and highlighted more than most theologians.

This is exactly the move that Mackintosh makes in his discussion of the person of Jesus Christ in his massive *The Doctrine of the Person of Jesus Christ*.[42] Christ's person is to be studied in the medium of redemption (otherwise we are dealing with an abstraction), and in such a manner that person and work, identity and purpose, mutually cast light one upon the other. Especially at the Reformation, Mackintosh suggests, and for Luther and Calvin in particular, redemption was cast in personal form as a relation historically mediated between God and a person.

> Salvation is fellowship with [God]. It rests on the forgiveness of sins, it is appropriated by faith as grateful self-surrender to an infinite object. And Christ is conceived in forms suitable to and worthy of this function. He is the Revealer of God; He is man's Surety and Representative. In Him the eternal Divine truth and love touch us; in Him we are led to the Father; and these two sides of the relationship—God in Him for us, and we in Him for God—at each point condition and harmonize with one another. Thus the great problem re-appears . . . —How must we think of His intrinsic nature in the light of this new conception of His work? Who is Christ, if He thus embodies to sinful men the redeeming grace of the Eternal?[43]

In a stunning phrase, Mackintosh commends his procedure: "His work is but His person in movement."[44] Thus the stage is set for a brief discussion of the person of Christ cast in kinetic soteriological form.

Mackintosh offers four conceptions as the best sort of intuitive guidance regarding the person and place of Jesus Christ in this regard: his ethical supremacy, atonement, union with Christ and revelation.

The discussion of Christ's ethical supremacy appears dated to the contemporary reader, especially with its appeal to conscience. Insofar as the conscience is a socially/culturally mediated construct, it may be an unreliable

---

[42]Ibid., p. 325.
[43]Ibid.
[44]Ibid., p. 326.

guide to eternal virtues. But we can leave it as said, surely, that Christ undoubtedly teaches a way of life and a compendium of values that have divine
authority as the self-revealing speech of the Son of God. To say such, of course,
is to allow that Jesus speaks as God, which directly points us to his person.

Of more interest, I think, are Mackintosh's reflections on the further three
points. Thus, to begin with, the atoning work of Christ is a decisive index—
perhaps we should say *the* defining index—of his person. Mackintosh begins
his brief discussion with a long citation from James Denney's great book *The
Death of Christ*, published in 1902, in which he argues that the doctrine of
the atonement is the proper evangelical foundation of Christology.[45] Thus,
according to Denney, "It is the doctrine of the Atonement which secures for
Christ His place in the gospel, and which makes it inevitable that we should
have a Christology or a doctrine of His Person."[46] The love and mercy that
we see in the gospel record of Jesus, in other words, is the love and mercy of
God. This claim constitutes the ground of the gospel. Faced with Jesus living
and dying, we are faced with the divine sacrifice poured forth in him.
However we may unpack this, the conviction of faith is "that in the sufferings of Christ for our sake God suffered. . . . The impression we receive at
the cross is unintelligible save as in Jesus we behold very God 'in loving
communion with our misery.'"[47]

Now, with echoes of John McLeod Campbell in his ears perhaps, Mackintosh notes the obvious point, that Jesus' condemnation of sin is God's condemnation of sin. In Jesus sin is exposed, reprobated, doomed and sentenced—
what a wonderful series of verbs Mackintosh employs! In doing this and as
such, says Mackintosh, this man is God, for here, as the man Jesus of Nazareth,
there is the meeting of sin with the Eternal. "Only He can forgive sin who
expiates it";[48] this surely is getting near to the mystery of the person of Jesus
Christ, of God acting for us as the man Jesus. There is a divine judgment and
saving action pronounced and enacted at the same time through the medium
of the humanity of Jesus. Thus the great christological question arises as to
how to speak of the miracle of his person as God and human being.

---

[45]Ibid., p. 329.
[46]Ibid., p. 330. Mackintosh merely references "317ff" of Denney's book with no other detail.
[47]Ibid., p. 331.
[48]Ibid.

Mackintosh is briefly at pains to reflect on how the suffering of one person can benefit or savingly embrace and comprehend any other. His answer is to follow Paul and John's Gospel by declining to conceive of Christ as an isolated person and of the Christian as another. Anticipating the next point, union with Christ, Mackintosh suggests that the false step in many theories of the atonement is to abstract the Christian from Christ, thus to emphasize the objective aspect of the atonement at the expense of the subjective. "But if by its very nature all Christian theology is an interpretation of believing experience from within, this oneness with Christ, of which we are conscious, is our [place to stand]; and the attempt to put it even temporarily in abeyance must be ruled out as illegitimate."[49] We will see later how McLeod Campbell tried to hold the objective and subjective aspects of the atonement together (although he is routinely criticized for collapsing the objective into the subjective); there was undoubtedly a dominant tendency in post-Reformation Scottish theology to lean toward the objectivity of the atoning work of Christ interpreted in forensic terms, which was then applied by way of imputation. Although Mackintosh does not cite Calvin, familiar sentences may not have been far from his mind: "As long as Christ remains outside of us, and we are separated from him, all that he has suffered and done for the salvation of the human race remains useless and of no value for us. Therefore, to share with us what he has received from the Father he had to become ours and to dwell with us."[50] Like McLeod Campbell, and Denney for that matter, Mackintosh declines to treat the atonement apart from his own experience of the saving Christ and his confession of faith in him. For Mackintosh, there is no adequate and satisfying doctrine of the atonement that is not also the account of the Christian experience of forgiveness. This is a theme to which I will devote a chapter in due course.

For now, Mackintosh leaves us with the bold affirmation of faith that God meets us savingly with forgiveness of sins in, through and as the man Jesus, who joins us to himself in such a manner that there is no Christian understanding of ourselves apart from union with Christ as the work of the Holy Spirit, and no understanding of Christ and his work apart from the experience of being forgiven and of our being gathered into one body in him. With this before us, we turn now to the third of Mackintosh's four conceptions as the

---

[49]Ibid., pp. 332-33.
[50]Calvin, *Institutes* 3.1.1.

best sort of intuitive guidance regarding the person and place of Jesus Christ: what he refers to as the Christian experience of vital union with Christ.

Mackintosh had already published an essay on union with Christ three years before he published his Christology,[51] and the two discussions are more or less identical with respect to content, although the latter is shorter. The repetition surely suggests the importance of the conception in his theology. In the Christology Mackintosh surfaces the conception of union with Christ in his discussion of the Christology of Paul, commenting that "no part of the apostle's teaching has a more vital bearing on his thought of the Exalted One than his mystic conception of the believer's union with Christ."[52] What follows appears to be a brief account of Adolf Deissmann's early work on the New Testament formula "in Christ Jesus," published in 1892, although it is not cited. Mackintosh, who was fluent in German and was a frequent visitor to Germany, may be supposed to have been familiar with this work and seems to have so appropriated it for himself that he can now claim the concept as his own. It is as if Christ were the air or element within which the Christian moved and lived. And this intimate sense of being in relationship with the living Christ, as we will see fully later on, is a marked, even a dominant, feature of both his theology and piety. The Christian lives in intimacy with Christ, as in a relation of spirit to spirit, yet this is not individualistically realized, for in such relationship the Christian is part of the corporate body of Christ. This "faith-mysticism" reflects a new order of being characterized equally by transcendence and mystic vital union. It is not putting it too strongly, Mackintosh argues, to say that for Paul, "union with Christ" is a brief name for all that the apostles mean by salvation.[53]

The locus classicus is Galatians 2:19-20: "I have been crucified with Christ, and it is no longer I who live, Christ lives in me" (from the translation used by Mackintosh). He comments, "No doubt the verse was written at a white heat. . . . Language has broken down under the intolerable strain, and . . . words which at their best must always be general are unequal to expressing a fact that is totally unparalleled. . . . [Paul] stands for a truly spiritual union;

---

[51]H. R. Mackintosh, "The Unio Mystica as a Theological Conception," in *Some Aspects of Christian Belief* (New York: George H. Doran, n.d. [preface, 1923]), pp. 99-120. The essay is a reprint of its publication in *The Expositor* 7 (February 1909): 138-55.

[52]Mackintosh, *Doctrine of the Person*, p. 56.

[53]Ibid., p. 334.

a reciprocal appropriation and interpenetration of spirit by spirit."[54] Thus far has Mackintosh moved away from any thought of a legal transference of status before God to the thought, rather, of personal incorporation into Christ. This now is the entirely dominant motif.

But also in John, Mackintosh finds that union with Christ is the secret of redemption. Thus, for example, he cites 1 John 2:24: "If that which ye heard from the beginning abide in you, ye also shall abide in the Son and in the Father." Christ is "the Vine," onto which believers are grafted as living branches; he is "the Bread of Life," by eating which believers live forever. As with Paul, Mackintosh argues, union with Christ can be contemplated from either side: "you in me" and "I in you."[55] "In all such passages we feel that the distinction between Christology and soteriology, never more than provisional anyhow, has simply disappeared. . . . [Christ] is definable as the Person who can thus be our inward Life, while on the other hand it is because He is this universal Person that His relation to us can be of this interior kind."[56]

What does this mean for our understanding of the person of Christ? For Mackintosh, it means this: "To have the Son is to have the Father also. Union with Christ is in no sense a preliminary step to union with God, or a preparation for it which may be ignored subsequently to the attainment of the real goal; it is union with God *per se*."[57] Mackintosh answers the question "Who is the incarnate Savior of the world?" with this conception of union with Christ. "Christian experience, then, as summarily described by the term mystic union, implies a Saviour at once Divine and human."[58]

The final insight into the person of Christ arises from the conviction that Christ is the perfect revelation of the Father. Here Mackintosh, in a mere handful of pages, swoops down on his subject matter with speed and acuity. His major move we might call the aggressive statement of the christological doctrine of God. In Christ, God is revealed in terms of Christ's humanity. "When we inquire as to the precise content of the term 'God' for our minds, and ask how it has been authenticated, we discover, it may be with some surprise, that without reasoning we have transferred to God the features of

---

[54]Ibid., p. 335.
[55]Ibid., p. 337.
[56]Ibid.
[57]Ibid., p. 338.
[58]Ibid., pp. 339-40.

Christ—holy and almighty love."[59] Calvin's axiomatic statement in this regard comes to mind: "God is comprehended in Christ alone."[60] What does this tell us of the person of Christ? "Only He can reveal perfectly who *is* what He reveals."[61] Otherwise, the corollary must follow: we do not know God. Christ does not reveal truths about God; Christ reveals God because he is God. There is no God hidden behind the back of Christ (an image often used by T. F. Torrance), a God other than the God we meet as the man Jesus, God as a general theistic assumption alongside of whom we might place Christ, as in the phrase "God and Christ." Christian faith attests that when we deal with Jesus, we are dealing with God personally present in the power and mystery of the Holy Spirit. Christ is one with God, whom he revealed. Thus the Christian experience of revelation leads Mackintosh to a certain interpretation of his person.

Mackintosh, rightly in my view, argues that if the work of Christ illumes his person, the converse also holds good.[62] Especially we find this to be the case in John's Gospel. The life of Jesus is presented in terms that by "nature" he was the Son of God, the eternal Logos: the Word became flesh (Jn 1:14).

> If, as we have seen, the work is the *ratio cognoscendi* [something by means of which a thing is known] of the nature, not less true is it that the nature is the *ratio essendi* [the ground of the existence of a thing] of the work. . . . Hence the positivism which insists only on the facts of Jesus' recorded life, but will tolerate no Christology, does not even apprehend the facts in their proper fulness and significance.[63]

The ground of knowledge of Christ in his life and ministry and the ground of his being (given as the answer to the "Who?" question) have concrete and intelligible reality only as they define each other in the unity of his person as that is given for us to know and experience. Only in this way can we know the Father's heart, and only a person, Jesus Christ, can show us a personal God, as the Father is known only in the Son.[64] "Eternity or time— do we have to choose? What if Christ belongs to both at once! What if he

---

[59]Ibid., p. 340.
[60]Calvin, *Institutes* 2.6.4.
[61]Mackintosh, *Doctrine of the Person*, p. 341.
[62]Ibid.
[63]Ibid., p. 342.
[64]Mackintosh, *Person of Jesus Christ*, p. 46.

is as old as the saving love of God, yet emerging into history at a definite spot in the long past!"[65]

This brings our conversation with Mackintosh to a close for now. We have before us a fusion of piety and theology, of experience and thought, regarding the person of Christ. There is nothing of cold analysis, of deduction, of play with scholastic constructs. There is rather the closest relation between the narrative and experience of faith in Christ and the argument concerning his divine person as God with us and for us in the flesh of his humanity. At all points it reads as a theology of the church at work in its thinking and preaching and not as an academic task for its own sake. We will find this fusion in each of our conversation partners as we work our way along, though each one, of course, speaks in his own voice. This manner of doing our theology is here commended as faithful to the subject of faith. Throughout, Mackintosh's voice has been calm, quietly thoughtful and mostly noncombative.

T. F. Torrance. As Mackintosh was mostly brief in length and gentle in tone, Torrance is fecund, lengthy to the point of prolixity, and relentlessly intense and encyclopedic (and exhausting) in style. With Torrance we enter a world where the theologian is ferociously battling for the integrity and faithfulness of theology, but not against the detractors of Christian faith and theology. His is a combat on behalf of the classically construed faith of the church catholic, most certainly critically received, but also under attack from the very theologians whose job it is to speak the truth of Jesus Christ into the present world with energy, intelligence, imagination and love, but many of whom he regards as failing to do so. With Torrance we enter a world of theological science (his image), of theology as *kata physin*,[66] theology developed according to the nature of the subject of inquiry: God as Father, Son and Holy Spirit, given for our salvation and known through Jesus Christ. This theology is assertive and kergymatic, abundant with confidence and conviction, prone to soaring flights of generality, yet with close attention to detail.

Since this book is not about Torrance's theology but is a contemporary construction of Christology and atonement as that arises in consideration with our three theologians, what follows here and elsewhere is not a com-

---

[65]Ibid., p. 48.

[66]Torrance often uses the Greek notion of *kata physin*, knowledge according to the nature of something.

prehensive account of Torrance on the subjects under discussion. It is, rather, a reflection on representative selections, but selections that intend to be faithful cross sections and that introduce his way of theology. To that end we will look at Torrance on procedure in Christology to gain a sense of his theology as dogmatics, and at his discussion of the incarnation, which will include his remarks on the virgin birth. Subsequent chapters will also deal with Torrance on the person of Christ, but under different headings as we continue to construct our interlocking circles.

First, we look at Torrance on procedure in Christology. Torrance published widely on the nature of theology, its methods of inquiry and on theological epistemology, in conversation especially with the history and philosophy of science current during his lifetime. The opening sentence to his book *Incarnation* provides a basic theme note found in much of that work: "Our task in christology is to yield the obedience of our mind to what is given, which is God's basic self-revelation in its objective reality, Jesus Christ."[67] In general terms, then, knowledge is a work of obedience as the object of our knowledge gives itself to be known insofar as it is unveiled under investigation. Especially when we seek to know God, however, that knowledge can be only on God's terms, given for us in its own authority and self-sufficiency. We cannot batter or coerce God, as it were, demanding that God tell us what we want to know. Neither can God's self-revelation be subject to an external or independent foundation for knowledge. To what outside the lordship of Jesus Christ could one appeal for a warrant for knowledge, as if his lordship entailed an epistemological frontier beyond which it did not apply? Knowledge of God through God's self-revelation in its objective reality, Jesus Christ, is, we might say, its own thing, without any corresponding analogy in human experience or knowledge. It fits no prior category for understanding, for the remarkable thing is that God gives himself to be known out of pure grace and freedom. "We have no capacity or power in ourselves giving us the ability to have mastery over this fact. In the very act of our knowing Christ he is the master, we are the mastered."[68] Revelation, above all else, is received in faith, and the mode of reception is gratitude and wonder.

---

[67]Thomas F. Torrance, *Incarnation: The Person and Life of Christ*, ed. Robert T. Walker (Downers Grove, IL: IVP Academic, 2008), p. 1.
[68]Ibid., p. 2.

Thus the starting point for Christology, according to Torrance, is the self-givenness of Jesus Christ, and this event has mystery as its essential character. How we know him is beyond our powers to grasp. In faith, which is an act of the Holy Spirit upon us yet also an act of trusting obedience of heart and mind, we confess that when we are encountered by Jesus Christ, he confronts us as God and a man in the unity of his one person. This is the fundamental mystery of Christian faith, to be adored rather than picked apart. Torrance says,

> Our theological task is to begin with awareness and acknowledgement of that mystery as the actual object which we seek to know theologically. That is, we seek to clarify our knowledge of this mystery—but if we are to be true and faithful to it, if we are to be scientific and rational, that is, to behave in terms of the nature of this mystery that confronts us, we must not begin by denying its mystery character or by transmuting it into something non-mysterious.... We must wrestle with it, inquire of it, be obedient to it, and seek in every way to let it *declare itself* to us.[69]

Scientific thinking, whether in theology or the natural sciences, is thinking in the way that that which is before us compels us to think, in order to think according to its nature and activity as they are disclosed under questioning that is appropriate to what it is. Thus science, in a general way, "refers to the kind of knowledge which is forced upon us when we are *true* to the facts we are up against.... In science we ask questions and answer them under the compulsion of what is 'over against us,' and so let our thoughts take shape *in accordance with the nature of what we experience* and under its pressure upon us."[70] Such thinking, then, is bound to its subject of inquiry, while our conclusions, given that our expressions of it always in some manner fall short of its reality, are open-ended, ever revisable as our knowing penetrates more deeply into that which is known. There is something here with which we have to do but that is never reducible to our sentences, for truth in real knowledge resides in that to which we refer rather than in the references themselves, in that which is signified rather than in the sign that signifies. A scientist cannot just invent a universe to his or her liking—

---

[69]Ibid., p. 3. It is helpful perhaps to lay alongside this statement the observation by David Willis that the mystery of the incarnation means it grows in hiddenness the more we know it, while the more we are engaged by the hiddenness, the more we are encountered by its disclosive power (*Clues to the Nicene Creed: A Brief Outline of the Faith* [Grand Rapids: Eerdmans, 2005], p. 78).

[70]Torrance, *Incarnation*, pp. 4-5.

that rightly is called science *fiction*. In theology too we operate within the bounds of God's self-disclosure, within the parameters laid down by God concerning both what we can know and how we can know the things of God. Knowledge of God is grounded in God's own action, God's self-presentation toward us, for God does not reveal things about God; rather, God reveals God. Knowledge from revelation is not data, but rather has at its heart knowledge of our being in relationship with God. Because God is God and God reveals God, the possibility for knowledge of God cannot be discussed apart from actually knowing God in an attitude of faith and worship and service.

Theology is bound to its given object, Jesus Christ, God's Word addressing us, and we are required to think about this in a manner appropriate to the way in which he is given for us in history.[71] In theology, as in any science, reason is under obedience; but in this case, reason is under obedience to God's grace and the way of that grace incarnate in history as the man Jesus of Nazareth. Thus, "We can only start from the given, where the historical and the theological are in indissoluble union in Christ."[72] This given is of cardinal importance for Torrance: Jesus Christ is wholly God; Jesus Christ is fully human; Jesus Christ is one person. This is the fundamental mystery of his person.

In the next chapter we will dwell at some length on the homoousial relation[73] between Christ and the Father in Torrance's theology. For now, I emphasize that we must start with the whole mystery of Christ, not from one aspect of his mystery, neither cutting off his divinity from his humanity in order to apprehend the "historical" Jesus nor cutting off the historical Jesus in order to apprehend him in his transcendence, forgetting that even in his ascension he carries his "self-same body," his history, into the presence of the Father (Scots Confession [1560]). We have before us, in Jesus Christ, God in time, God as a man, and God active in history,[74] thereby disavowing any deistic disjunction between God and history. Thus the whole gospel is entailed with this Jesus Christ, and what we have to deal with in Christology first of all, then, is incarnation, in which the unity of God and humankind comes into history as the man Jesus, established from the side of God, for our salvation

---

[71] Ibid., p. 6.
[72] Ibid., p. 7.
[73] This is a Torrance construction found throughout his writing. The term refers to the Nicene *homoousios tō Patri*, where the Son is stated to be one in being with the Father.
[74] Torrance, *Incarnation*, p. 8.

and knowledge of God through revelation. All attempts to start Christology somewhere else than with the given person of Jesus Christ fail to deal seriously with this God-established unity as wholly God and fully human. We begin with its "thusness" in history, so to say. In sum: "We must face with utter and candid honesty the New Testament presentation of Christ to us, not as a purely historical figure, nor as a purely transcendental theophany, but as God and man."[75] Torrance will often say that what we have before us in Christology, in other words, is the dogmatic Christ, Christ as he is, at once the historical and theological Christ, and to whom we offer the obedience of our minds. The New Testament knows of no other Jesus than Jesus within the complex personal unity of historical man and spiritual event.

In an early account Torrance makes a similar point when he refers to the ontic and noetic (being and knowing) aspects of Christology wherein Christ, clothed with his humanity, proclaims his message in word, life and deed. Ontically, Christ is in his humanity not only the author and agent of our salvation, but also in *himself in our flesh* the source and substance of it.[76] Here the reference is to the saving significance of his person given as the humanity of Christ, to who he is as God and Savior as the man Jesus. Jesus Christ himself is the atonement. Noetically, however, Christ comes to us with his own Word and self-revelation, as his grace toward and love of us are lived out amid human history. Here Torrance is referring to knowledge of Christ insofar as we know him as the Christ who offers up himself in his ministry of revelation and reconciliation. Following Calvin, Torrance insists that "Christ cannot be separated from His mission of Revelation and Reconciliation or His Mediatorship, and therefore we cannot know Him 'naked,' as it were, without his 'clothing.' The only Christ we know is Christ clothed with His Gospel, and that is Christ with all His human life and historical acts and His self-communication to us through them."[77] It is in the unity of Christ and his ministry that knowledge of God is bounded by the manner in which God gives himself to be known in Christ for us and for our salvation. "It is precisely in that very togetherness of Christ and His graces in

---

[75]Ibid. p. 10.

[76]Thomas F. Torrance, introduction to *The School of Faith: The Catechisms of the Reformed Church* (New York: Harper, 1959), p. lxxxii.

[77]Ibid., p. lxxxiii.

the constitution of His own Person as the incarnate Son and Saviour that we have the foundation for a full and proper Christology."[78]

For Torrance, we know the mystery of Christ according to the way in which he presents himself through the apostolic kerygma *kata Pneuma*— the apostolic testimony according to the Spirit.[79] The dogmatics of Christology is the knowledge of Christ in this way. Thus, while the language and tone here are very different from those of H. R. Mackintosh, we find in Torrance once again the combination of thought and piety, theology and faith, conjoined as the mode of approach to the mystery of Jesus Christ.

Before we move on to Torrance on the incarnation, a few words of review are appropriate, for he is not without his critics. Torrance is rightly called a theological realist.[80] For him, this means that theology makes truth claims about God. Our language about God in some manner corresponds to God, and as such it reaches beyond, but surely not away from, traditions of faith and personal experiences of God. Torrance believes that theological knowledge is more than the phenomenology of church tradition or personal experience. Truth claims are made, and there is some kind of connection between our language and the subject under discussion. Torrance believes, and argues passionately, that the theologian can break through the cultural constrictions that limit us to stubborn contextuality, and even through the theologian's sin, because in Christ God has come redemptively and revealingly to us in history. Rationality, for Torrance, is not limited to inventive categories of mind, but rather resides in God, who as Logos incarnate has made God known, and to whom we must give the obedience of faith. That phrase, "the obedience of faith" (*hypakoē pisteōs* [Rom 1:5; 16:26]), plays like a backbeat in Torrance's theology. The ground for coherence in theology does not lie in the humanly logical arrangements of arguments, but neither is coherence confounded, for God reveals God, who graciously chooses to be known by us. And that really is the point: God chooses to be known by us.

Torrance, it can be said, exhibits a tendency toward a kind of revelational positivism, while acknowledging the subject-object relations insisted on by

---

[78]Ibid.

[79]Torrance, *Incarnation*, p. 30.

[80]Sue Patterson, *Realist Christian Theology in a Postmodern Age*, Cambridge Studies in Christian Doctrine 2 (Cambridge: Cambridge University Press, 1999), p. 1.

critical postmodernity, in which the Kantian "turn to the subject" means that our experience in the world includes a degree of description from which we cannot escape.[81] To put that differently, Torrance, on the ground of union with Christ, believes that we can penetrate far into the being of God insofar as God gives himself to be known by us in Christ, without being irretrievably trapped in all-too-human cultural and linguistic creations. We know more than we can say. The question is whether Torrance has gone too far in the direction of objectivism.[82] Is there a lack of epistemological restraint, even of epistemological humility? Perhaps, at times, Torrance can seem to go where angels fear to tread. Yet, given the subject-object relations of a knower and something known, which always include contextuality and the limits of language, given that God seeks to be known as God and not remain tangled in a knot with us in which neither God nor ourselves can be distinguished, and given that the ground of rationality is the Logos incarnate as the man Jesus, must we not dare to say that our theology can really speak more rather than less faithfully of God? As such, our theological constructs are never the truth of God; they are offered repentantly insofar as they fall short. Even so, there is a moving forward in knowledge because, once again, God wills to be known by us. Is not the very concept of revelation, granted that it is never received absent interpretation, up for sale otherwise? Is not the alternative danger that God in fact remains mute? That revelation is given in a context- and language-constructed world does not mean that it is somehow less than revelation. Or to put that differently, God is a living God who intrudes into our place that we may know God as God who breaks through to us, even if our words about God remain inadequate and, as often as not, sinful. Surely to say otherwise would be a sin against the Holy Spirit, who joins us to Christ and mediates to our minds knowledge of God.

Now we turn to look at Torrance on the incarnation. Jesus Christ himself is the atonement, and there is no knowledge of a Christ who is not Savior—knowledge, that is, of a "merely" historical Jesus. When we come to reflect on his conception and birth as the beginning of his incarnate person, we do so recognizing that this is as much about God's saving purpose as it is Christology. As I have said, there is no Christ, in any aspect, who is not at once

---

[81]Ibid., p. 14.
[82]See George Hunsinger, cited in D. Paul La Montagne, *Barth and Rationality: Critical Realism in Theology* (Eugene, OR: Cascade Books, 2012), pp. 173-74.

revelation and atonement. Atonement is not to be left for the end of the christological account but rather belongs in the account from the beginning.

Torrance begins his teaching on the incarnation with a discussion of the incarnation and the old Israel,[83] and in this way he interprets Israel's story from the perspective of the incarnation. It would take us farther afield than is needful to recapitulate Torrance's presentation in detail. But a couple of brief notes are in order. First, the discussion shows Torrance's intention to be a biblical theologian. His review of the Old Testament background to the incarnation sets the discussion of Jesus' birth in the long context of salvation history, as "God selects one particular people, the Jews, and in that people he works within humanity, preparing for the incarnation of the beloved Son of God. Thus the story of Israel is *the prehistory of the incarnation* of the Son of God. Jesus is born through the womb of Israel and within Israel through the womb of the virgin Mary."[84] Torrance presents us with Jesus the son of Israel, who must be apprehended within that context. "Thus the knowledge of God, of Christ, and of the Jews are *all bound up inseparably together.*"[85] The knowledge of God in Christ comes to us through the Jewish Scriptures of the Old Testament, as well as through the Jewish Scriptures of the New Testament church. "The supreme instrument of God for the salvation of the world is Israel, and out of the womb of Israel, Jesus, the Jew from Nazareth . . . very God himself, come in person."[86]

Christology surely must yield to the fact that Jesus' textbook was the Hebrew Scriptures that came from a people and shaped a people, in a kind of continuous dialectical dance, reflecting their sense of God with them, amid all the travails of obedience and disobedience. Jesus' identity was shaped by that history and the interpretation of that history through a living library that formed their central, people-defining worship of God. Luke's account of the beginning of the Nazarean ministry in Jesus' home synagogue sums this up with the familiar words following the reading of the scroll of Isaiah 61: "Today this scripture has been fulfilled in your hearing" (Lk 4:21).

The second point that Torrance makes regarding the incarnation and the

---

[83]Torrance, *Incarnation*, pp. 37-56.
[84]Ibid., pp. 40-41.
[85]Ibid., p. 43.
[86]Ibid., p. 44.

old Israel is an extended reflection on the Christian doctrine of Israel that has the form of a systematic attempt to hold together Christology, atonement and Israel with Romans 9. This material appears in a number of places in Torrance's published writings, spanning his career.[87] One must judge it to have been of some importance for him. In his book *Incarnation* the argument is developed through twelve headings, though other presentations of the same material omit these. Nevertheless, this represents some penetrating theological reflection that at times edges toward being disturbing. I will not here lay out the detail of the argument, but I will note the conclusion (to do otherwise would take us too much away from the trajectory of this chapter).

Israel was elected by God to be the instrument of divine love for the redemption of the whole world. That election reached its climax in the incarnation, for in Christ election and substitution combined with a view to universal redemption.

> In Jesus Christ, it is revealed that the *election* of one for all becomes salvation for all in the *rejection* of one for all. . . . The election of Israel as an instrument of the divine reconciliation, an instrument which was to be used in its very refusal of grace so that in its midst the ultimate self-giving of God might take place, meant . . . that Israel was elected to act in a representative capacity for all people in its rejection of Christ. The consequent rejection of Israel is to be understood in the light of the substitution of Israel for all other people.[88]

That statement, on any reckoning, is quite remarkable in its theological audacity and is a summary of Torrance's argument. There is something terrible here about the utter awfulness of sin, and Israel's terrible burden borne for us. Israel carries humanity's sin vicariously. Jesus' incarnation means not just the judgment of God on human sin, and God's salvation, but that this happened within Israel such that "Israel could only fulfill the gracious purpose of God by rejecting Christ."[89] Israel, as it were, especially at the crucifixion, stands in for all human hatred of God's grace as Christ bore the guilt of Israel, who here represents humankind at its very worst in rebellion against God.

---

[87]Ibid., pp. 44-56; Thomas F. Torrance, *Conflict and Agreement in the Church*, vol. 1, *Order and Disorder* (London: Lutterworth, 1959), pp. 287-98; idem, *The Mediation of Christ* (Grand Rapids: Eerdmans, 1983), chap. 2.

[88]Torrance, *Incarnation*, p. 52.

[89]Ibid., p. 53.

Torrance nevertheless insists that even in Israel's rejection of Christ, God's covenant with Israel remains: "The rejection of Israel as a people is only to be understood in the light of the substitutionary nature of the cross, for Israel's rejection is bound up with the atoning rejection of the man on the cross, or rather in his acceptance of the sentence of our rejection."[90] Torrance comments that Paul did not hesitate to speak of the rejection of Israel as the reconciling of the world in a manner almost identical with the assertion that by the death of Jesus we were reconciled to God. God used Israel's rejection of Christ in order to bring forth salvation for all. In all this, however, Israel is held fast by God's covenant, albeit in the shadow of the cross. As such, Israel's rejecting Christ in our place—rejecting Christ for us as a substitute for our rejection of God—also means Israel's restoration to life as through the darkness the people of God's terrible election will come to behold the light of the resurrection, and all Israel will be saved. Thus God is faithful to God's covenant with Israel. In this way, says Torrance, Israel has a unique mission from God for the world, "for by his election of Israel God has once and for all bound up the salvation of mankind with Israel."[91] But, we might add, at a terrible cost to Israel.

What are we to make of this? In his travel commitments, conversation partners, as well as throughout his writing, Torrance was a stubborn opponent of anti-Semitism. His task here is a *theological* account of Israel with respect to understanding the incarnation. In fact, Torrance never mentions the Jews in his discussion, only Israel, and as a theological concept, albeit they remain real people. Further, he seems to be following Paul's lead, especially in Romans 9–11. And there is virtue in a theological interpretation of Israel; in fact, it should not be avoided in any attempt at a complete theology of the incarnation. One ventures to wonder, however, if Torrance has just gone a bit too far into a mystery that may be best left opaque. On the other hand—and this is the point of briefly outlining this discussion—what Torrance has done is use the dogmatic foundation intrinsic to Christology: as the man Jesus Christ, God is at work personally and directly in redemption, and this means at every turn having to take that history with utter seriousness. Israel is not a spectator to God's redemption, either throughout their history or through incarnation and atonement. Israel was not sidelined

---

[90]Ibid., p. 54.
[91]Ibid., p. 56.

to serve merely as a passive context for the person and work of Christ. On-tologically, we might suggest, Israel, then as now, is a theological entity, and not only to be apprehended phenomenologically as a religious, racial, ethnic or political entity. Israel's election, and here, election vicariously to reject Christ and be judged by God, is deeply and terribly woven into the divine mystery of redemption. Torrance, I believe, has here been faithful to his dogmatic instinct and tried to bring light to bear in a place where there still remains the darkness of unknowing. When we pose the question "Who is the incarnate Savior of the world?" Torrance has reminded us that Israel is always part of the answer, even if Israel's role is only dimly understood.

As we turn from Israel to Torrance's teaching on the Word made flesh, once again we are confronted with a huge amount of detail in Torrance's account of the incarnation, and selection is required. But some overarching themes are detected and can be mentioned briefly as an introduction.

First, the act of God the Son and the act of God the Word is one act, for revelation and reconciliation belong indissolubly together.[92] This theme re-peats throughout Torrance's work. As Son, God comes to effect reconciliation; as Word, God comes as revelation. The hypostatic or personal unity between reconciliation and revelation is a point of cardinal importance. Second, God comes as reconciliation and revelation in Jesus Christ by taking on sinful human flesh. By way of exchange, *katallagē*, substitution, he who knew no sin in the flesh becomes sin-bearer for us. This is the heart of the atonement, and it begins with the incarnation.[93] Note that Christ in the incarnation assumes not some kind of ideal humanity, but precisely humanity under judgment by God because of sin. This is humanity in its rebellion and alienation from God.

Third, following an Athanasian Christology, Torrance argues that in being made flesh for us, Christ is both the Word of God addressed to us and God's Word received, obeyed and lived out in active answer and response to God's truth. Thus from God and from within humanity Christ is God for us and humankind faithfully for God in the unity of his person. Correspondingly, too much in atonement theology has been made of the passive obedience of Christ and too little of the active obedience of Christ. For if salvation is in Christ, it must mean much more than the distillation of atonement into his death, but

---

[92]Ibid., p. 57.
[93]Ibid., p. 63.

must include his life as well. We will come back to this bidirectional or dual-action Christology more fully in due course. Fourth, the whole incarnational movement is represented as the descent and ascent of Christ, from incarnation to ascension. For Christ is at once the descent of God into our midst and the ascent from within our humanity back to communion with the Father.

And fifth, God becomes flesh, but does so without ceasing to be the eternal Word and Son of God. Clearly this is a miraculous event in which the eternal becomes temporal for us. Christ does so under the form of a servant, under the form of veiling himself. The locus classicus is Philippians 2:5-11. According to Torrance, there is no ground for suggesting a metaphysical change in God the Son.[94] *Kenōsis* (Phil 2:7: *heauton ekenōsen*, "he emptied himself") designates the redemptive descent of the Son into the flesh of our humanity, and in becoming human, even in his veiling, the Son did not empty himself of all of his divine properties and attributes. At this point Torrance is right, I believe, not to answer how the Word became flesh. "*How* recedes into the divine nature of the Son of God and is beyond our observation and understanding."[95] We must be prepared to leave this as mystery, for the New Testament itself offers no explanation. The point is that in the incarnation God comes among us as the man Jesus, as wholly God and fully human.

The heart of the matter in answer to our question "Who is the incarnate Savior of the world?" clearly is Christ's birth into our humanity, and Torrance gives it a whole chapter in his book *Incarnation*. The eternal Word and Son became human without ceasing to be God, and on this ground we know God and are delivered from our sins. Torrance presents the once-for-all union between God and humankind in Jesus Christ in a remarkable theology of the virgin birth, and to this we now turn to bring this chapter to a close.

Torrance begins by reasserting the mystery of Christ's birth into our humanity.[96] The conception and birth of Jesus, given what I have presented regarding the person of Christ, is inconceivable by human thought. However we approach this, we are confronted stubbornly with a miracle. It may be acknowledged with wonder and thankfulness, but not explained, for explanation requires some degree of sympathetic connection with that which we

---

[94]Ibid., pp. 75-76.
[95]Ibid., p. 95.
[96]For this account, ibid., pp. 87-104.

apprehend. If we may understand it at all in some manner, it will be in terms of its own light.

Both Matthew and Luke give an account of Jesus' miraculous conception and birth, while clearly noting his human origin through Mary. In Matthew, Jesus is son of Joseph at the direction of God, thus setting him as a son of David. Genealogically, both Gospels, however, make clear that Jesus was not the biological son of Joseph. Thereafter, Joseph mostly is of little importance in the account, and there is no mention of him in Mark. Mark also makes no mention of the virgin birth. In fact, Torrance notes that after the completion of the accounts of the birth of Jesus, no mention is made of the virgin birth again, and Luke records no account of it in the preaching of the early church in the book of Acts.

Torrance does not address directly what we can make of this, but in his discussions of John and Paul he seems to suggest that the doctrines of the divine generation of Jesus and of the virgin birth were deeply, although subtly, woven into the mind of the church from the earliest days. When Torrance turns to John, he refers to a verse where explicit reference is made to the virgin birth, but not often noted as such, John 1:13. The whole sentence reads, "But to all who received him, who believed in his name, he gave power to become children of God, who were born, not of blood or of the will of the flesh or of the will of man, but of God." "Who were born" or "Who was born"—singular or plural? A literal translation might read, "born not of *bloods* [a reference to Ezek 16:6], nor of the will of the flesh, nor of a husband [*andros*, not *anthrōpou*, which would indicate humankind], but of God." While most manuscripts going back to the fifth century record a plural reading, likely referring to all who believe in Jesus Christ, Torrance argues that there is considerable patristic evidence, going back to the second and third centuries, that records a singular reading. In this case the reference is to Jesus,[97] and that singular reading seems to make more sense of the whole sentence. Torrance makes explicit reference to Tertullian (*On the Flesh of Christ* 19, 24), who suggests that the Valentinians had corrupted the text, for they did not like the idea of the virgin birth.

> If the text is to be read in the singular, then we have here in the fourth Gospel
> quite explicit reference to the virgin birth of Jesus. It must be in line with this

---

[97]Ibid., p. 90.

that the Johannine "only-begotten Son" [Jn 1:14, 18; 3:16] is to be understood, as well as the references in John 3 to being "born from above" (*anōthen*) which has primary objective reference to Christ himself.[98]

Further, Torrance briefly discusses 1 John 5:18 to add to his argument: "We know that those who are born of God do not sin, but the one who was born of God protects them." The last reference is certainly to Christ. It is upon Christ's unique conception and birth that our own spiritual conception and birth depend, for we are given to share in his birth. Overtones of the doctrines of baptism and the atonement are clear to hear. Torrance makes the connection here that baptism rests upon the virgin birth of Christ as well as upon his death and resurrection. Here he follows Irenaeus, who used John 1:13 in the singular, in reference to Christ, and there also gave us the earliest doctrinal account of infant baptism.[99] We do not have here a watertight argument for the doctrine of the virgin birth in John, but a case is put forward that seems to have merit.

Coming to a brief discussion of Paul on the matter, Torrance begins with the Adam-Christ relation. Christ is the second Adam. But while Adam came into existence from the earth *but* at the hand of God (the Septuagint has *ginesthai* at Gen 2:7), Christ came into existence from heaven sent from God (1 Cor 15:47), while his humanity was formed on earth. Torrance goes on to cite Galatians 4, where three times Paul uses the verb *gennaō* of human generation (Gal 4:23, 24, 29), but when in that context he speaks of the generation of Jesus he uses *ginesthai,* thereby disavowing ordinary human generation (Gal 4:4). This is repeated at Romans 1:3 and Philippians 2:7. Torrance concludes that Paul's theology is consonant with the doctrine of the virgin birth.

We may sum up the discussion thus far, stressing both the continuity (born from Mary) and the discontinuity (born from above) with our humanity that we find in the doctrine of the incarnation. This brief presentation of biblical themes must now be developed into a theological construal as we continue to inch our way forward, via our conversation with Torrance, keeping in mind our programmatic question, "Who is the incarnate Savior of the world?"

Turning to the doctrine of the virgin birth,[100] Torrance rightly states that it must not be understood as a theory of explanation. It was a transcendent act

---

[98]Ibid., p. 91.
[99]Ibid., p. 92.
[100]Ibid., pp. 94-104.

of free, divine grace involving a miracle of God's creative agency within human existence. It is an event with two sides to it; it is both an outward visible event and an invisible supernatural act: born of the virgin Mary and conceived by the Holy Spirit. Here the *how* of the event is an act of the Holy Spirit that recedes back into the mystery of God and is beyond human observation and understanding. As such, the virgin birth cannot be understood in terms of human biology, for it is an act of God the creator, creating not out of nothing but within human existence. It is both a physical and a metaphysical event. It is a theological event in which God is creatively at work in a new, indeed singular, way within history. Says Torrance, remarkably, the virgin birth is "the sign, in fact, that he who is born of Mary is the creator himself."[101]

In this way, the virgin birth cannot be separated from the mystery of Christ—that is, from the union of divine and human nature in personal existence. As a sign, the virgin birth points to this dogmatic reality, to the hypostatic union, in which inward reality and outward form constitute the incarnation, and as such is the atoning union. The virgin birth corresponds as sign to the nature of that which it signifies, the mystery of Christ. The mystery of his birth and person belong together, and our knowing of this mystery similarly forces the inevitable tension upon our minds when we recognize that both the inward act and the outward event must be allowed their place in our thinking.

Torrance now goes further, perhaps following a soteriological impulse. Because it is at the resurrection that the mystery of the person of Christ is fully revealed, the virgin birth and the resurrection belong together as the twin signs that mark out the mystery of his person (born of the virgin Mary, raised from the virgin tomb, where no one had ever been laid [Lk 23:53]). In this way, the resurrection reveals the meaning of the birth. As at the birth the Son is veiled in flesh, at the resurrection the Son is unveiled, resurrected out of human sin and death to the glory of his perfect union. Thus Torrance insists, somewhat dramatically, that "to deny the virgin birth involves a denial of the resurrection, and vice versa."[102]

What does all this mean? First, it means that the secret of Jesus' existence, and especially here the secret of his origin, lies wholly in God's sovereign

---

[101]Ibid., p. 95.
[102]Ibid., p. 97.

freedom, will and grace. In the virgin birth God is revealed as Creator and Redeemer. Second, Jesus' birth from Mary means that he was a human being. Torrance notes that the virgin birth was inserted into the creed in order to combat Docetism, the view that in some manner Jesus was not really human.[103] Third, it also excludes Ebionism, the notion that the Son united himself with another man who was adopted by the Son of God, taken over, as it were, to become the man Jesus. Fourth, the virgin birth excludes synergism, the notion that God and Mary somehow worked together or cooperated in some way.

To expand briefly this last point: The virgin birth is the doctrine that the whole initiative in redemption is from God. This implies the disqualification of human spiritual capability unto salvation and also the exclusion of understanding Jesus either as a product of the causal-historical process or as the product of cooperative grace from the side of Mary. It was the entry of eternity into time, grounded in God alone. As such, it was a re-creative act, not *ex nihilo* but creation *ex virgine*, presupposing the first creation, says Torrance, and beginning the new creation.[104] For out of Mary, a sinner, comes the sinless man, who bears upon himself the sin of the whole world. And as Mary is sanctified by her son, so too we are given to share in his holiness through union with Christ as the gift of the Holy Spirit. Thus the pattern of redeeming grace is revealed: God takes the initiative to do what for us is impossible to do, as we are given to share in the life of Christ and thereby in the new creation that he inaugurates. We become children of God (Jn 1:12) dependent upon the *egeneto*, the "became," of the Word in our flesh (Jn 1:14).

Who is the incarnate Savior of the world? The answer is Jesus, conceived by the Holy Spirit, born of the virgin Mary, of whom, the Christmas Lord, we can say, "clothed in flesh the Godhead see; hail the incarnate Deity." This is the miracle, mystery and reality of our salvation.

---

[103]Ibid., p. 98.
[104]Ibid., p. 100.

CHRISTOLOGY

The Mystery of Christ—the *Homoousion* and the Hypostatic Union

IN THIS CHAPTER WE WILL PUSH as far as possible into the mystery of Christ, bringing the focus of attention to two classical christological categories. The *homoousion*, which is the Nicene Creed's confession of the oneness of being between the Father and the Son, and the hypostatic or personal union, wherein Jesus is confessed to be one person who is wholly God and wholly a man, are relational theological constructs that address, respectively, the Father-Son relationship and the personal union of God and humankind in the Word become flesh, whose name is Jesus. The discussion of the classical christological categories intends to make as clear as possible the dogmatics contained within the previous discussion of the person of Jesus Christ. Thus we enter the worlds of Nicaea and Chalcedon as we continue to be in discussion with our Scottish theologians where they have addressed the issues.

There should be no doubt about the force of the mystery that confronts us as we make our way forward. For McLeod Campbell, Mackintosh and Torrance, bearing witness rather than explanation is the aim. And in view of the mystery before us, we enter a field of inquiry that must be approached with humility. Who are we to speak of such things? Yet in the obedience of faith, for God calls the church to preach and teach the gospel, we try to make some sense of what is meant when we confess that the Word by which the creation was spoken into being has become flesh. When he ventured into this kind of discussion, Torrance on occasion used the image of us having to clasp our hands over our mouths, for we must speak of holy and wondrous things that are beyond us—indeed, that have their truth in God. Constrained by the limits of our creatureliness, nevertheless, in union with Christ, true human as well as true God, we stand on the threshold of heaven, where, in the becoming flesh of the Word of God, the veil between the creator and the creature in some manner is pulled aside for us to apprehend the glory of God's redeeming love for us in Jesus Christ.

This chapter is divided into two parts, treating respectively the *homoousion* and the hypostatic union—that is, the Father-Son relationship and the personal union in Jesus Christ in which he is wholly God and wholly human.

NICENE CHRISTOLOGY AND THE *HOMOOUSIOS TŌ PATRI*

> We believe . . . in one Lord Jesus Christ, the only begotten Son of God, be-
> gotten of the Father before all worlds, God of God, Light of Light, Very God
> of Very God, begotten, not made, being of one substance with the Father
> [*homoousios tō Patri*] by whom all things were made. (Nicene Creed)

We are seeking now to say something faithful concerning the mystery of the being of Jesus Christ in terms of the Father-Son relationship, but not first of all as an intratrinitarian relationship within God's eternity. How, in any case, would we aspire to that knowledge outside of the Word becoming flesh? Rather, we come to this issue through the only opening given for us to enter, through the church's confession of the incarnate Son, whose name is Jesus, in his relationship to the Father. This fundamental point is made by Torrance: "The consubstantial or homoousial relation of the Son to the Father was asserted [by the Nicene Fathers] to be between the *incarnate* Son, Jesus Christ, and the Father. Both ends of the *homoousion*, the divine and the human, had to be secure."[1] In this way, the intrinsic soteriological thrust embedded within the Christology of the oneness in being or substance is both affirmed and protected.

John McLeod Campbell on the Father-Son relationship. John McLeod Campbell was not a professional theologian. He never held a university ap-

---

[1]Thomas F. Torrance, *The Trinitarian Faith: The Evangelical Theology of the Ancient Catholic Church* (Edinburgh: T & T Clark, 1993), p. 146. Alister E. McGrath has noted that for Torrance, Christology and soteriology are held together in an inseparable union, for each is grounded in and articulates the *homoousion*. In fact, Torrance regarded the *homoousion* to be the ontological ground of all Christian theology. See Alister E. McGrath, *T. F. Torrance: An Intellectual Biography* (Edinburgh: T & T Clark, 1999), pp. 154, 158.

pointment (although the University of Glasgow awarded him a Doctor of Divinity degree in later life). His adult life was spent in pastoral ministry, first in the Church of Scotland parish of Rhu, on the east shore of the Gare Loch in Dumbartonshire, until his deposition in 1831, then in an independent congregation in Glasgow. His theology was developed within the context of pastoral ministry rather than that of lecturing to students and of academic research. Perhaps that is in part the reason for his decidedly cumbersome, periphrastic writing, and also for his inventive theological categories. There is no mistaking a McLeod Campbell sentence! But it is to the categories summoned to his task of rethinking atonement theology that attention is drawn, for they are not those of the textbooks or of the creeds. Rarely in *The Nature of the Atonement* does he attain to equivalence in language to the Nicene or Chalcedonian christological definitions.[2] Rather, in seeking to find a path away from the penal theology of the Federal Calvinists, either of Westminster or as recently modified (as he puts it), more often than not he invents christological and atonement language to carry the force of his argument. Thus, as we turn to reflect on the mystery of Christ, dealing first with the relationship between the Father and the Son, we begin by engaging the theology of McLeod Campbell. I will devote a later chapter to a detailed discussion of his whole atonement theology, but here I will borrow a slice of it with regard to Christology as we listen to what he has to say on this first topic.

Programmatically, McLeod Campbell states, "Assuming the incarnation, I have sought to realise the divine mind in Christ as perfect Sonship towards God and perfect Brotherhood towards men, and, doing so, the incarnation has appeared developing itself naturally and necessarily as the atonement."[3] This means no less than that Jesus savingly is God,[4] and this is Campbell's idiosyncratic expression of orthodox two-nature Christology. How, then, must we understand the mystery of Christ in this regard? Insofar as at its core the mystery of the hypostatic union is the predicate of the incarnation,

---

[2]See Peter K. Stevenson, *God in Our Nature: The Incarnational Theology of John McLeod Campbell*, Studies in Evangelical History and Thought (Carlisle: Paternoster, 2004), p. 255. Stevenson's book is an outstanding contribution to Campbell studies, and what immediately follows is at points indebted to it.

[3]John McLeod Campbell, *The Nature of the Atonement* (1856; repr., Grand Rapids: Eerdmans, 1996), p. 19.

[4]Ibid., p. 50.

representing in particular the mystery of his person, of who it is who becomes flesh, we expect to have some access toward understanding this
mystery through Campbell's treatment of Christ's perfect sonship on earth
toward the Father. That is, we will try to learn what we can of the divine side
of the *homoousion*[5] as we have it before us in Jesus' attested relation with the
Father. In order to do this we recognize that we make a distinction that is
for working purposes only and does not imply a Docetic separation of
Christ's divinity from his humanity. After all, we only know of the Son's relation with the Father insofar as the Son is incarnate. But I will leave aside
for now discussion of the hypostatic union and what that means for soteriology.[6] In taking this course, we begin to probe more deeply into the
subject matter of the previous chapter, while recognizing that what is said
here belongs inseparably with the discussion in the following chapter.

We have already had occasion to note the importance of Matthew 11:27 for
Christology. In McLeod Campbell's *Thoughts on Revelation* he remarks that all
we know of the grace of God to us in the dispensation of the Spirit is contained
in these words of Christ's communion with the Father, which precede his invi-
tation to come to him for rest. "All things are delivered unto me of my Father:
and no man knoweth the Son but the Father; neither knoweth any man the
Father save the Son, and he to whomsoever the Son will reveal Him" (the
translation from McLeod Campbell's text). McLeod Campbell comments,
"These words reveal the Divine circle into which we have to be taken up, that
the love of God may accomplish its desire in us. We are to know the Son by the
teaching of the Father: we are to know the Father by the teaching of the Son.
The Father drawing us to the Son, the Son revealing the Father;—these are
Divine actings in the Holy Spirit."[7] In *The Nature of the Atonement*, and in a
soteriological vein, commenting on 1 John 4:14 ("And we have seen and do
testify that the Father sent his Son as the Savior of the world"), McLeod

---

[5]Thus Stevenson, *God in Our Nature*, p. 256.
[6]"We do not expect to understand what is on the divine side, and pertains to the acting of God as
God. As to that ultimate mystery which our faith receives in believing in God the Father, the Son,
and the Holy Spirit, while in itself eternal, and irrespective of all finite existence, *we* can only be
called to the study of it *in its manifestation in connection with man*" (McLeod Campbell, *Nature of
the Atonement*, p. 260). That is, we can only know a God who acts in history, and who has given
himself to be apprehended as such.
[7]John McLeod Campbell, *Thoughts on Revelation: With Special Reference to the Present Time*, 2nd
ed. (London: Macmillan, 1874), pp. 134-35.

Campbell says that the words shed light on the whole scheme of redemption: its origin, its end, and the means by which the end is accomplished.[8] What he means, and he cites other New Testament verses in support, is that attention must be given to the relation of the revelation of the Father by the Son to our being reconciled to God. And in a summary of his whole argument, he goes on to say, "Fatherliness in God originating our salvation: the Son of God accomplishing that salvation by the revelation of the Father; the life of sonship quickened in us, the salvation contemplated; *these* are conceptions continually suggested by the language of scripture if we yield our minds to its natural force."[9] This, exactly, is the nature of the atonement. And those understand this who know the experience of orphans who have found their lost Father. It is as we acknowledge our orphan state as the deepest contradiction of the law of our being that we yield "to the teaching of the Father drawing us to the Son who alone reveals the Father," fulfilling the apostle Philip's sigh, "Show us the Father, and it sufficeth us" (Jn 14:8).[10] The Father's sending of the Son, whom the Father knows, to be the Savior of the world, and that the Son, who knows the Father, would reveal the Father to us, is the whole truth of the gospel. In sum: "The Son should propose to save us by the revelation of the Father, and that our salvation shall be participation in the life of sonship."[11]

Details of this atonement scheme I will leave until a later chapter. For now, the intent is to highlight the oneness in being between the Father, and the Son that these summary soteriological affirmations entail. In order to fully reveal the Father, the Son in the body of his flesh must be wholly God and one in will with the Father. This oneness in will, assuming as it does a prior oneness in being between the Father and the Son, is central to McLeod Campbell's teaching. This oneness in will is the place where the homoousial relations between the Father and the Son are perceived to be redemptive for us. Thus McLeod Campbell picks up on Hebrews 10:4-10, and in particular the psalmist's words (Ps 40:8) "Lo, I come to do thy will, O God." In commentary he writes,

> The will of God which the Son of God came to do and did, this was the essence
> and substance of the atonement, being that in the offering of the body of Christ

---

[8]McLeod Campbell, *Nature of the Atonement*, p. 241.
[9]Ibid., p. 241.
[10]Ibid., pp. 241-42.
[11]Ibid., p. 242.

once for all which both made it acceptable to Him who in burnt offerings and sacrifices for sin had no pleasure, and made it fit to "sanctify" those whose sin the blood of bulls and of goats could not take away. Let us then receive these words . . . as the great key-word on the subject of the atonement.[12]

The will of God immediately contemplated is what God is, God's eternal will of love toward us, which by doing it—or, better, embodying it—the Son has perfectly declared the name of God: "Father."[13] Even at the point of Christ's deepest suffering unto death, McLeod Campbell sees Christ remaining faithful to the Father's will, which he had come forth to reveal and, put emphatically by the theologian, "TO REVEAL BY TRUSTING IT."[14]

Thus, according to McLeod Campbell, Psalm 40:8 and Hebrews 10:4-10 supply the light that reveals the nature of the atonement, as the Son hears the Father's voice, abides in the Father's love, remains strong in the life that is the Father's favor, drinks the cup of suffering, commends himself to the Father's care, and thus from first to last does nothing of himself. All is done and said in oneness with the Father, and even in his desolation Christ is not alone, for the Father is with him. Everything that Christ bore was borne also upon the Father's heart. What we were to Christ's heart in his sorrow and suffering over our sin, we were also to the Father's heart. "Therefore His separating between us and our sins, His intercession, 'Father, forgive them; for they know not what they do,'—a separating, an intercession, in the assurance of the response of the Father's righteous mercy:—in all this I say is unity, and harmony, and divine simplicity. We can trace all this back to the purpose, 'Lo, I come to do thy will.'"[15]

This brief discussion of McLeod Campbell concludes with reference to the closing paragraph of the introduction to the second edition of *The Nature of the Atonement*. There, setting his proposal in the context of what he rejects (the will of God understood as the reign of law), he suggests that we must go beyond the words "he that hath seen me hath seen the Father." These words, as such, shed no light on the fatherhood of God or the sonship to which the grace of God in Christ would raise us. "But the words 'He that

---

[12]Ibid., p. 111.
[13]Ibid., p. 158.
[14]Ibid., p. 206.
[15]Ibid., p. 227.

hath seen me hath seen the Father' are explained by the words, 'I am the way and the truth and the life, no man cometh unto the Father but by me.' We see the Father when we see the Son, not merely because of identity of will and character in the Father and the Son, but because a father as such is known only in his relation to a son."[16]

Commenting on this, Peter Stevenson is surely right when, while noting that McLeod Campbell does not develop the relational language further, he suggests that McLeod Campbell's language points in the direction of a relational ontology.[17] It would be a harsh reading indeed to give only a noetic interpretation of McLeod Campbell's understanding of the oneness of will between the Father and the Son at the point of the Son on earth revealing the will of the Father. Relational imagery ripples through *The Nature of the Atonement*, and the filial life of the Son toward the Father is emphasized again and again, not least in the end contemplated in the atonement, our restoration to sonship, which arises through the Son revealing the will of the Father to love us. The point of everything is precisely the perfect connection between the oneness of will, the will to love, and the revelation of the Father. As far back as the theological orations (480)[18] of Gregory of Nazianzus it has been recognized that the Father-Son language is relational language in which neither the Father not the Son can be spoken of in isolation. The Father is the Father of the Son; the Son is the Son of the Father. This is the meaning of the oneness in being between the Father and the Son, which is the ground for the oneness of will, and as such we are now anticipating the deeper understanding of *homoousios tō Patri*, which has played such a major role in the affirmation of the mystery of Jesus Christ.

H. R. Mackintosh: Nicaea, a position gained. According to Mackintosh, "Nicaea is a position gained once for all."[19] Even so, "Christological theory is in truth like a great cathedral. 'It is ever beautiful for worship, great for service, sublime as a retreat from the tumult of the world, and it is for ever

---

[16]Ibid., p. 34.

[17]Stevenson, *God in Our Nature*, p. 259.

[18]Gregory of Nazianzus, *On God and Christ: The Five Theological Orations and Two Letters to Cledonius*, trans. Frederick Williams and Lionel Wickham, Popular Patristics Series (Crestwood, NY: St. Vladimir's Seminary Press, 2002).

[19]H. R. Mackintosh, *The Doctrine of the Person of Jesus Christ*, 2nd ed. (Edinburgh: T & T Clark, 1913), p. 292.

unfinished.' The Christ whom any mind or group of minds can reproduce is not the infinite Redeemer of the world."[20] That Christology is always en route is a theme that we have encountered already, and it reminds us that even the most celebrated christological categories should not be walled off from review, criticism and revision, if necessary. The task of interpreting Christ is ongoing; indeed, faithfulness to that task is part of our theological service to God lest our formulations become ossified and reified. We will find as we progress, however, that Mackintosh is not only interested in christological theory critically received. Almost in a way in which he cannot do otherwise, christological theory folds out into a doxological discussion of living faith. This interplay between theology and piety is a marked, and wonderful, characteristic of Mackintosh's theological writing.

Why do Christology? Mackintosh suggests that four motives may be found in the New Testament itself.[21] (1) It was believed that Jesus was the fulfillment of Old Testament prophecy, and that God's revelation ended with him. If so, who was/is he? (2) Jesus' exaltation and his gift of the Spirit mean that he is Lord, begetting in believers a transcendent life and a hope in his coming again to be revealed as central and omnipotent. If so, who was/is he? (3) The apostolic church, extending the mission beyond the Jewish circle, discovered that Jesus was for the whole world. His significance was universal. If so, who was/is he? (4) The self-witness of Jesus quickened the thought of his awareness of a unique sonship, which raised all manner of questions concerning his relationship to God. If so, who was/is he?

Mackintosh argues that the study of our Lord's filial consciousness must keep always in mind Matthew 11:27. This text keeps coming up, and now is the time to allow Mackintosh to address it directly. This is the text Mackintosh had before him: "All things are delivered unto Me of My Father, and no one knoweth the Son, save the Father; neither doth any know the Father, save the Son, and he to whomsoever the Son willeth to reveal him." These words, he asserts, are "the most important for Christology in the New Testament"[22] and "the climax of Jesus' witness to Himself."[23] Of supreme

---

[20]Ibid., p. 300.
[21]For these, see ibid., pp. 2-4.
[22]Ibid., p. 27.
[23]Ibid., p. 415.

significance is the unqualified correlation of the Father and the Son, which is a relation of "absolute intimacy and perfect mutual correspondence."[24] Not only does Jesus know the secret of the Father's being, beyond anything known by the prophets, and not only is this knowledge complete, final and inaccessible to all except those to whom the Son is mediator, but also the Father alone knows the secret of Jesus' identity and person. That is to say, we are confronted here with mutuality in knowing to the very depths of identity and person between the Father and the Son. The revealing medium is in total harmony with what is revealed, for Jesus is Son of the Father and knows the Father. Thus our knowledge of the Father is at Jesus' discretion, indebted entirely to him. If this is the case, Jesus' sonship is constitutive of his being, and neither the Father nor the Son can be known without the other. The Father and the Son can be known only in the other.[25] To know the Father is to know the Son; to know the Son is to know the Father. We are encountered, then, by something utterly new in religious experience, something wholly other, for, as Mackintosh cites James Denney, "the sentence as a whole tells us plainly that Jesus is both to God and to man what no other can be."[26] Jesus' sonship to the Father is the ontic ground of his being.[27]

Mackintosh wants to make his point on the ground of Jesus' unconditioned self-consciousness. In doing so, we note, he is making a theological rather than a psychological point. On the one hand, the Jesus of the Synoptic Gospels makes no reference to his preexistence; on the other hand, however, every attempt to conceive of him *becoming* Son to the Father, Mackintosh believes, founders on the basis of this self-consciousness with respect to the identity of his person. The origin and secret of his filial identity are not open to our inspection; his identity is nevertheless the supreme reality, and the ground of his vocation lies in the uniqueness of being the Father's Son. As such, he does and can do God's work.[28] Referring once again to Matthew 11:27, Mackintosh later in the book insists, "The knowledge of God professed by Jesus is conceived exclusively as given in and with His filial consciousness. . . . He is

---

[24]Ibid., p. 27.
[25]Ibid., p. 28.
[26]Ibid.
[27]Alister McGrath rightly notes that the *homoousion* played a foundational role in Mackintosh's thinking on the identity of Christ and the nature of God (see McGrath, *T. F. Torrance*, p. 164).
[28]Mackintosh, *Doctrine of the Person*, p. 31.

speaking of a knowledge possessed by the Son *qua* Son. . . . This Sonship signified for Jesus' own mind a unique and incommunicable relation to God and man."[29] The name "Son" signifies Christ's inherent and personal unity with the Father, something known to him and that he can reveal to those to whom he chooses to be let in on his knowledge of the Father.

With this in view, Mackintosh concludes that Jesus is the proper object of faith. We are not called to believe *like* him, but to believe *in* him.[30] And in thus believing, we have faith in God.

> God and Christ are not held apart, or connected merely by inferential reasoning; they are apprehended together in a single movement. In laying hold of Christ we lay hold of God personally present to Him, but nowhere else offered to us in this personal fashion, nowhere else certified and conveyed to us as Redeemer. . . . Trust in God and trust in Christ are vitally correlative.[31]

This is a remarkable statement that takes us deeply into the central mystery of Christian faith. Here faith is thrust in a trinitarian direction, though as yet there is no developed doctrine of the Holy Spirit. But, note, Mackintosh is not dealing in otiose doctrine. Mackintosh's piety now suddenly bursts forth as he exults in the direct, personal, experiential and vital encounter with the living Christ. Commenting first on the experience of the apostles, Mackintosh observes that faith is the confession of Christ's Godhead, which is an intuition that arises directly from encounter with him: "Everything grew out of the living contact of Jesus with their souls; all doctrine was but the confession that in that human life God Himself was turning to sinners and opening His heart to them."[32] Doctrine is confessional doxology, perhaps more to be sung than argued. It is no less so with us today. Faith is not reducible to assent to doctrine. Much more surely faith is wrung from us as the person of Jesus wins dominion over us in an experience that transforms our lives. We feel ourselves in the presence of the supreme reality, God himself, and faith is submission, capitulation, obedience and, in terms of time, loyalty.[33] Acknowledging the admonition that faith has many varying stages of maturity, Mackintosh still insists

---

[29]Ibid., pp. 415-16.
[30]Ibid., p. 345.
[31]Ibid., p. 348.
[32]Ibid., p. 351.
[33]Ibid., p. 352n1.

that faith in the Christian sense is this knowledge of Christ as living, present and divinely strong to save. As such, faith is the fruitful soil of doctrine.[34]

Mackintosh has argued that for Jesus there was an unmediated relation with the Father. Such a relationship of undimmed filial consciousness is not possible for us, and its nature remains Jesus' secret. Our relation to the Father, rather, is mediated in and through him.[35] We are sinners, and that makes our access to God unattainable when left to ourselves. The gospel is not the demand for us to have a faith like Jesus. If we are to enter the presence of God, it will be because we are led there by Jesus, who in himself is in perfect and uninterrupted union with the Father. In this way, Jesus is faith's creator, not faith's illustration.[36] And he can do this because he is a living and exalted Lord who binds us to himself. "Union with [Christ], not assent to doctrine, is redemption."[37] That affirmation serves to capture the center of Mackintosh's dialectic between theology and piety/faith, just as it is also the central work of the Holy Spirit upon us. And the basis for this is his unyielding conviction of the real presence of a living Lord who is with us now and here and with whom we have immediate relations.[38] While this proposition can be the subject of argument and defense, it is even more an instinct of the soul in which believers are joined to the Lord in a spiritual fellowship. It is trust in a living person.[39] Christology, if it is to speak of this Lord and this relationship with him, must be careful to speak always of a living and transcendent Lord. To cut loose from this measure would mean the dissipation of Christology, as it becomes mere teaching, a poor substitute for the life-giving influence of a present Lord.[40]

To bring this section to a close one further point, already suggested, may be noted briefly in order to give coherence to this account. The relation of the exalted Christ to those who confess faith in him is through his gift of the Holy Spirit.[41] All along this gift has been assumed; it is now made explicit. A quotation gives Mackintosh's position: "It is only as the Spirit—one with Christ Himself—comes to perpetuate the spiritual presence of the Lord, and to cast

---

[34]Ibid., p. 353.
[35]Ibid., p. 360.
[36]Ibid., p. 361.
[37]Ibid., p. 364.
[38]Ibid., pp. 364-65.
[39]Ibid., p. 365.
[40]Ibid., p. 369.
[41]Ibid., pp. 373-76.

light on the unending significance of His work, that we are quite liberated from the impersonal and external, whether it be lifeless doctrine or the historically verified events of an ever-receding past. Only through the Spirit have we contact with the living Christ."[42] This cardinal point could not be made plainer.

The Spirit is given neither as substitute nor as compensation for an absent Christ; rather, it is in the Spirit that Christ is made present to us. No experiential distinction may be made between Christ and the Spirit in this case. The Spirit is the method of Christ being present to us.[43] The exalted Christ is identical with the earthly Jesus, and his work on earth continues through the Spirit. The coming of the Spirit, then, is one form of Christ's return, though now unseen but still abiding and present.[44] In this way, there is no disjunction between the exalted Christ and Jesus. But neither, it seems right to comment, is the Spirit a kind of deus ex machina, conjured up to fill in the gap between an absent Christ and us. As the form of Christ's return in this age, the Spirit is intrinsic to Christology, to the doctrine of God, and to our experience of the real presence of Christ in our lives.

T. F. Torrance on **homoousios tō Patri.**[45] The Council of Nicaea (325) was faced with having to sort out the fundamental or core mystery at the center of Christian faith: Who is Jesus Christ in his relation to God? The answer given is that Jesus is truly God, one in being with the Father. In order to understand what was, and is, at stake here, we must understand the question in its proper setting. Torrance insists that the early church was faced—as the church continues to be faced today—with a cosmological and epistemological dualism of immense proportion that threatens the heart of the gospel. The theological development of the Christian doctrine of the incarnation occurred over and against the philosophical notion of a fundamental disjunction or separation (*chōrismos*) between the "real" world of the intelligible realm and the phenomenological or less "real" or shadowy world of the sensible realm.[46] That is, a profound distinction is made between the

---

[42]Ibid., p. 373.

[43]Ibid., p. 374.

[44]Ibid., p. 375.

[45]An earlier version of this section was part of my essay "The Christology of Thomas F. Torrance," in *The Promise of Trinitarian Theology: Theologians in Dialogue with T. F. Torrance*, ed. Elmer M. Colyer (Lanham, MD: Rowman & Littlefield, 2001), chap. 3.

[46]This is the distinction between the *kosmos noetos* and the *kosmos aisthetos*, the *mundus intelligibilis* and the *mundus sensibilis*. For the impact of this on the doctrine of the church, see Thomas F.

realm of ideas and the realm of things, the former being real, while the latter has only a derivative reality. This disjunction is found in one form or another in ancient times in the middle dialogues of Plato, in Aristotle, Clement, Origen and Augustine, and in modern times in Descartes, Newton and Kant. In short, "The Church found itself struggling with two powerful ideas that threatened to destroy its existence: (a) the idea that God himself does not intervene in the actual life of men in time and space for he is immutable and changeless, and (b) that the Word of God revealed in Christ is not grounded in the eternal Being of God but is detached and separated from him and therefore mutable and changeable."[47] If this disjunction holds, Christianity falls apart because on both counts there can be no incarnation of God, no *egeneto sarx*. This disjunction drives a vicious wedge between God as Creator and God in redemption in such a way that it cuts into the unity of the incarnation by separating Christ's divinity from his humanity. In so doing, this dualism also destroys the atonement and renders impossible the Christian doctrine of God. "This created a real problem for the Church's understanding of the Incarnation as a real *egeneto sarx* on the part of the Logos, for it inhibited a serious consideration of the real *becoming* of the intelligible in the sensible, or the eternal in the contingent."[48]

The effects of this deistic disjunction between God and creation are to shut God out of the world and to conjure a Jesus without divinity. This means that God has not really come among us as the man Jesus Christ; the corollary is that God remains mute and unknown. Incarnation, in this case, is illusory, not real, for God only seemed to become a man, which is Docetic. Incarnation is equally illusory when Jesus is considered to be only a godly man, even the most godly, but not God. This is the Ebionite heresy (seeing Jesus as an ordinary man but not God as this man).[49] In either case, God and creation remain separated. The consequences are the collapse of redemption into my-

---

Torrance, *Theology in Reconstruction* (London: SCM Press, 1965), pp. 34, 175, 211; idem, *Space, Time and Incarnation* (London: Oxford University Press, 1978), pp. 15, 43; idem, *The Ground and Grammar of Theology* (Charlottesville: University of Virginia Press, 1980), p. 21; idem, *Reality and Evangelical Theology* (Philadelphia: Westminster, 1982), pp. 28, 55; idem, *Trinitarian Faith*, pp. 47, 275. With regard to Athanasius, see Thomas F. Torrance, *Theology in Reconciliation: Essays Towards Evangelical and Catholic Unity in East and West* (London: Geoffrey Chapman, 1975), p. 224.
[47]Torrance, *Theology in Reconstruction*, p. 261.
[48]Ibid., p. 175.
[49]Torrance, *Trinitarian Faith*, pp. 112-13.

thology and theological language into symbol. There are two reasons for this: the first is that salvation has now no historical or empirical dimension; the second is that Jesus is not ontologically grounded in God. This leads to the loss of meaning in christological and soteriological speech because it has no objective reference in God corresponding to it.

This absolute separation between God and the world (what Torrance means when he refers to a "cosmological dualism" or a "cosmological disjunction"), between eternity and temporality, has come into modern thought in a most damaging way through Immanuel Kant. Kant argued for an axiomatic distinction between unknowable things in themselves (what he called *noumena*) and what is scientifically knowable—things as they appear to us (what he called *phenomena*). Thus Kant limited knowledge to what we can make out of these appearances, insisting on a bifurcation between the realm of hypothetical entities, or noumena, and the realm of phenomenal objects and events. According to Torrance,

> This implies a deep split in human experience: between the experience of man as a being in the world of phenomena, where he has no freedom, and the experience of man as a subject of the supersensual, or noumenal, world, where his only freedom belongs. . . . Kant severed the connection between science and faith, depriving faith of any objective or ontological reference and emptying it of any real cognitive content. . . . The whole history of nineteenth- and twentieth-century theology demonstrates that so long as people operate with an axiomatic disjunction between a noumenal realm of ideas and a phenomenal realm of events, nothing more than a merely moral or poetic or symbolic or mythological meaning can be given to the biblical account of the saving intervention of God with us in the world of space and time.[50]

For Torrance, then, the assumption of this cosmological dualism into Christology drives a wedge between Jesus' divinity and humanity, destroying the basic faith of the church by cutting Christ into two aspects.[51] The false question that arises for Christology is this: On which side of the duality are we to think of Jesus Christ? Thus it became clear to the Greek theologians of the fourth

---

[50]Torrance, *Ground and Grammar*, p. 27. This is the basis also for the distinction between *Geschichte* and *Historie* found in much mid-twentieth-century Protestant theology (see Torrance, *Space, Time and Incarnation*, p. 63).

[51]Thomas F. Torrance, *The Mediation of Christ* (Grand Rapids: Eerdmans, 1983), p. 63.

century especially that a very different, unitary approach to the doctrine of Christ was needed, one in which they understood him right from the start in his wholeness and integrity as one person who is both God and human being.[52]

In view of the dualism between God and creation (which is not to be confused with the distinction between the Creator and his creation), Torrance argues that we must start off on a different foot altogether. In order to know Christ aright it is necessary to know him as he discloses himself to us on his own terms, in the light of his being as the Logos of God and the Son of the Father. Thus, as we know Jesus Christ on the ground of his intrinsic being as he reveals that to us, our knowledge is reconciled to the truth of who he is in the unity of his incarnate personhood. In this way, he is known according to his nature (*kata physin*) within the objective frame of meaning that he has created for the church, through the apostolic testimony to him. Such knowledge proceeds to understand Jesus Christ in the light of his internal relations with the Father, as far as we can apprehend them, and within the matrix of interrelations out of which he came as a son of Israel and the Son of Man. This, according to Torrance, is to know him as he is in his own being and according to his own nature.

For Torrance, then, the historical answer to "this menace" of dualism was, and for us today still is, the *homoousion* of the Nicene Creed: the doctrine that Jesus Christ, the son of Mary, belongs to the divine side of reality and is very God come into our world to redeem us.[53] The primary heuristic theological instrument by which a realist, unitary knowledge of Jesus Christ was developed was the doctrine of the *homoousion*, through which the church confessed the nature of the incarnation and atonement for our salvation.

What is the nature of the relation between Jesus Christ and God the Father? This, according to Torrance, was the decisive issue set before the church in the fourth century, as it still is. It was in answer to this question that the Nicene Fathers formulated their response, ratified by the Council of Constantinople, that we believe in God the Father, "And in the one Lord Jesus Christ, the Son of God, begotten from the Father, only-begotten, that is, from the being of the Father, God from God, Light from Light, true God from true God, begotten

---

[52]Ibid.

[53]Torrance, *Theology in Reconstruction*, p. 261; also idem, *The Christian Doctrine of God: One Being, Three Persons* (Edinburgh: T & T Clark, 1996), p. 21.

not made, of one being with the Father, through whom all things were made."[54]
The central concept here is "of one being with the Father"—*homoousios tō Patri*. It intends to express the oneness in being between the Father and the Son, making explicit also the identification of the Son with the Creator through the reference "through whom all things were made."[55] In this way, says Torrance, the Nicene Council "decided to cut away all ambiguity and remove any possibility for misunderstanding by inserting the crucial expression 'of one being with the Father' . . . which meant that the Son and the Father are equally God within the one being of God."[56] Although *homoousion* is not a biblical term, it is a purely theological (i.e., scientific) construct or instrument[57] by which the church has been able to apprehend and henceforth to protect the central evangelical truth of the gospel. In sum: (a) "It is the self-same God who is revealed to us as the Son and the Father";[58] and (b) "if the Son is eternally begotten of the Father *within* the being of the Godhead, then as well as expressing the oneness between the Son and the Father, *homoousios* expresses the distinction between them that obtains within the oneness."[59]

Interpreting this, Torrance says that "the [*homoousios tō Patri*] was revolutionary and decisive: it expressed the fact that what God is 'toward us' and 'in the midst of us' in and through the Word made flesh, he really is **in himself**; that he is in the **internal relations** of his transcendent being the very same Father, Son and Holy Spirit that he is in his revealing and saving activity in time and space toward mankind."[60] The *homoousion* crystallizes the view that while the incarnation falls within the structures of our humanity, the church confesses that it also falls within the life and being of God.[61] This is the important point, both theologically and pastorally, for this is the ground and content of faith. In this way, Torrance understands that the *homoousion* protected the integrity of the gospel, being the hinge upon which the Nicene Creed turned, and it remains still the cardinal concept to

---

[54]Torrance, *Trinitarian Faith*, p. 116.
[55]Ibid., p. 117. This point is brought out also by David Willis, *Clues to the Nicene Creed: A Brief Outline of the Faith* (Grand Rapids: Eerdmans, 2005), p. 61.
[56]Torrance, *Trinitarian Faith*, p. 122; see also idem, *Mediation of Christ*, p. 64.
[57]Torrance, *Christian Doctrine of God*, p. 80.
[58]Torrance, *Trinitarian Faith*, p. 124.
[59]Ibid., p. 125.
[60]Ibid., p. 130; bold is original.
[61]Torrance, *Ground and Grammar*, p. 160.

which the church has returned again and again in the understanding, proclamation and ministry of the gospel.

Two points may be noted. First, we note the epistemological significance of the *homoousion*.[62] According to Torrance, without the *homoousion*, if Jesus Christ were not wholly God (*totus Deus* but not *totum Dei*, wholly God but not, as it were, the whole of God), being only externally related to God in some manner, God would remain utterly unknowable, for there is then no access for us to the Father through the Son and in the Holy Spirit.[63] Jesus Christ would then have only a transient symbolic relation to God.[64] But confessed as central to the Nicene Creed, the *homoousion* means that

> the Son of God in his incarnate Person is the place where we may know the Father as he is in himself, and know him accurately and truly in accordance with his own divine nature. The *homoousion* asserts that God *is* eternally in himself what he *is* in Jesus Christ, and, therefore, that there is no dark unknown God behind the back of Jesus Christ, but only he who is made known in Jesus Christ.[65]

In this case, Jesus Christ is the mediating center of revelation whereby all of our knowledge of God is controlled.[66]

There is, second, a soteriological significance to the *homoousion*.[67] When Jesus Christ is detached from God, his word of forgiveness is the word only of one man to men and women.[68] According to Torrance, "It is quite a difference when the face of Jesus is identical with the face of God, when his forgiveness of sin is forgiveness indeed for its promise is made good through the atoning sacrifice of God in Jesus Christ."[69] The *homoousion* grounds the reality of our Lord's humanity and all that he revealed and did for our sakes— "for us men and for our salvation"—in an indivisible union with the eternal being of God.[70] The point is, "*Only God can save, but he saves precisely as man.*"[71] For Torrance, "The incarnation is to be understood, then, as a real

---

[62]Torrance, *Theology in Reconstruction*, p. 34.
[63]Torrance, *Trinitarian Faith*, p. 133.
[64]Torrance, *Mediation of Christ*, p. 69.
[65]Torrance, *Trinitarian Faith*, p. 135; see also idem, *Mediation of Christ*, p. 70.
[66]Torrance, *Mediation of Christ*, p. 65.
[67]For the relation of the *homoousion* to grace, see Torrance, *Theology in Reconstruction*, pp. 182-83.
[68]Torrance, *Mediation of Christ*, p. 68.
[69]Ibid., p. 70.
[70]Torrance, *Trinitarian Faith*, p. 135.
[71]Ibid., p. 149.

becoming on the part of God, in which God comes *as man* and acts *as man*, all for our sake—from beginning to end God the Son acts among us in a human way."[72] In this case, "The work of atoning salvation does *not* take place *outside* of Christ, as something external to him, but takes place *within* him, *within* the incarnate constitution of his Person as Mediator."[73] This point is central to the whole argument being made throughout these chapters.

Over and against the view of the dualist or disjunctive outlook in religion and thought that pervaded the ancient world, and that is still extant today in the vague deism characteristic of generic civil religious theism, the church has committed itself to the gospel of the incarnation of the Son of God, the Word made flesh, in which God in Christ has really come among us into time and space for our salvation. For Torrance, "The linchpin of this theology, the essential bond of connection that held it together in its foundations, as it was formulated in the great ecumenical creed of all Christendom at Nicaea and Constantinople, is the so-called *homoousion*, the confession that Jesus Christ the incarnate Son is of one being or of one substance with God the Father."[74] The proclamation of this gospel is the primary homiletical responsibility of the church today.

It must not be thought, however, that in Torrance's mind the term *homoousion* is in some way sacrosanct and beyond reconsideration. As he repeatedly insists, all theological terms and concepts fall short of the realities that they intend and are open to further modification in light of them. The truth lies not in the concepts and words, but rather in the reality to which they refer. It is important to register this methodological humility before the self-presentation of God. God cannot be captured within our sentences and concepts. Torrance should not be accused of constructing a closed rationalistic system of theology based deductively upon fourth-century Greek theology. Nevertheless, he argues that "the formulation of the *homoousion* proved to be of astonishing generative and heuristic power, for it was so well rooted in the source of the Church's faith that it was pregnant with intimations of still profounder aspects of divine reality in Jesus Christ pressing for realisation within the mind of the Church."[75]

---

[72]Ibid., p. 150.
[73]Ibid., p. 155.
[74]Torrance, *Ground and Grammar*, pp. 39-40.
[75]Torrance, *Christian Doctrine of God*, p. x.

The formation of the *homoousion* was, then, a turning point of far-reaching significance for the church, in which "it was recognised as uniquely constitutive for all subsequent theological and conciliar activity."[76] That is to say, the *homoousion* "took on the role of an interpretative instrument of thought through which the Church's general understanding of the evangelical and apostolic deposit of the Faith was given more exact guidance in its mission to guard, defend, and transmit the Faith in its essential truth and integrity."[77] In Torrance's assessment, it became the all-important hinge upon which turned not only the Nicene Creed itself, but also the development of the Christian doctrine of God and an understanding of the assurance of the salvation of humankind.

THE HYPOSTATIC UNION

McLeod Campbell, Mackintosh and Torrance, each in his own way, have shown that the mystery of Christ is rightly unfolded by reflection on the Father-Son relationship. From this we turn now to the cognate doctrine of the mystery of Christ in his personal union as wholly God and wholly human.

H. R. Mackintosh: Chalcedon, a tendency to theorize. In what is perhaps an odd statement Mackintosh notes, "Christology is only a reasoned account of how the Man Jesus has for us the value and reality of God."[78] I say this is perhaps an odd statement because it seems to devalue Christology. But his intent, I think, is to direct us to Jesus Christ, about whom we think, rather than to the church's formulations themselves, for in laying hold of Christ we lay hold of God himself. That is his point, and in multiple ways he makes the case for an experiential faith again and again. According to Mackintosh, faith is a matter not of reasoning (and here I think he means deductive reasoning) but of intuition, as we have seen.[79] *Intuition* certainly is an ambiguous term that has something of an old-fashioned feel. Perhaps Mackintosh intends something of the nature of apperception, a way of understanding through awareness whereby a whole reality is recognized and about which we can think. Surely he does not intend intuition to imply

---

[76]Ibid., p. xi.
[77]Ibid., p. 80.
[78]Mackintosh, *Doctrine of the Person*, p. 410.
[79]Ibid., p. 350.

fideism, where faith is independent of reason. Nevertheless, whatever Mackintosh means precisely, christological formulations have their place. God has not chosen to save us by argument, yet still we are called to give a good account of what we believe. "Dogmatics is called to fix in lucid conceptual forms the whole rich truth of which faith is sure."[80] To that end Mackintosh rightly recognized that all manner of questions may need to be answered at the beginning of a constructive statement of christological doctrine, but one question in particular demands attention: the validity of the doctrine of the two natures of Jesus Christ.[81] This concern offers a fruitful place to begin the second part of the chapter.

We start with reference to Cyril of Alexandria (d. 444). In opposition to those who denied a real union of the natures of Christ, Cyril argued that Christ not only assumed but also became flesh, to form the personal subject of the God-man. Cyril coined the phrase "one out of two natures" to express this. Before the incarnation, two natures existed, God and humankind—although what is meant by "God's nature" remains very obscure, and even the common term "human nature" has an uncertain meaning. These ambiguities recognized but put aside for a moment, we note that with the incarnation only the one divine-human nature of the Lord existed in a hypostatic or personal union.[82] The danger in this formulation, clearly, is that this union could be seen to absorb the two natures so that they are no longer distinct within the union. It was to address that problem that the Fourth Ecumenical Council at Chalcedon was convened in 451. The important sentence of the resulting Chalcedon Creed includes the famous four adverbs. Confessing the one Lord Jesus Christ, perfect in Godhood and manhood, the council fathers acknowledged him in two natures, *without confusion, without change, without division and without separation*, the distinction of natures not being annulled by the union, but coming together as one person.

Undoubtedly, this was a remarkable formulation of the central Christian conviction concerning Jesus Christ, and it has served the church well for a long time. Mackintosh, however, observes the obvious: all four of the adverbs fixing the two natures relative to one another are negative, while the

---

[80]Ibid., p. viii.
[81]Ibid., p. 293.
[82]Ibid., p. 206.

unity of the person of Christ is positively emphasized.[83] With the religion of the creed he has no argument; with the theology it is otherwise.

With respect to the religion of the creed, the reality and integrity of the two natures are upheld, and the incarnation has not created a being somehow neither divine nor human, or either one exclusively. And the two natures are indeed intended to be hypostatically or personally one. With respect to the theology of the creed, however, Mackintosh is less charitable: "Thus it may be pointed out that Christological relations which, in essence are ethical and personal, have been too much expressed in terms imbued with a certain mechanical and even material flavor. This is particularly true of the term 'nature' [*physis*], which is not an ethical word at all."[84] For Mackintosh, the result of the Chalcedonian definition—and, if correct, this conclusion is catastrophic for Christian faith—is a suspicion of dualism entailed in the parallelism of the two natures in a relation to each other that is not personally mediated. God and human nature are yoked together, not exhibited in the singleness of a personal life such as we find presented of Jesus in the New Testament.[85] Further, Mackintosh judges that the unity affirmed by Chalcedon is so marvelous and wonderful that Christ's humanity is overshadowed by his divinity. Christ's humanity appears to be an organ of the divine Word. It becomes impossible to think then of Jesus Christ as the new human. In a cutting, dismissive judgment Mackintosh argues that "the Council did not so much reconcile or synthesise the opposing theories put before it, as conceal their opposition under extremely careful phrases."[86]

So Mackintosh will not travel down the road of literal fidelity to the definition of Chalcedon. "Nicaea is a position gained once for all. Chalcedon, on the other hand, betrays a certain tendency not merely to define but to theorise."[87] According to Mackintosh, the chief defect in traditional Christology, it appears, is its insistence in principle on the doctrine of the two natures. That is a remarkable conclusion!

Mackintosh: the human life of God and kenotic Christology. Mackintosh develops his positive statement on Christology over many hundreds of

---

[83]Ibid., p. 213.
[84]Ibid., p. 214. By "ethical" Mackintosh appears to mean "relational," and it is the correlate here of "personal."
[85]Ibid.
[86]Ibid., p. 215.
[87]Ibid., p. 292.

pages. In particular, his reflections on the humanity of Christ are evident on virtually every page. It would be both tedious and unbearably long to recite all of his arguments. Instead I will cut a cross section that seems to take us to the heart of his positive proposal regarding the relation between the humanity and divinity of Christ and its corollary, according to Mackintosh, the doctrine of kenosis or self-emptying that he espoused. As I do this, it is helpful to bear in mind Mackintosh's central methodological move: at every turn he begins with the Jesus Christ of history, with the actual Jesus as the Gospels reveal him, who is attested to be God in word and act, and whom we know (not just know about, but know intuitively and personally) as risen and ascended Lord. Mackintosh will have nothing to do with theories concerning God, or human beings for that matter, or with philosophical prolegomena, or even with discussion regarding the nature of Scripture.[88] Jesus as he encounters us and as we lay hold of him (for Mackintosh, the work or agency of the Holy Spirit, who joins us to Jesus Christ as he is attested in Scripture, proclaimed in the sermon, and celebrated in the sacraments)— that is the starting point, and a deeper apprehension of that is the goal.

Jesus was not simply human in some general sense (whatever that might mean); he was a man. The second part of that sentence is very important. However, it was in view of a weakening emphasis on Jesus' individuality, on his particular humanity, in part stimulated by the fights against Arianism and Adoptionism, that the notion of Christ's impersonal humanity took hold. Two theological words were used to try to overcome the problem: *anhypostasis*, which refers to the divinity of Jesus' person, and *enhypostasis*, which insists that, nevertheless, Jesus was truly a human being. The *anhypostasis* was meant to protect the view that if the Word had not become flesh, Jesus would not have existed. The person of Jesus, in other words, lay in the Logos. The truth in this is the insistence that Jesus is God. The danger is that his humanity and, even more, his life as a man are overwhelmed by his divinity. In response to Chalcedon, with its doctrine of abstract natures, and to the *anhypostasis*, which tends to suppress Christ's singular, actual humanity, Mackintosh starts with the oneness of Jesus Christ in history. He places emphasis on Jesus' life, and in particular on the Jesus who meets us

---

[88]See the remarkable statement (ibid., p. 317) about knowing Christ, as it were, beyond Scripture, knowing him independently.

in the pages of the New Testament. We do not read of Jesus in the New Testament with Chalcedonian adverbs and philosophical abstractions concerning the meaning of the word *nature* playing a dominating hermeneutical role in the foreground of our minds.

The true humanity of Jesus as a particular man is important for four reasons.[89] First, it guarantees the incarnation. If Jesus' particular humanity is unreal at any point, then God has not become incarnate. The faith of the church is that God in Christ is fully, totally, really a man. Mackintosh gives full play to the doctrine of *enhypostasis*. Second, Christ's full humanity is an essential basis for atonement. Jesus Christ can act as God for us only from within our humanity, entering into the existential hell of our rebellion and separation from God and bearing its consequence on our behalf. In order to be the atonement Jesus has to be a man. Third, because divinity is the source and basis of Jesus' perfect particular human being, he is our pattern in faith and prayer in his sinless life. (We will see later, in a way not fully developed by Mackintosh, that there is a need here for the doctrines of the vicarious humanity of Christ and of our union with Christ.) And fourth, because Jesus the man was resurrected, we, in him, have a future of transcendent life with God.

Now, faith apprehends Jesus Christ, a man, as the personal presence of God. Mackintosh identifies three aspects of Christ's humanity that are intelligible only if construed in terms of his Godhead.[90] First, because Jesus was God, he lived a sinless life. As God incarnate, Jesus did not have the disposition to sin. His sinlessness reveals his inward and essential relationship with God. (His all-too-human finitude will be addressed shortly.) In Christ we behold the human life of God. Second, the Gospels reveal an intense relationship between Jesus and the Father, a relationship of singular intimacy. This has already been discussed. And third, Mackintosh notes Christ's exaltation. By his resurrection, Jesus is declared to be who he was in life, God with us as this man. Thus Mackintosh advances the conviction that "Christology as such is meaningless save on the presupposition of Christ's Godhead, while on the other hand His Godhead is no random or arbitrary postulate, but the reverse side of the assurance that He is the proper object of saving faith."[91]

---

[89]Ibid., pp. 404-6.
[90]Ibid., pp. 412-18.
[91]Ibid., p. 423.

Jesus Christ, the man in history, in will, word and deed, is God. In him is salvation and blessedness because we see in his human life the love, holiness and redeeming grace that, as such, define who God is. Christology properly sighted, with thoroughgoing reference to the particular humanity of Jesus, and with faith that he is the medium of redemption of which as believers we have direct or experiential knowledge[92] (for there is no other way to know Jesus qua Jesus), leads irresistibly in a soteriological direction. Salvation *is* fellowship with Jesus, for in him God's love touches us and through him we are led to the Father.

It was precisely the wish to interpret the divinity of Christ through his particular humanity that inspired the kenotic theories of his person. I will close this discussion on this point because it is long identified as a characteristic aspect of Mackintosh's Christology.

Somehow—this word is used advisedly, for we are now outside the human possibility of knowledge—God in Christ has brought the reality of divine life to us. On the one hand, Christian faith must speak of the self-abnegating descent of God; on the other hand, it must at all points keep its feet on the ground of history and deal with the man Jesus. Says Mackintosh, "God in Christ, we believe, came down to the plane of suffering men that He might lift them up. Descending into poverty, shame, and weakness, the Lord was stripped of all credit, despoiled of every right, humbled to the very depths of social and historical ignominy, that in this self-abasement of God there might be found the redemption of man."[93] Christology, however, has often found this too much to believe and has fudged the doctrine of Christ's true humanity. "Christ's point of departure was Godhead, no doubt, yet in his descent He stopped half way."[94]

According to Mackintosh, four assertions are required for the Christian view of Jesus: (1) Jesus is divine, the object of faith and worship with whom believers have a relationship; (2) in a personal sense, Christ's divinity is eternal and his preincarnation being is real; (3) Jesus' life on earth was truly human; (4) Jesus did not have two consciousnesses or two wills. The unity of his life is a given truth.[95] To avoid adopting a Docetic Christology in order

---

[92]Ibid., p. 322.
[93]Ibid., p. 467.
[94]Ibid.
[95]Ibid., pp. 469-70.

somehow to protect God from mutability and passibility, Mackintosh suggests that kenoticism in some form cannot be avoided.[96] In some manner Jesus' incarnation entailed the surrender of the glory and prerogatives of divinity, no less than "a Divine self-reduction."[97] In order to become human the Son must empty himself in an act of divine self-adjustment. And this now is the mystery: in this man Jesus, God is revealed. Only by contracting himself in his divine fullness could God in Christ draw near to us as truly a man. Thus Mackintosh refers here to "the human life of God."[98] In Jesus we have the personal presence of God as a man who is not omniscient, ubiquitous or almighty, but whose immutability is precisely given as perfect in love and holiness and freedom as the true man.

Kenotic theories tend to be attempts at explanation, in answer to the question "How did God become human with the incarnation?"[99] At times Mackintosh seems to fall into explanation, drifting across the line between christological affirmation and theorizing, succumbing to the very problem that he found with Chalcedonian Christology. The point at issue is the translation of *ekenōsen* at Philippians 2:7, the locus classicus text for this subject in the New Testament. The NRSV puts it that Christ Jesus "emptied himself, taking the form of a slave." As Torrance points out, the Greek does not say that Christ emptied anything out of himself, as if out of a container. Rather, he emptied himself of his glory, his heavenly *morphē* or form, taking an inglorious, earthly form.[100] For Torrance, there can be no metaphysical change in the Son. If Torrance is correct, then Mackintosh seems to be claiming too much when he argues for a divine self-reduction. It is enough to say that kenosis refers, as Mackintosh rightly says, to the self-abnegating descent of God the Son, but there appears to be no textual basis for arguing that God the Son somehow poured divinity out of himself. That is to say, following Torrance—and I think this is helpful—*how* the Son became human while remaining wholly God is a matter about which the New Testament remains silent. It is a mystery. The most we can say is that

---

[96]Ibid., p. 469.

[97]Ibid., p. 470.

[98]Ibid., p. 486.

[99]Thomas F. Torrance, *Incarnation: The Person and Life of Christ*, ed. Robert T. Walker (Downers Grove, IL: IVP Academic, 2008), p. 76.

[100]Ibid., p. 74.

it is a miracle of the Holy Spirit.[101] The danger in Christology is that in our attempts to understand we are tempted toward explanation, when in the nature of the case there is nothing in the New Testament on which we can build that explanation. The mystery here is to be confessed by faith and adored with thanksgiving.

One more observation needs to be made to complete Mackintosh's account. Mackintosh continues his discussion of kenosis in a new direction, for kenosis has a moral correlate, plerosis—the fullness of the Redeemer's person. This is now a remarkable and enduring contribution. According to Mackintosh, we have a double movement in Christ, as it were.

> The unification of Divine and human life in Christ may be regarded as the focus and meeting-point of two great spiritual movements of an essentially personal character. From above comes the creative initiating movement of God towards man, directed by the saving purposes of Holy Love. From beneath comes the yearning movement of man toward God, in faith and love and hope. These two personal currents—of salvation held forth and communion longed for—join and interpenetrate in the one person, Jesus Christ.[102]

In God all things begin from his eternal divine purpose to make the Son the means to salvation; in Jesus that uniquely human life of his is lived open to relationship with the Father, being a progress in personal unity with God rather than progress toward God from outside. The Father's gift is humanly actualized.[103] "The moral glory of the *kenosis* points to the almighty consummation of the *plerosis* or re-ascent."[104] The humanward and Godward movements of self-limitation and faith, hope and love, respectively, correspond. "As [Jesus Christ] stooped to save, He grew in the stature of Divine humanity."[105] In Christ, in the unity of his person, divine self-limiting and human self-acquisition combine and synthesize and in so doing are mutually correlative. For Mackintosh, in the Christian conception, Godhead is self-renounced and self-fulfilled in Christ.[106]

What are we to make of Mackintosh's discussion beyond Torrance's cri-

---

[101]Ibid., p. 76.
[102]Mackintosh, *Doctrine of the Person*, p. 500.
[103]Ibid., p. 502.
[104]Ibid., p. 504.
[105]Ibid., p. 505.
[106]Ibid., p. 507.

tique? I offer three brief points. First, in this teaching Mackintosh has clearly tried to move far away from classical theism, with its notion of an immutable and impassible deity. And yet, is not the lingering presupposition of such a philosophical construal of divinity the ground for kenotic theories? They seem to be necessary because we still work with the axiom of an unchangeable deity. If, on the other hand with Calvin, we argue that God is comprehended in Christ alone, then there is no need to appeal to divinity behind the back of Jesus, as it were. Mackintosh has suggested that God's immutability is God's eternal purpose to love and save.

The ethical, personal and relational attributes of divinity replacing metaphysical construals is not such a novel idea today, but in 1912 surely it was a bold move. I am left wondering in general about the leftover metaphysics of deity that still casts a pall over the radical doctrine of God that emerges from Christology, and Mackintosh's at times apologetic tone with respect to kenosis makes me wonder if that is still the case with his presentation. Mackintosh is not thoroughgoing enough, perhaps, in pushing kenosis backwards into God such that Christ, the servant Son who though he was rich for us became poor (2 Cor 8:9), is the criterion for divinity and the critique of divinity that is not christologically construed.

Second, the dialectic posed between kenosis and plerosis, between self-emptying and self-fulfilling or fullness, is stunningly provocative and insightful. Mackintosh's brief chapter on the self-realization of Christ prefigures my next chapter, where I will take up the dual-action Christology that is put forward strongly by McLeod Campbell and Torrance in their own ways. Mackintosh could have done more to develop this, and especially the doctrine of the vicarious humanity of Christ, but it is here nonetheless and is something to build on.

Third, while Mackintosh has little to say on the ascension as such, his doctrine of plerosis must surely be pushed in that direction. In this way, the plerosis of Christ can be seen to match Mackintosh's vigorous treatment of the exalted Lord as a living, reigning and acting Lord. His theological intuition of the living Christ—of the Christian consciousness of him and of trust in him in a personal relationship—and his doctrine of union with Christ point to the truth and reality of the ascension and the role that it surely played in the background to his theology.

T. F. Torrance on the hypostatic union. In the field of theology done in the English language, T. F. Torrance is *the* modern theologian of the hypostatic union. The doctrine is laced through almost everything he wrote and is indicative of and determinative for his Christ-centered approach to theology at every turn. Regarding his systematic treatment, he intends to

> state the doctrine of the hypostatic union of the two natures in the one person of Christ in such a way that we are faithful throughout to the whole biblical account of his person and work as the incarnate Son of the Father. . . . We have to see that reconciliation is the hypostatic union at work in expiation and atonement, and therefore that hypostatic union cannot be expounded aright except in terms of Christ's active ministry . . . bringing revelation and reconciliation to bear revealingly on one another.[107]

Reconciliation depends upon the central Christian claim that one person, Jesus Christ, acts both from the side of God and from the side of humankind and in such a way that these acts are identical in the person of the mediator.

Recording every nuance of Torrance's exposition of the hypostatic union would be a mammoth task that would extend this chapter far beyond reasonable limits, especially if I were to include his erudite discussions on the historical development of the doctrine. Thus, again, I must cut a cross section of what presents as the central argument. In doing this I will keep in view the central thesis of the whole discussion: an account of the relations between Jesus Christ, who is the incarnate Son, and the Father, the result of which is the atonement. In the incarnate Son the relation between God and humankind is savingly established. We cannot reflect on who Christ is, on his person, without having to reflect on his purpose and work.

I begin this discussion by noting three introductory points that Torrance makes. First, Torrance insists on emphasizing on the reality of the humanity of Christ. (Perhaps his teacher Mackintosh is in the front of his mind.) If Jesus were not really a man, God would not have come among us, but in some sense would have stopped short. On the other hand, the deity of Christ guarantees that in Jesus Christ we have to do with the full reality of God. In laying hold of Jesus Christ we lay hold of God. It would be hard to overemphasize this point for Torrance. Thus Christ's humanity means that God

---

[107]Torrance, *Incarnation*, p. 184.

has come to *us*, while Christ's deity means that *God* has come to save us.[108]

Second, the humanity of Christ is essential for revelation in such a way that his creatureliness constitutes and guarantees revelation within creation and thereby made accessible to us.[109] On the other hand, the deity of Christ is essential to revelation, ensuring that knowledge of God is grounded in God. "The humanity of Christ guarantees the actuality of revelation, but the deity of Christ guarantees its nature as revelation of *God*. Jesus Christ is the Son of the Father, and as such he *is* the revelation he brings."[110] Revelation is not information about God; rather, it is God giving himself to be known in personal relations with us in Jesus Christ.

Third, the humanity of Christ is essential for reconciliation. As truly a man, his death in particular is not only an act of God himself in human nature, but also an act of a man in response to God. Salvation is not worked out "above our heads," as it were, or in some manner external to us. It is worked out from within our humanity through the life and death of Jesus. On the other hand, salvation must be an act of *God*, an event anchored in God. The whole of Christ's life is identical with the course of God's action toward us. "He who reveals God to man, and reconciles man to God, must be both God and man, truly and completely God, and truly and completely man."[111] The ground is now set for the presentation of Torrance on the hypostatic union.

To begin with an obvious point: our topic is the hypostatic *union*. The divine acts in Christ's human nature, and the human acts in Christ the Son, are acts of one person in which divine and human acts and natures are united.[112] The worship and acknowledgment of Christ in his divine and human acts and natures is the doctrine of the hypostatic union. Divine and human acts and natures are united in one person or *hypostasis*.[113] The mystery is the unity of divinity and humanity as a singular personhood. And here we are confronted with the particularity that is the central Christian claim, for it is in this union that both revelation and reconciliation have their truth. Following Chalcedonian categories, Godhead and true humanity are

---

[108]Ibid., p. 188.
[109]Ibid., p. 186.
[110]Ibid., p. 188.
[111]Ibid., p. 190.
[112]Ibid.
[113]Ibid., p. 191.

united in Christ in such a way that they cannot be separated, yet are not to be confused; one does not absorb the other, neither is a third entity formed. Says Torrance, "In the hypostatic union, God remains God and man remains man, and yet in Christ, God who remains God is for ever joined to man, becomes man and remains man. In this union God has become man without ceasing to be God, and man is taken up into the very being of God without ceasing to be man. That is the mystery of Jesus Christ in whom we have communion through the Holy Spirit."[114]

We see emerging here the theology of Christ as mediator of revelation and reconciliation. First, with regard to revelation, through the hypostatic union we can know God in Christ in human terms. Christ is the sole locus of theological speech. Specifically, our language of God must repose upon, and derive from, this union. Only in Christ, the Word who has become flesh, is there a relation of correspondence between God speaking and human hearing, and human capacity to speak about God and God as he is as God. Apart from Christ's speech about God all other speech about God is empty, for it is not within our capacity otherwise to speak of God. In Christ, then, we know God and have communion with God.[115]

Two brief observations may be made. First, on the ground of the hypostatic union Torrance has entirely swept aside theism as a theological scheme for knowing God. "God talk" that is not in Christ, with specific reference to the content and substance of the person of Christ in his hypostatic union, comes near to being a blasphemy against God's choice to become flesh as the man Jesus in order that we would know God and speak faithfully of him. Further, and now positively, the Christology of the hypostatic union is the single epistemological category given for us by which we may know God. This is a huge point to make, not only with regard to other systems of faith and claims to knowledge of God, but also with regard to the status of nonchristological philosophical warrants for theological knowledge. Torrance spent considerable time throughout a number of books and essays exploring the epistemological significance of the hypostatic union. And it is worth observing that he was "antifoundational" before that word became fashionable. Here I want to note especially that

---

[114]Ibid., pp. 191-92.
[115]Ibid., p. 193.

this calls forth a trinitarian knowledge of God as the yield of the Father-Son relationship and Christ's conception by and sending of the Holy Spirit. That is to say, the doctrine of the Trinity is ontologically embedded within the hypostatic union, and it is not thinkable outside of differentiated relations within the Godhead. In this case, we are required to think of God in his revelation in trinitarian terms first of all, only then moving from the Trinity to the unity of God, although we must hold equally to both at once.

Second, with regard to Christ as the mediator of reconciliation, the hypostatic union is the enactment of God's reconciling purpose. As Jesus Christ, God has entered into human being and existence to be one with us, and to act from within our humanity to yield to the Father the obedience of a true and faithful Son, and doing so vicariously to lay hold of God.[116] This is in correspondence with the Nicene Creed: "for us and for our salvation." In an important summary statement Torrance highlights that Jesus himself is the atoning union:

> The significance of that atonement lies not merely in that Jesus Christ as man offered a perfect sacrifice to God, nor does it lie merely in that God here descended into our bondage and destroyed the powers of darkness, sin, death and the devil, but that here in atonement God has brought about an act at once from the side of God as God *and* from the side of man as man: an act of real and final union between God and man.[117]

Clearly, if we reflect soteriologically on the hypostatic *union*, we are impressed by the one action of Christ that is both humanward and Godward, an action that at once takes place within human life and yet is God's atonement for us. "The atonement is the work of the God-man, of God and man in hypostatic union, not simply an act of God in man, but an act of God *as* man. And so the hypostatic union and atonement belong together."[118]

Thus Torrance is at pains to urge the centrality of the union over and against the separation of the human and divine natures of Christ. In fact, he seems to be little interested in speaking of "natures," preferring always to emphasize the personal christological union. In this way, he avoids getting trapped in abstractions concerning definitions of divine and human natures,

---

[116]Ibid., p. 194.
[117]Ibid., p. 195.
[118]Ibid.

all the while continuing to take the historicity of Jesus Christ with enormous seriousness as the "place" where the divine economy is being worked out. As such, then, the hypostatic union as the personal event of Jesus Christ is both the ground and the actuality of the atonement.

But another point also now comes into view: seen through the lens of the hypostatic union, the atonement is not an end in itself.

> The purpose of atonement is to reconcile humanity back to God so that atonement issues in union between man and God, but it issues in union between man and God because the hypostatic union is that union already being worked out between estranged man and God, between man's will and God's will in the one person of Christ. It is the hypostatic union, or hypostatic atonement, therefore, which lies embedded in the heart of atonement.[119]

With this statement we see Torrance's dogmatic intuition at work. Insisting that atonement must be worked through in terms of the person of Christ in view of the hypostatic union vis-à-vis some other frame of reference (we could think here, for example, of the relations between God and us in legal or forensic terms), Torrance has broken away from thinking of atonement as only forgiveness of sins or amelioration of God's wrath or substituted punishment. The heart of atonement does not lie in these interim steps. Rather, judgment of sin, expiation of guilt, and the oblation of Christ's filial obedience are in order to bring us back to union with God, a union anchored within the eternal union of the Father and the Son, and of the Son and the Father, through the communion of the Holy Spirit.[120] The mention of the Spirit here, however, serves to remind us that the hypostatic union is the predicate of the act of the Holy Spirit at Jesus' conception and subsequent sonship in the flesh in his relationship with the Father. It is through awareness of the work of God the Spirit that we are forced back again and again to the historical Jesus in his hypostatic unity.

It is not yet salvation that our sins are forgiven. We must be restored to communion with the Father, and through Christ, in union with him, to enter into the life of the Holy Trinity itself. Perhaps Torrance could have developed this further, and especially perhaps robustly in the direction of a

---

[119]Ibid., p. 196.
[120]Ibid.

deeper understanding of the doctrine and process of sanctification.[121] Language that Julie Canlis applies to her interpretation of Calvin applies equally well to Torrance: he refuses to collapse mediation into expiation.[122] In short, atonement theory has too much held to too small a vista of salvation. But when enjoined through the doctrine of the hypostatic union, a wholly amazing and wonderful salvation comes before us: communion. Especially with the Western church in mind, we can say that salvation in Christ is more glorious than has often been imagined.

---

[121] This point is very well made in Alexandra Radcliff, "The Claim of Humanity in Christ: Salvation and Sanctification in the Theology of T. F. and J. B. Torrance" (PhD diss., University of St. Andrews, 2014).

[122] Julie Canlis, *Calvin's Ladder: A Spiritual Theology of Ascent and Ascension* (Grand Rapids: Eerdmans, 2010), p. 56.

CHRISTOLOGY

The Magnificent Exchange
and Union with Christ

SURELY SOME OF THE MOST GLORIOUS WORDS penned by John Calvin
are found in his *Institutes of the Christian Religion* 4.17.2, where he writes on
union with Christ as the special fruit of the Lord's Supper. Of interest are his
comments on the magnificent exchange (*mirifica commutatio*), picking up a
theological heritage that can be traced back to Irenaeus, Athanasius and Gregory
of Nazianzus,[1] and that was noted also by Luther. Thus Calvin's words:

> This is the wonderful exchange which, out of [Christ's] measureless benevo-
> lence, he has made with us; that, becoming Son of man with us, he has made
> us sons of God with him; that, by his descent to earth, he has prepared an
> ascent to heaven for us; that, by taking on our mortality, he has conferred his
> immortality upon us; that, accepting our weakness, he has strengthened us
> by his power; that, receiving our poverty unto himself, he has transferred his
> wealth to us; that, taking the weight of our iniquity upon himself (which op-
> pressed us), he has clothed us with his righteousness.[2]

It is the aim of this chapter to show that Christ himself is the magnificent
exchange. The magnificent exchange is one way of saying who Christ is in the
personal unity of his divinity and humanity, in the unity of his person and

---

[1]Irenaeus, *Five Books of S. Irenaeus Against Heresies*, trans. John Keble, Library of Fathers of the Holy
Catholic Church 42 (Oxford: James Parker, 1872), book 5, preface; Athanasius, *On the Incarnation*,
trans. John Behr, Popular Patristics Series (Crestwood, NY: St. Vladimir's Seminary Press, 2011),
paragraph 54; Gregory of Nazianzus, *On God and Christ: The Five Theological Orations and Two Letters to Cledonius*, trans. Frederick Williams and Lionel Wickham, Popular Patristics Series (Crestwood, NY: St. Vladimir's Seminary Press, 2002), oration 1:15.

[2]John Calvin, *Institutes of the Christian Religion*, ed. John T. McNeill, trans. Ford Lewis Battles, 2 vols.
(Philadelphia: Westminster, 1960), 4.17.2. For references to Luther, see p. 1362n8.

work, in which case, union with Christ is the undoubted, indeed, the required corollary. The magnificent exchange, in other words, *is* Jesus Christ as he unfolds himself in saving ministry, by which he becomes as we are so that we might share in what he is. Union with Christ is embedded as one work within the magnificent exchange as by the Holy Spirit he binds us to himself to share his benefits. In Calvin's words, "The Holy Spirit is the bond by which Christ effectually unites us to himself."[3] The significance of this work of the Holy Spirit can hardly be overemphasized. In putting the two doctrines together in this way we show the atoning exchange and union with Christ as essentially one event, having a personal, relational and participatory character. To say otherwise would be to characterize Christ and his work in only external relations to us, with Christ remaining at a distance from us in some manner. As Calvin said, as long as Christ remains outside of us, all that he has done for us remains useless and of no value to us. It is precisely through union with Christ that we receive the grace of Christ, know his benefits and, by participation in the Spirit (2 Cor 13:14), become persons of faith.

The locus classicus for the doctrine of the magnificent exchange is 2 Corinthians 8:9. "For you know the generous act of our Lord [*tēn charin tou kyriou*, "this grace of our Lord"] Jesus Christ, that though he was rich, yet for your sakes he became poor, so that by his poverty you might become rich." T. F. Torrance suggests that "the whole doctrine of the incarnation is summed up here."[5] Christ exchanged his place with our place in an atoning reversal of our status, making an atoning exchange.[6] Christ puts himself in our place so that we in him might be put in his place. This is the meaning of reconciliation, which is an act effected on the basis of exchange.[7] Of course, the reference here is not to worldly wealth or poverty, although the apparent economic categories fit the immediate context of the collection of money in 2 Corinthians 8. The reference is to Christ's entry into a lower estate by virtue of his incarnation and to our entry into a higher estate by virtue of the incarnation

---

[3]Calvin, *Institutes* 3.1.1.
[4]Calvin, *Institutes* 3.1.1.
[5]T. F. Torrance, *Incarnation: The Person and Life of Christ*, ed. Robert T. Walker (Downers Grove, IL: IVP Academic, 2008), p. 74.
[6]T. F. Torrance, *Atonement: The Person and Work of Christ*, ed. Robert T. Walker (Downers Grove, IL: IVP Academic, 2009), p. 3.
[7]Ibid., p. 151.

and atonement, through our union with him. We are called, through the Holy Spirit, to participate in Christ's sonship (Gal 4:5), for as Son of the Father he takes our sin, enmity and death in order to give us what is his in exchange: his righteousness, love and eternal life.[8] It is in this way that we understand our election, redemption and sanctification as the one work of God. We "have been chosen and destined by God the Father and sanctified by the Spirit to be obedient to Jesus Christ and to be sprinkled with his blood" (1 Pet 1:2).

It is a fruitful theological exercise to hold together as one event, as one person-act, these two cardinal doctrines as they relate to Christology and atonement: the magnificent exchange and union with Christ. It is a curious omission that little has been written on the magnificent exchange. If it is as important as Torrance has suggested, with which judgment I concur, it is surely worthy of our attention. Union with Christ, on the other hand, is a doctrine that is making something of a comeback.[9] This is a gratifying retrieval. The distinction of the approach to my share in that retrieval is to highlight the vicarious humanity of Christ, a doctrine much loved by our Scottish theologians. In that way, the intended unity between the magnificent exchange and union with Christ will be secured even more firmly.

My task now is to discuss the magnificent exchange and union with Christ in engagement with our selected Scottish theologians. As we follow this path, we begin a slow turn toward reflection on the atonement. The atonement has never been far from sight; now it begins to come closer to our purview. The discussion once again will be in two parts, dividing for the sake of exploration what really must not be separated. In the first part we will engage the christological structure of the magnificent exchange, looking especially at the mediatorial dual-action or bidirectional Christology. In the second part we will take our bearings from our Scottish theologians as they have reflected on union with Christ.

THE CHRISTOLOGICAL STRUCTURE OF THE MAGNIFICENT EXCHANGE

The magnificent exchange must be set in the context of the whole movement

---

[8]James B. Torrance, introduction to John McLeod Campbell, *The Nature of the Atonement* (1856; repr., Grand Rapids: Eerdmans, 1996), p. 16.

[9]See, for example, J. Todd Billings, *Union with Christ: Reframing Theology and Ministry for the Church* (Grand Rapids: Baker Academic, 2011).

of Christ in his descent and ascent. That is what is intended by the reference to the christological structure of the magnificent exchange. From this we see that the magnificent exchange is not at its core something that Christ does; rather, it is the working out *of who he is* in his history in our flesh. Christ is the magnificent exchange as God's gracious saving movement toward us. In himself Christ is the word/act of God to us, *and* he is the responding and acceptable filial human movement toward God. In himself he is the word/act of humankind to God. While, given the limits of language, we have to speak of these analogically as downward and upward movements, suggesting a kind of dual character they are the living forth of the one Lord Jesus Christ and must be thought of as united in Christ in a manner similar to the unity of the hypostatic union. As in Christ his person and work cannot be partitioned, neither in the consideration of his ministry for our salvation can his humanity and divinity be separated.

The theology of the dual mediatorial ministry of Jesus Christ can certainly be found already in Athanasius of Alexandria. In a major work, *Contra Arianos*, written between 356 and 360 (which we only have in a nearly two-hundred-year-old English translation that is virtually unreadable at times), Athanasius makes the cardinal point toward the end of his treatise: "We must say that our Lord, being Word and Son of God, bore a body, and became Son of Man, that, having become Mediator between God and men, *He might minister the things of God to us, and ours to God.*"[10] For Athanasius, the consequence of this dual mediatorial ministry of Christ is, in the well-known words from his *De Incarnatione*, written before Nicaea, that the Savior "became human that we might be made divine."[11] This refers to the transition of humankind from one state into another, which the theological tradition came to call "the magnificent exchange," as we have seen. Out of the measureless love of God, Jesus Christ became what we are in order to make us what he is.[12] Our "divinization," of course, is "in Christ." We do not become gods. As Athanasius says in *Contra Arianos* 1.38, "He descended to effect [man's] promotion, therefore He did not receive in reward the name of the

---

[10]Athanasius, *Four Discourses Against the Arians* 4.6, in *The Nicene and Post-Nicene Fathers*, ed. Philip Schaff and Henry Wace, 2nd series, vol. 4 (repr., Grand Rapids: Eerdmans, 1998) (italics added).

[11]Athanasius, *On the Incarnation* 54.3.

[12]Thomas F. Torrance, *The Trinitarian Faith: The Evangelical Theology of the Ancient Catholic Church* (Edinburgh: T & T Clark, 1993), p. 179.

Son and God, but rather He Himself has made us sons of the Father, and deified men by becoming Himself man." This for Athanasius is the glorious conclusion to Christ's ministry to the Father on our behalf.

The bidirectional structure of Christology in John McLeod Campbell. The center of McLeod Campbell's soteriology is the Christology of Christ's mediatorial ministry from the Father and to the Father. "The active outgoing of the self-sacrificing love in which the Son of God wrought out our redemption presents these two aspects, first, His dealing with men on the part of God; and, secondly, His dealing with God on behalf of men. These together constitute the atonement equally in its retrospective and prospective bearing."[13] In the next chapter, I will treat McLeod Campbell's atonement theology in detail. For now I will limit attention to the structure of his Christology as the setting for the full development of his theology of the atonement. This will nevertheless be our first sustained look at his soteriology, as that is unavoidable when I discuss his Christology in some detail.

Arguably, chapters 6 and 7 are the most famous chapters in *The Nature of the Atonement.* And rightly so, because they are the central planks on which McLeod Campbell builds his argument. They are entitled respectively, "Retrospective Aspects of the Atonement" and "Prospective Aspects of the Atonement." These chapters carry great force. The first third of the book sets the context for them; the second half of the book negotiates around problems raised by them, while working out their implications. It is now time to have an extended conversation with John McLeod Campbell, recalling once again that his theological language is both idiosyncratic and, at times, highly convoluted.

McLeod Campbell offers a fourfold christological structure, somewhat in the manner of four open-ended boxes created by two intersecting perpendicular lines. Retrospectively, Christ deals with people on the part of God *and* deals with God on behalf of humankind. Thinking visually, we have here the downward movement of God in Christ toward us *and* the upward movement of God in Christ toward God with respect to our past sins and how they are dealt with. Prospectively, the Son honors the Father in the sight of humankind *and* the Son deals with the Father on our behalf with respect

---

[13]John McLeod Campbell, *The Nature of the Atonement,* 2nd ed. (1867; repr., Eugene, OR: Wipf & Stock, 1999), p. 11.

to our future life in God. Again thinking visually, we observe that Christ reveals the life of sonship in response to God's fatherhood as the downward movement of God toward us *and* Christ offers the true human response to the Father as the upward movement of Christ toward the Father, into which life we participate. Thus we have two parallel movements from and to God, looking backwards and forwards, respectively.

McLeod Campbell defended the gospel of the love of God precisely at the point where the atonement is actual—that is, in and through the mediatorial bidirectional priesthood of Christ, from which light alone he sought to expound it. Thus he developed the dual nature of Christ's priestly ministry, which reached both backwards to deal with our separation from God, the retrospective aspect, and forwards to bring us into communion with God, the prospective aspect. With regard to the prospective aspect of the atonement, he broke with the conventional pattern, which was to see atonement only retrospectively. He developed each aspect in view of a dynamic understanding of the dual movement of classical Christology that we have been considering. Thus, in an Athanasian mode: "The active outgoing of the self-sacrificing love in which the Son of God wrought out our redemption presents these two aspects, first, His dealing with men on the part of God; and, secondly, His dealing with God on behalf of men. These together constitute the atonement equally in its retrospective and prospective bearing."[14] God in Christ acts in this twofold way in the flesh of our humanity as our atoning priest, bringing God to us and us to God, to bridge the gulf that stood between what sin had made us and what it was the desire of God's love that we should become.[15] The redemption of us who stand condemned in our sins through a broken communion with God is truly and fully seen only in its relation to the results contemplated: our participation in eternal life through our adoption as "sons" of God.[16] I will now fill in some of the content of this mediatorial bidirectional Christology.[17]

The atonement in its retrospective aspect. Retrospectively, in Christ dealing with humankind on the part of God, Christ bears witness for God, revealing

---

[14]Ibid., p. 113.

[15]Ibid., p. 127.

[16]Ibid., p. 128.

[17]For some of what follows in a briefer form, see Andrew Purves, *Reconstructing Pastoral Theology: A Christological Foundation* (Louisville: Westminster John Knox, 2004), chap. 3.

God, and as such suffering in his body the divine judgment against and sorrow over our sin. Here McLeod Campbell lays heavy emphasis on Christ's witness-bearing—witnessing, to vindicate the Father's name, to the excellence of the will of God against which we were rebelling, to the trustworthiness of the Father's heart in which we were refusing to put confidence, and to the unchanging character of God's love. This witness-bearing was part of the self-sacrifice of Christ, for here we see him as the man of sorrows. Perhaps we must speak of the profound sadness of God and the terrible burden of that sadness that Jesus suffered as he took it upon himself.

It is important to note that McLeod Campbell develops this in line with the love of God and not in line with a penal theology of punishment. The sadness that is Christ's suffering shows that our sins break God's heart and bring God's condemnation upon our heads; Christ, as it were, is in full sympathy with God's condemnation of sin. Insofar as sin involves suffering the judgment of God, Jesus suffers that judgment. Christ's suffering is on account of human fault and God's judgment upon it. But this suffering arises from God's love for us. God in Christ has entered into humanity's sinful separation from God because it is the nature of divine love to suffer with humanity. What Christ suffered on the cross was not a punishment for imputed sin, but rather the revelation and bearing of God's judgment of sin in that suffering. This, however, is not yet the atonement.

It is in Jesus Christ as the righteous man dealing retrospectively with God on our behalf (the upward movement, as it were) that McLeod Campbell's originality first really shines through in what has come to be called his doctrine of "vicarious penitence" (although he does not use the term).[18] As God with us, Jesus Christ sees and knows sin for what it is. He knows the judgment of God upon it and bears the consequence. Yet it was in his humanity that Christ, as the priest of all in the body of our flesh, turned to the Father and offered to God what we were unable to. In the words of some famous sentences,

> That oneness of mind with the Father, which toward man took the form of
> condemnation of sin, would in the Son's dealing with the Father in relation to

---

[18]See also Karl Barth, *Church Dogmatics* 4.1, trans. G. W. Bromiley, ed. G. W. Bromiley and T. F. Torrance (Edinburgh: T & T Clark, 1956). Barth writes of Christ's "perfect repentance" (p. 172).

our sins, take the form of a perfect confession of our sins. This confession, as
to its own nature, must have been *a perfect Amen in humanity to the judgment
of God on the sin of man.* . . . He who would intercede for us must begin with
confessing our sins.[19]

How does this "Amen" overcome God's judgment?

> He who responds to the divine wrath against sin, saying, "Thou art righteous,
> O Lord, Who judgest so," is necessarily receiving the full apprehension and
> realization of that wrath, as well as of that sin against which it comes forth
> into His soul and spirit, into the bosom of the divine humanity, and, so re-
> ceiving it He responds to it with a perfect response—a response from the
> depths of that divine humanity—and *in that perfect response He absorbs it*. For
> that response has all the elements of a perfect repentance in humanity for all
> the sin of man—a perfect sorrow—a perfect contrition—all the elements of
> such a repentance, and that in absolute perfection, all—excepting the per-
> sonal consciousness of sin—and by that perfect response in Amen to the
> mind of God in relation to sin is the wrath of God rightly met, and that is
> accorded to divine justice which is its due, and could alone satisfy it.[20]

This is a dogmatically controlled intuitive insight into the nature of the
atonement that illustrates both the task and the risk of theology—the task
because McLeod Campbell thinks through or beyond the narrative of the
scriptural texts, seeking to apprehend the reality of God to which they bear
witness; the risk because he ventures into the mystery of God and our redemption, where there is always the danger of saying too much. Bearing
witness to God is one thing, speculation and theory-building are something
else, and sometimes it is a fine line that separates them. According to
McLeod Campbell, then, Christ responds to the judgment of God as the true
priest with a perfect response, a perfect sorrow, and an adequate repentance
on behalf of all, which alone can satisfy God's judgment. Our sin has been
borne away not by an equivalent punishment and pain, as required by the
penal theory, but by an equivalent repentance in our stead and on our behalf.[21] Christ as God knows the awful sorrow of sin upon the heart of God.

---

[19]McLeod Campbell, *Nature of the Atonement*, p. 118 (italics original).
[20]Ibid. (italics original).
[21]This notion of vicarious repentance had already been found in Scottish theology in Samuel Ruth-
   erford's *Christ Dying and Drawing Sinners to Himselfe; or A Survey of Our Saviour in His Soule-
   suffering, His Lovelynesse in His Death, and the Efficacie Thereof* (London: n.p., 1647), p. 79, cited

His perfect "Amen" is from a heart broken by the burden of sin and the need for repentance acceptable to God. In this way, similar to the theology of Athanasius, in the interceding life of Jesus itself, by the virtue of his vicarious active obedience in the flesh of our humanity, the atonement is not only rendered possible by the incarnation, but also is itself a development of the incarnation.[22] That is to say, the incarnation as such is not the atonement, for here the active obedience of Jesus toward the Father on our behalf is greatly stressed. Further, McLeod Campbell saw that the atonement was not something done "above our heads" or as an external act removed at a distance from us, as it were, but was an act of God's grace from within Christ's vicarious humanity that entailed both God for us and us for God in the unity of his person and as lived out through his ministry and death.

It is a matter of considerable debate whether so-called vicarious repentance or vicarious penitence is a valid theological construct. H. R. Mackintosh did not directly discuss this construct or McLeod Campbell's atonement theology in either of his major works. He did, however, publish a brief essay on the topic in 1916, with some detailed reference to McLeod Campbell. It is helpful to look briefly at this essay.[23] Initially, the construct strikes Mackintosh as the fruit of devout and spiritual thought, avoiding all strains of a legal interpretation of the gospel. Regarding McLeod Campbell in particular, Mackintosh has high praise. No one, he judges, would be more rewarded than to sit at the feet of McLeod Campbell when reflecting on the deepest problems of the cross of Christ.

Nevertheless, there are objections to the notion of vicarious penitence. Mackintosh notes first that there is no New Testament account that resembles the view that Christ repented of our sins vicariously. Second, with respect to application to Jesus, the sinless man, the idea of vicarious peni-

---

in T. F. Torrance, *Scottish Theology: From John Knox to John McLeod Campbell* (Edinburgh: T & T Clark, 1996), p. 305. McLeod Campbell used the expression "perfect repentance" to refer to an aspect of Christ's response to divine judgment against sin, meaning by it Christ's expiatory confession of our sin. Subsequently, commentators tend to refer to this either as "vicarious repentance" or "vicarious penitence." It is difficult to differentiate between these references. Repentance suggests something of an inner disposition of sorrow or regret, while penitence seems to carry the notion of an outward act corresponding to that sorrow or regret. I judge that McLeod Campbell is intending both references, insofar as Christ suffered in both his soul and his body.

[22]McLeod Campbell, *Nature of the Atonement*, p. 122.

[23]H. R. Mackintosh, "The Vicarious Penance of Christ," in *Some Aspects of Christian Belief* (New York: George H. Doran, n.d. [preface, 1923]), pp. 79-98.

tence is not true to life. One repents only for one's own sin. It makes no sense, says Mackintosh, to repent for another's sins. Third, the most obvious criticism is that the term *penitence* not just implies but includes guilt. Can this be transferred to Jesus, who did not commit moral evil? The same question, of course, sits at the door of the doctrine of penal substitution. How can someone be justly punished for something that he or she did not commit? A final objection is that the notion of atonement as something provided by God, as an expression of divine purpose and love, means that the nature of atonement must be predicable of God. Can we predicate penitence of God? Does that make any sense?

On the other hand, what can be learned from McLeod Campbell at this point? Mackintosh identifies promising contours for atonement theory. First, vicarious penitence points us to a great inward experience of Jesus, a terrible spiritual anguish, where perfect holiness and love meet sin's malice and passion against God. McLeod Campbell has opened a window to a deep truth. Our sins bore down upon Jesus in a terrible way such that any theory of the atonement must keep in mind that he bore our sins deeply within himself, and not merely in some way external to himself in an imputed manner. Second, vicarious penitence leads us to be aware of Christ's true oneness with us. His identifying presence with us must lead him to know the shame for our dark wrongdoing and to take responsibility for it. If, says Mackintosh, "vicarious penitence" is the wrong term for this, the reality still must be acknowledged. Third, vicarious penitence is suggestive of the truth that our Lord's acknowledgment of God's righteous judgment and bearing of it must have its place in an account of the atonement.

What McLeod Campbell's position finally lacks, according to Mackintosh, is a satisfying account of Christ's death. Why was a verbal contrition not enough? Why must blood be drawn to make an atonement? We must return to this later, in the next chapter on McLeod Campbell's atonement theory, because this seems to be the nub of the critique, and he tries to answer it head on. For now, an alternative question in support of McLeod Campbell can be posed (I find it inexplicable that McLeod Campbell did not discuss this in support of his approach): If baptism by John was a baptism unto repentance, why was Jesus, the sinless man, baptized by John if not for us in a vicarious repentance? To suggest otherwise would be to give Jesus' baptism some manner of symbolic but empty significance only, turning it into an example for us to follow. But what is the example we are to follow? Jesus' baptism as an example for us to follow really makes no sense, insofar as we will never receive the baptism of John.

Before taking leave of Mackintosh for now, we should note that he makes some very McLeod Campbell–like comments in his chapter on the atonement in *The Christian Experience of Forgiveness*, although the latter's name is not mentioned. This book was published in 1927, and it leads one to wonder if Mackintosh had overcome some previous doubts over McLeod Campbell's approach. Writing of Christ's death, Mackintosh says, "For us, with us, He there bowed under the Father's judgment on sin, confessing the sinfulness of wrong and its utter evil in God's sight. His bowing thus, in perfect love, *was* His sacrifice. . . . We take His confession as our own, pronouncing our Amen to His utter acceptance of the righteous will of God."[24] Christ thus identified himself as making the sacrifice for sin through the mind and spirit of perfect sonship, which satisfied the Father's heart. This confession of sinfulness by which we are forgiven for Christ's sake does not mean that Christ propitiated God such that wrong was remitted; rather, the love of the Father is the font of redemption, and the atonement is the manner, flowing from his love, in which pardon is given.[25]

We now turn briefly to the response of T. F. Torrance to McLeod Campbell's doctrine of Christ's retrospectively confessing our sin to the Father. Torrance notes that McLeod Campbell intends Christ's "perfect Amen" to have been yielded out of the ontological depth of his humanity.[26] That is, McLeod Campbell intends us to see that the atonement takes place within the incarnate constitution of the mediator. This is a point that I emphasized before. It means here that we are not just externally, imputationally justified, but personally, in such a way that through Christ's incarnation vicarious sorrow lay at the heart of his atoning sacrifice.[27]

What really did McLeod Campbell mean by Christ's "perfect repentance," the term that he employed? Torrance ventures that McLeod Campbell was

---

[24]H. R. Mackintosh, *The Christian Experience of Forgiveness* (New York: Harper & Brothers, 1927), pp. 224-25.
[25]Ibid., p. 225.
[26]Torrance, *Scottish Theology*, p. 300.
[27]Ibid., p. 305.

feeling after the meaning implied in the patristic Latin term *poenitentia*, correlated with *poena*.[28] The latter is used of penalty or satisfaction; the former of repentance or penitence. *Poenitentia*, then, is the internal counterpart to *poena*. In this sense, says Torrance, vicarious penitence makes sense. Further, in view of Christ's inseparable oneness with God, Christ's "Amen" to God is the actualization of incarnation, the expression of Christ's submission to God's judgment on sin.

Clearly we are wading in deep water, where the sheer mystery of which we are trying to speak demands that we try to put out a little farther. Whatever else McLeod Campbell was trying to do with his notion of Christ retrospectively dealing with God on the part of humankind, he was reaching for something ineffable yet wonderful, no less than the Christian confidence in God's love and mercy revealed in Jesus Christ. Thus Torrance, I think, for all of his technical brilliance and complexity, gets it about right when he puts McLeod Campbell's intentions into pastoral form. "'Perfect repentance,' in McLeod Campbell's deeply spiritual sense, means that when the sinner confesses his sins, all too unworthily, the Gospel tells him that *Christ has already answered for him*, and that *God in Christ has already accepted him*, so that the sinner does not rest on any repentance of his own, but on what Christ has already offered to the Father not just in his place but on his behalf."[29] I will discuss Torrance's views on representation and substitution later in the book. With that, we will turn now to the prospective aspect of the atonement to illustrate further the bidirectional mediatorial Christology at the heart of the magnificent exchange.

The atonement in its prospective aspect. The gospel of the atonement not only deals with our past sins and the judgment of God upon us. For McLeod Campbell, Christ's confession of our sin in response to divine condemnation of it must have contemplated our own participation in that confession and its consequence for us. Atonement is not just appeasement of the past; it must look also to our future life with and in God, to restoration to a life of communion with God. Atonement must be seen in the light of the end contemplated: the meaning of communion with God is our participation in eternal life through union with Christ. To this end McLeod Campbell favorably cites

---

[28]Ibid., pp. 305-6.
[29]Ibid., p. 308.

1 Peter 3:18: "For Christ also suffered for sins once for all, the righteous for the unrighteousness, in order to bring you to God." Thus the remission of sins is directly related to the gift of eternal life.[30] This end contemplated is, for McLeod Campbell, not the legal title of an imputed righteousness but rather life in Christ, nothing less than participation in the mind and life of Christ in his life of sonship to the Father.[31] Once again we make note of the astonishing creativity that McLeod Campbell brought to soteriology when he gave such weight to the eschatological aspect and its impact on the sanctified life of sonship that is ours in Christ and through the Holy Spirit.

In order to develop this general perspective of the ends contemplated in the atonement, McLeod Campbell once again appeals to the bidirectional mediatorial Christology that we are examining, but now in prospective aspect. First, McLeod Campbell reflects on the Son's honoring the Father in the sight of people, which is the "downward" or God-toward-human aspect. This revealing of the Father has as its object our participation in the life of sonship, knowing, enjoying and inheriting the Father as our Father. "We are called to hear the Son that we may know the Father through knowing the Son in whom He is well pleased, and so may know what is the Father's desire as to ourselves, and what He has given to us in the Son, that that desire of His heart for us may be fulfilled in us."[32] Thus we are called in Christ to enjoy the Father as our Father, making us heirs of God and joint heirs with Christ. The deep truth to which McLeod Campbell would direct us here is that in Christ we truly know the Father's heart toward us. We now see the sin that made us godless, thereby becoming orphans, but even more, much more, we see the intended restoration of our orphan spirits to the Father and the Father of spirits to his lost children.[33]

Prospectively, dealing with God on our behalf, what Christ desires for us is nothing less than our sharing in his human fellowship with the Father.[34] And it is here that the full nature of the atonement shines through to us. Christ has offered to the Father the true and perfect response to the Father's love, which is

---

[30]McLeod Campbell, *Nature of the Atonement*, p. 128.
[31]Ibid., p. 129.
[32]Ibid., p. 137.
[33]Ibid., p. 139.
[34]Ibid., p. 141.

accepted and is now to be reproduced in us.[35] Gloriously, "what God has accepted for us in Christ, is also what God has given to us in Christ."[36] This is the power to confess our sins with our "Amen" to Christ's confession of them. It is knowledge of our adoption as "sons." This leads to worship of the Father, which is true "sonship," our access into the holiest of all, the Father's heart. Thus we are established in a filial relation to the Father of our spirits. Thus is fulfilled the teaching of John 14:6: "No one comes to the Father except through [the Son]." This is the great and all-including necessity that is revealed by the atonement.

We who are called to repentance, to say "Amen" to Christ's righteous "Amen" to God's judgment upon us, are not to be abandoned at the last minute to our own devices and ostensible spiritual capacities. In fact, we who are called to respond make our "Amen" to Christ's "Amen" by the grace of our union with Christ through the Holy Spirit. The relational character of this is reflected in McLeod Campbell's move from the retrospective to the prospective aspects of the atonement, where he moved mostly from theistic language, with its reference to God, to filial language, with its reference to the Father, as befits the goal of the gospel. The atonement is not just a sharing in Christ's benefits, but even more it is a sharing in his filial love for the Father, a sharing in a relationship that is uniquely his. Jesus reveals God precisely as Father, and only in that revelation do we know who the Father is and what is the desire of the Father's heart. This knowledge teaches us of our loss through sin and of the Father's will to restore us from our orphan state to communion through adoption. In order to do this, Christ, who has made the perfect confession, now presents his own righteousness in humanity expressed as perfect love toward and in service of God. Christ has consecrated a way into the holy company of God through the purification of his blood, enabling us, in his name—that is, in union with him through the Holy Spirit— not only to worship God in truth and to draw near to God, crying, "Abba, Father," but also to serve God as we are called to do. We come to God as God's children or not at all,[37] and that alone in union with the priestly sonship of Jesus Christ, in his revealing of the Father as our Father, and in his offering of us in his own human nature to share in his divine sonship.

---

[35]Ibid., p. 142.
[36]Ibid., p. 143.
[37]Ibid., p. 243.

Two aspects of Calvin's theology deeply influenced McLeod Campbell at this point: our union with Christ (to be considered shortly) and the notion of the wonderful exchange that lay at the center of Calvin's understanding of the Eucharist (as we have already seen). As argued, the two concepts must be interpreted together. Christ, who has joined himself to us in his incarnation, joins us to his ascended human nature through the Spirit, and, by his continuing priestly intercession for us, he makes us to share in his filial communion with the Father, effecting a wonderful exchange, a glorious substitution, taking to himself our sin, enmity and death, giving us what is his—his righteousness, love, eternal life—leading us to pray, "Our Father, who art in heaven." This is salvation.

The foregoing may be summed up by the wonderful statement of McLeod Campbell: "Therefore Christ, as the Lord of our spirits and our life, *devotes us to God* and *devotes us to men* in the *fellowship of his self-sacrifice*."[38] This one sentence is surely the sum of all practical theology. The dogmatic development of practical theology within an ecumenical, catholic and evangelical perspective, in other words, is based on a comprehensive doctrine of the atonement.

A comment is now in order. McLeod Campbell's theology of the atonement, developed precisely in line with the priestly ministry of Jesus Christ, opens up fresh vistas of theological insight. In view of his reflection on the nature of the atonement, the doctrine never looks quite the same again. Yet its strength is also a problem: it suffers from single-mindedness. He has taken one soteriological metaphor—our restoration to communion with the Father—and allowed it to open up the whole of the gospel. Other metaphors, of course, must also be included and developed to open up the soteriological vista in a comprehensive way. His arguments leave atonement theory incomplete, in part because of his unremitting pastoral resistance to penal atonement and its perceived negative effect upon the spiritual well-being of his people. It may be too that he pushed his reflections into speculations because he took the risk of thinking theologically as far as he thought he could penetrate into the truth of the gospel. Nevertheless, because his theology is before us, even in a partial form, as a corrective to what he took to be a diminished view of the gospel, we

---

[38]Ibid., p. 255.

can look again at the biblical metaphors that express the majesty and holiness of God in legal terms and allow them an appropriate, though not a controlling, place. For our purposes, however, the priestly ministry of Christ is both illustrated and deepened in our awareness as an integral aspect of the gospel. And the christological structure of the magnificent exchange is before us in its architectonic grandeur.

The bidirectional mediatorial structure of Christology in T. F. Torrance. As Torrance indicates again and again, he is deeply indebted to Athanasius in many ways. This indebtedness is found, for example, in his development of what Athanasius spoke of as Christ exercising a twofold ministry, as we have seen, in which he "ministered not only the things of God to man but ministered the things of man to God."[39] This is a vigorously developed theme in Torrance's Christology. It is especially important to explain how Torrance understands the role of Jesus Christ as the true human in his response to God on our behalf, for that is an aspect of Christology that is often left undeveloped. When this is thought through in relation to the doctrine of union with Christ, Torrance introduces directly his understanding of our specific forms of response that are called forth by the gospel. It is in this way that we can rightly speak of Torrance as a practical theologian.

Following Athanasius, and in keeping with what we have seen with McLeod Campbell, Torrance asserts that in the incarnation there is both a humanward and a Godward direction, in which Christ mediates God to us and us to God in the unity of his incarnate personhood. This is the direct correlate of the hypostatic union. Thus Torrance refers to the

> double fact that in Jesus Christ the Word of God has become man, has assumed a human form, in order as such to be God's language to man, and that in Jesus Christ there is gathered up and embodied, in obedient response to God, man's true word to God and his true speech about God. Jesus Christ is at once the complete revelation of God to man and the correspondence on man's part to that revelation required by it for the fulfilment of its own revealing movement.[40]

---

[39]Thomas F. Torrance, "Athanasius: A Study in the Foundations of Classical Theology," in *Theology in Reconciliation: Essays Towards Evangelical and Catholic Unity in East and West* (London: Geoffrey Chapman, 1975), p. 228.

[40]Thomas F. Torrance, "The Place of Christology in Biblical and Dogmatic Theology," in *Theology in Reconstruction* (London: SCM Press, 1965), p. 129.

Torrance insists that because the Word of God has been addressed to us, and has actually reached us because it has been addressed to us in Jesus Christ, we have the Word that has found a response in our hearing and understanding. That is, we do not begin with God alone or with humankind alone,

> but with God and man as they are posited together in a movement of creative self-communication by the Word of God. . . . A profound reciprocity is created in which God addresses His Word to man by giving it human form without any diminishment of its divine reality as God Himself speaks it, and in which He enables man to hear His Word and respond to it without any cancellation of his human mode of being. . . . Thus the Word of God communicated to man includes within itself meeting between man and God as well as meeting between God and man, for in assuming the form of human speech the Word of God spoken to man becomes at the same time the word of man in answer to God.[41]

Torrance identifies the foundation for the christological development of the incarnate reciprocity between God and humankind in the nature of the covenant partnership between God and Israel, found, for example, in the covenant established between God and Israel at Mount Sinai.[42] God, within the covenant established and maintained unilaterally by God, freely and graciously gave a covenanted way of response so that the covenant might be fulfilled. Israel was given ordinances of worship designed to testify that God alone can expiate guilt, forgive sin and establish communion. This was not just a formal rite to guarantee propitiation between God and Israel. By its very nature, the covenanted way of response was to be worked into the flesh and blood of Israel's existence in such a way that Israel was called to pattern their whole life after it.

Later, in the prophecies of the Isaiah tradition especially, the notions of guilt-bearer and sacrifice for sin were conflated to give the interpretive clue for the vicarious role of the Servant of the Lord. "The hypostatised actualisation within the flesh and blood existence of Israel of the divinely provided way of covenant response [was] set forth in the cult. . . . A messianic role was evidently envisaged for the servant in which mediator and sacrifice,

---

[41]Thomas F. Torrance, "The Word of God and the Response of Man," in *God and Rationality* (London: Oxford University Press, 1971), pp. 137-38.

[42]For the following, see Thomas F. Torrance, *The Mediation of Christ* (Grand Rapids: Eerdmans, 1983), pp. 83-86.

priest and victim were combined in a form at once representative and substitutionary, corporate and individual, in its fulfilment."[43] As the Servant of
the Lord and the Redeemer, the Holy One of Israel, were brought together
in the prophetic mind, "and yet held apart only by a hair's breadth,"[44] it
seems that there was the dawning awareness that the Servant of the Lord is
to be the Lord himself, who comes to redeem Israel. It would take the incarnation to actually bring that to pass, however, for Jesus Christ was recognized and presented in the New Testament both as the Servant of the Lord
and as the divine Redeemer, not now only of Israel, but of all people.

> As the incarnate Son of the Father Jesus Christ has been sent to fulfil all righ-
> teousness both as priest and as victim, who through his one self-offering in
> atonement for sin has mediated a new covenant of universal range in which
> he presents us to his Father as those whom he has redeemed, sanctified and
> perfected for ever in himself. In other words, Jesus Christ constitutes in his
> own self-consecrated humanity the fulfilment of the vicarious way of human
> response to God promised under the old covenant, but now on the ground of
> his atoning self-sacrifice once for all offered this as a vicarious way of response
> which is available for all mankind.[45]

Jesus Christ has fulfilled the covenant from both sides—from God's side
and from our side. In the incarnate unity of his person he is the divine-human
Word, "spoken to man from the highest and heard by him in the depths, and
spoken to God out of the depths and heard by Him in the highest."[46] "Expressed otherwise, in the hypostatic union between God and man in Jesus
Christ there is included a union between the Word of God and the word of
man."[47] In which case, concludes Torrance, the gospel is not to be understood
as the Word of God coming to us, inviting our response, but as including "the
all-significant middle term, the divinely provided response in the vicarious
humanity of Jesus Christ."[48] Our response in faith, then, is made, through the
Spirit, in Christ, as by God's grace we lay hold of Christ's response for us.

Torrance was fond of citing Hebrews 3:1-6, where reference is made to

---

[43]Ibid., p. 85.
[44]Ibid., p. 86.
[45]Ibid.
[46]Torrance, "Word of God," p. 138.
[47]Ibid., p. 142.
[48]Ibid., p. 145.

Christ as "the apostle and high priest of our confession." Says Torrance, "Here we have described Christ's twofold function in priestly mediation. He is the Apostle or *Saliah* of God, and He is also our High Priest made in all points as we are, but without sin."[49] As high priest, Jesus is contrasted with Moses, who was faithful in all God's house as a servant (Num 12:7; Heb 3:5), while Jesus is Son over his own house (Heb 3:6).

> In this particular passage the work of Christ as Apostle and High Priest, both in the sense of "the Son over the House," is described in terms of confession, *homologia*, a word which occurs in three other passages (3.1; 4.14; 10.23). In each case it sets forth primarily the confession made by the High Priest as he enters within the veil. It is the confession of our sin before God and the confession of God's righteous judgement upon our sin. As Apostle Christ bears witness for God, that He is Holy. As High Priest He acknowledges that witness and says Amen to it. Again as Apostle of God He confesses the mercy and grace of God, His will to pardon and reconcile. As High Priest He intercedes for men, and confesses them before the face of God.[50]

The confession of Christ as apostle and high priest is not in word only, but includes the actual judgment of God at the cross and the actual submission of Christ in full and perfect obedience. But this obedience of Christ to the judgment of God must not be limited to his passive obedience only, in which, he was "made under the law" to bear its condemnation in our name and on our behalf. For he lived also to bend back the will of humankind into a perfect submission to the will of God through a life lived in active filial obedience to his heavenly Father. Torrance understands, therefore, that the humanity of Christ was not external to the atonement, and that the atonement cannot be limited only to his passive obedience. Rather, Jesus Christ, "bone of our bone, flesh of our flesh," "*is* our human response to God."[51] In Christ's passive *and* active obedience he not only suffered the judgment of God on the cross for us, but also fulfilled the will of God in an obedient life of filial love. In view of this development of the vicarious humanity of Christ, it is clear why Torrance insists that incarnation and atonement must be thought together, and

---

[49]Thomas F. Torrance, *Royal Priesthood: A Theology of Ordained Ministry* (Edinburgh: T & T Clark, 1955), p. 11.

[50]Ibid., p. 12.

[51]Torrance, *Mediation of Christ*, p. 90.

why revelation and reconciliation are inseparable, in order to have a full doctrine of justification and sanctification.

I close this discussion with brief reference to Torrance's discussion of the life and faithfulness of the Son toward the Father as he develops this in *Incarnation: The Person and Life of Christ*. There the bidirectional structure of the magnificent exchange is developed in one aspect—the human-to-God direction—in a manner that is concrete and specific.

In an astonishing thrust of grace, the Son of God descends into our communion-with-God-shattered world in order to live out from within it a life of filial obedience to the Father through which humanity is brought back into communion with the Father.[52] In order to understand this we have to think especially of the active obedience of the Son in terms of positive communion, filial love and worship. In language that echoes McLeod Campbell, Torrance writes of the Son's life of perfect sonship on earth toward the Father. As such, Christ lifts up humanity in himself to communion with the Father, restoring the image of God in alienated humanity.[53] In this regard Torrance considers the active obedience of Jesus Christ in three ways.

First, Jesus fulfills the divine covenant as the man of prayer. In the incarnation, as we have seen, Christ fulfills the covenant from the side of God *and* from the side of humankind. Thus it is in our place that Jesus prays to the God who hears prayer. From the side of human disobedience Jesus prays a prayer of obedience.[54] In his praying, God's will to be known as our Father is fulfilled, as also from within our alienated existence Jesus offers a childlike and filial obedience. Christ's prayers in effect bind God to us and us to God.

It is in the context of the double movement in Christ of God's faithful seeking and assuming humankind back into fellowship, and of humankind's faithful return to God, summed up in the Father-Son relationship characterized in Christ's life of prayer, that the powers of evil attack him.[55] Christ is faced with terrible temptations to break the bonds of fellowship with the Father, to destroy his life of prayer and obedience, and to render void the meeting between God and humankind in Jesus. Evil attempts "to destroy

---

[52]Torrance, *Incarnation*, pp. 114-29.
[53]Ibid., p. 115.
[54]Ibid., p. 118.
[55]Ibid., p. 119.

the ground of reconciliation, to disrupt the foundation for atonement being laid in the obedient and prayerful life of the Son of Man."[56]

Yet Christ was faithful over God's house as a son (Heb 3:6). Torrance does not cite this verse at this point, but it was often in his mind and serves well to sum up the theology before us. Jesus, under the attack of evil, remained faithful, continuing to present himself to the Father in worship and adoration as the perfect human self-offering to God. Torrance calls this "the great *palingenesia* [rebirth], the great conversion of humanity to God."[57] In and through Jesus Christ we have a mediator with the Father, bringing the Father to us and us to the Father, who works out this ministry as our substitute and representative before God through his life of prayer and worship. And supremely this is done by him drawing us into his own prayer. This happens, first, as we overhear his high priestly prayer at John 17, where he prayed for his disciples and us, where he presents himself and us to the Father. Then he went forth to Gethsemane fulfilling in deed and death the prayer of his incarnate life: "Not my will, but thine, be done."[58] And second, he gives us the prayer of his own filial life with the Father, so that in Christ we are bold to pray, "Our Father who art in heaven." In this way, we live the new life of fellowship with God in Jesus Christ.

Second, Jesus fulfills the divine covenant as the man of obedience. He offered the "Amen" of the godly life faithful to the will of God, the last Adam undoing the sin of the first Adam.[59] Christ stood in the gap created by human rebellion against God and lived the obedient life effecting our reconciliation with God. This is what we see in his baptism (is McLeod Campbell in mind?), where he "set himself to offer in our place contrition for our sin, acceptance of the divine verdict upon our guilt, and a holy life in amendment of ours."[60] Torrance calls this "the vicarious baptism unto repentance," no less.[61] Thus Christ offered to God in our name the perfect faith, confidence and trust through his life of thanksgiving and praise. For us, he was the faithful believer who gave the acceptable human response to God.

---

[56]Ibid.
[57]Ibid.
[58]Ibid., pp. 120-21.
[59]Ibid., p. 123.
[60]Ibid., p. 124.
[61]Ibid., p. 125.

Although it is not part of the discussion in this Torrance text, he was a vigorous advocate for the subjective genitive translation of *pisteōs Iēsou Christou*, the "faith *of* Jesus Christ," as found in the KJV translation (see, e.g., Rom 3:22, 26; Gal 2:16; 3:22; Phil 3:9).[62] Torrance undoubtedly found this translation congenial to his consistent conviction that it is the faithfulness of Jesus that saves us, not our appropriation of salvation through our faith. Nevertheless, and it remains a subtle point, Torrance believed that our faith was called for to be received as the gift of the Holy Spirit, and that rejection of this gift brought dire consequences, no less than rejection of salvation.

And third, Jesus fulfilled the divine covenant perfectly reflecting the divine glory. The structure of Christology is now familiar: Jesus Christ was at once the complete revelation of God toward humankind and the perfect correspondence on our part to that revelation. This means that the course of Christ's life was identical (*homoousios tō Patri*) with the course of the Father's action toward humankind.[63] Jesus was the image of the invisible God, present among us bodily (Col 2:9). Everything that he says and does rests entirely upon the mutual relation of the Son to the Father and the Father to the Son, a closed relation to which we have entry through our union with Christ. In this way, the life of Jesus is the specific place on earth and within history where revelation and reconciliation with God took place; Christ is the "place" where God and humankind meet and where the divine covenant is fulfilled.

In closing it might be enough to say that the magnificent exchange is the Father-Son relationship and the hypostatic union in action. For both John McLeod Campbell and Thomas F. Torrance, the magnificent exchange is the incarnation seen through the lens of atonement, even if it is not yet all that has to be said about atonement.

UNION WITH CHRIST

The magnificent exchange is to be thought of as Jesus Christ as he unfolds himself out in saving ministry by which he joins us to himself in his human nature and us to him. Union with Christ is embedded as one work within the magnificent exchange as by the Holy Spirit he binds us to himself in his human nature to share his benefits. It is important to be clear here that in

---

[62]For a bibliography, see ibid., p. 28n40.
[63]Ibid., p. 126.

union with Christ we are not somehow mystically swept up into his person so as to lose our personal identity such that dynamic interaction and relationship with Jesus are lost. Union with Christ does not mean that we become Jesus in some way; union requires and maintains a distinction of persons. But it does mean that through the Spirit's gift of union with Christ's exalted human nature we are transformed, made new people, which may be expressed as having baptismal identity. He takes what is ours, sinful and broken before God, and heals it, so that in Christ we are holy and blameless before God in love (Eph 1:4), and he gives us what is his, to share in his filial life with the Father. In putting the two together in this way we show the atoning exchange and union with Christ as essentially one event, having personal, relational and participatory character.

It is only through union with Christ that we partake of the blessings of his holy and obedient life.[64] Writing on the doctrine of deification through grace, Torrance notes that Reformed theology interprets participation in the divine nature as the union and communion we are given to have with Christ in his human nature. It is properly understood as participation in his incarnate sonship, and therefore as sharing in him in the divine life and love. That is to say, it interprets "deification" precisely in the same way as Athanasius does in *Contra Arianos*. It is only through "real and substantial union" (Calvin's expression) with him in his human nature that we partake of all his benefits, such as justification and sanctification and regeneration. Because in Christ human nature is hypostatically united to divine nature so that the Godhead dwells in him "bodily," in him we really are made partakers of the eternal life of God himself.[65]

Torrance has observed in a number of places that Scottish theology at the Reformation gave a place of centrality to the union of God and humankind in Christ, and to the understanding of the Christian life therefore as an offering to God only "by the hand of Christ" (John Knox).[66] Thus, "It is in and through our union with him, that all that is his becomes ours."[67] And again,

---

[64]Thomas F. Torrance, "Justification: Its Radical Nature and Place in Reformed Doctrine and Life," in *Theology in Reconstruction*, p. 158.
[65]Thomas F. Torrance, "The Roman Doctrine of Grace from the Point of View of Reformed Theology," in *Theology in Reconstruction*, p. 184.
[66]See Torrance, *Scottish Theology*, p. 42; idem, "Justification," p. 151.
[67]Torrance, "Justification," p. 151.

"It is only through union with Christ that we partake of the blessings of Christ, that is through union with him in his holy and obedient life. . . . Through union with him we share in his faith, in his obedience, in his trust and his appropriation of the Father's blessing."[68] In this way, through union with Christ Torrance's Christology moves on seamlessly to his exposition of the Christian life. Union with Christ is given to us through the gift of the Holy Spirit, and as such it is the ground of the church and ministry. However, there is nothing mechanical or automatic in this. By a real communion with Christ by the Holy Spirit we are turned back to God in freedom. But even in our response to God, in faith, life and ministry it is to Christ that we look and on him we depend in all things. According to Torrance, "The Christian Church is what it is because of its indissoluble union with Christ through the Spirit, for in him is concentrated the Church and all ministry. . . . [Thus], there is only one ministry, that of Christ in his Body."[69] It is the case, then, that the Holy Spirit constitutes the church in union with its Head, joining us to Christ to share in his communion with the Father and to bear faithful witness to him in the life of the world.

Although McLeod Campbell does not use the expression "union with Christ," something of the intent of the construct as we have it in Torrance may be found already in the earlier theologian. Importantly for what is excluded, McLeod Campbell notes, "The relation of our participation in the atonement to the atonement is radically a different thing from what the words 'following an example' suggest."[70] Positively put,

> Ascending upwards to the mind of God, into the light of which the atonement introduces us, and descending again to the ultimate fulfilment of that mind in men washed from their sins in the blood of Christ, and made kings and priests unto God, and reigning with Christ, we not only feel a harmony and simplicity and beauty in the natural relation of the atonement to Christianity, but we are also conscious to finding in that natural relation a chief and most sure ground for our faith in the atonement, and in remission of sins, and eternal life, as presented to us in connection with it. Every time we are enabled, in spirit and in truth, through participation in the spirit of Christ, to confess

---

[68]Ibid., pp. 158-59.
[69]Thomas F. Torrance, "The Foundation of the Church: Union with Christ through the Spirit," in *Theology in Reconstruction*, p. 208.
[70]McLeod Campbell, *Nature of the Atonement*, p. 232.

sin before God, and meet His mind towards sin with such a response as, in the faith of pardon and liberty of sonship, we are enabled to give, we have a clearer glimpse of the excellence of Christ's expiatory confession of our sins, and of the righteousness of God in accepting it on our behalf, to the end that we might thus share in it.[71]

That long, cumbersome quotation represents McLeod Campbell's fuller position. In summary fashion it is also expressed "as the quickening in us of the life of sonship."[72] For McLeod Campbell, union with Christ is the experience of orphans who have found their long-lost Father. The Holy Spirit, in which case, is the spirit of sonship, and with sonship, necessarily, comes knowledge of and confidence in the fatherliness of the Father. Thus the Father by the Spirit draws us to the Son[73]—union with Christ in all but name. The gift of faith is the fellowship of the Son's apprehension of the Father, which is sonship, and which utters itself finally and fully as "Abba, dear Father."[74] Surely to utter such is nothing else than our experience of living within the magnificent exchange.

Something of a similar intimacy with regard to the experience of union with Christ is found also with H. R. Mackintosh, and we have already taken notice of this. At the core of union with Christ is the intimate sense that we are forgiven,[75] and in that Mackintosh and McLeod Campbell share a similar theological intuition. As Mackintosh interprets the apostle Paul, this is not a vague feeling of forgiveness; it is tied directly to our relationship to Christ. More than justifying faith that lays hold of the imputed righteousness of Christ, union with Christ unites people to Christ, putting them right with God; but by the same token it makes people share in the fellowship of Christ's own life of divine power.[76] Says Mackintosh directly, "Christ takes us with Him, as it were, into communion with God."[77] Thus we must think of faith in terms of organic living relations: God in Christ for us, we in Christ for God—the magnificent exchange, in other words, in which Christ is one with us and we are one with him.

---

[71]Ibid., p. 236.
[72]Ibid., p. 238.
[73]Ibid., p. 253.
[74]Ibid., p. 166.
[75]Mackintosh, *Christian Experience of Forgiveness*, p. 123.
[76]Ibid., p. 125.
[77]Ibid., p. 225.

I conclude these reflections by giving attention to specific forms of response through participation in Christ's mediation of our human response to God, noting briefly how Torrance understands faith, worship and Christian service in terms of the vicarious humanity (his real humanity for us) of Christ.

Faith. For Torrance, before we refer to our own faith, faith must be understood first of all in terms of "Jesus stepping into the relation between the faithfulness of God and the actual unfaithfulness of human beings, actualising the faithfulness of God and restoring the faithfulness of human beings by grounding it in the incarnate medium of his own faithfulness so that it answers perfectly to the divine faithfulness."[78] In this way, according to Torrance, Jesus acts in our place from within our unfaithfulness, and by the gift and bond of the Holy Spirit we are given a faithfulness in which we may share. He is the truth of God and human being keeping faith, and also truth with God in the unity of God revealing himself and human being hearing, believing, obeying and speaking his Word.[79] In this way, our faith is grounded objectively yet personally in Christ, the one who believes for us; our faith depends upon the faithfulness of God in Christ for us. In fact, that is what faith is: trust in the faithfulness of Jesus Christ, to which we are joined. "Thus the faith which we confess is the faith of Jesus Christ who loved us and gave himself for us in a life and death of utter trust and belief in God the Father. Our faith is altogether grounded in him who is 'author and finisher,' on whom faith depends from start to finish."[80] Indeed, we are summoned to believe, but in such a way as "our faith is laid hold of, enveloped, and upheld by his unswerving faithfulness."[81] Thus, according to Torrance, we rely not upon our own believing, "but wholly upon [Christ's] vicarious response of faithfulness toward God."[82]

Worship. As above with regard to faith, so also with regard to worship, Torrance insists that Jesus Christ has embodied for us the response of human beings to God in such a way that henceforth all worship and prayer are grounded in him. "Jesus Christ in his own self-oblation to the Father *is* our

---

[78]Torrance, *Mediation of Christ*, p. 92.

[79]Torrance, "Word of God," p. 154.

[80]Torrance, *Mediation of Christ*, p. 94.

[81]Thomas F. Torrance, *Preaching Christ Today: The Gospel and Scientific Thinking* (Grand Rapids: Eerdmans, 1994), p. 31.

[82]Torrance, "Word of God," p. 154.

worship and prayer in an acutely personalised form, so that it is only through him and with him that we may draw near to God with the hands of our faith filled with no other offering but that which he has made on our behalf and in our place once and for all."[83] Thus all approach to God is in the name and significance of Jesus Christ, "for worship and prayer are not ways in which we express ourselves but ways in which we hold up before the Father his beloved Son, take refuge in his atoning sacrifice, and make that our only plea."[84] Christ has united himself to us in such a way that he gathers up our faltering worship into himself, so that in presenting himself to the Father he presents also the worship of all creation to share in his own communion with the Father. For Torrance, in worship, as in faith, Christ's takes our place, and we trust by the Spirit solely in his vicarious self-offering to the Father.

Christian service. The essential nature of the church, as of individual Christians, is participation in the humanity of Jesus Christ, who is the love of God poured out for us. That is, "the Church is Church as it participates in the active operation of the divine love."[85] As the Son is sent from the Father, so the being of the church in love involves a sharing in the mission of Jesus Christ. In this way, ministry is grounded upon a christological pattern (*hypodeigma*). Thus, "as the Body of which he is the Head the Church participates in His ministry by serving Him in history where it is sent by Him in fulfilment of His ministry of reconciliation."[86] The ministry of the church is not another ministry, different from the ministry of Christ or separate from it, but rather takes its essential form and content from the servant-existence and mission of Jesus. The mission of the church is not an extension of the mission of Jesus; it is a sharing in the continuing and now exalted mission of Jesus, by the grace of the Holy Spirit. "Thus Jesus Christ constitutes in Himself, in His own vicarious human life and service, the creative source and norm and pattern of all true Christian service."[87]

Torrance directs his readers to Galatians 2:20, and especially to the words "I yet not I but Christ."[88] In this the message of the vicarious humanity of

---

[83]Torrance, *Mediation of Christ*, p. 97; see also idem, "Word of God," p. 158.

[84]Torrance, *Mediation of Christ*, pp. 97-98.

[85]Torrance, *Royal Priesthood*, p. 30.

[86]Ibid., p. 35.

[87]Torrance, "Word of God," p. 162.

[88]Torrance, *Mediation of Christ*, p. 107; see also idem, *Preaching Christ Today*, p. 31.

Christ alone is the gospel on which we rely. The whole of the Christian life in all regards is included in the "I yet not I but Christ," for in Jesus Christ all human responses

> are laid hold of, sanctified and informed by his vicarious life of obedience and response to the Father. They are in fact so indissolubly united to the life of Jesus Christ which he lived out among us and which he has offered to the Father, as arising out of our human being and nature, that they are *our responses* toward the love of the Father poured out upon us through the mediation of the Son and in the unity of the Holy Spirit.[89]

A POSTLUDE TO CHAPTERS ONE, TWO AND THREE

Thus these reflections directly on Christology come to a close. We have been in dialogue with our Scottish friends, allowing them to lead and teach us, while trying en route to make our own way through the material in order as far as possible to offer a contemporary presentation. As noted at the beginning, we have proceeded by way of interlocking circles as the mystery of Jesus Christ has been presented to our minds through the theologies of McLeod Campbell, Mackintosh and Torrance. Undoubtedly, much has been omitted that was worthy of inclusion; but that which had to be lifted up, I trust, has been.

We turn now in a new direction and to a different style of presentation in what amounts to the second part of the book. Our topic now for three chapters will be the atonement directly considered. But rather than circle around soteriological themes and invite McLeod Campbell, Mackintosh and Torrance to make their contributions, each will be given a chapter. As we work our way through this somewhat massive and complex body of writing, I will be offering my side of the conversation. Again, not everything that can be said will be said, for mere reporting is not the task at hand. Rather, judicious selection is necessary to honor constraints of space. Further, not everything written by our Scottish theologians has equal merit. The attempt will be to lift up the central contributions and let lie the material that is not unimportant as such, but is not of primary interest.

---

[89]Torrance, *Mediation of Christ*, p. 108.

4

ATONEMENT

John McLeod Campbell's
Theology of Satisfaction

WE BEGIN THIS CHAPTER with a meditative reflection on the death of
Jesus that serves as a preface to these three chapters on the atonement doctrine of the three Scottish theologians with whom we are engaged. This reflection picks up a number of themes with which we are now familiar and
turns the corner, as it were, to our addressing the atonement head-on.

MARK 15:33-34: GOD-FORSAKENNESS IN GOD

Let us not sanitize Jesus' death by pretending that it was something other
than it was. Jesus died a lonely, desperate, God-abandoned death. He died
with the terrible opening words of Psalm 22 on his lips: "My God, my God,
why have you forsaken me?" The one who had lived his life seemingly in
such close and intimate relationship with Abba, dear Father, died as one who
felt that he was without hope. Unlike Jesus' cry, the cry of the psalmist led
to his rescue by God: "He did not despise or abhor the affliction of the af-
flicted; he did not hide his face from me, but heard when I cried to him" (Ps
22:24). For the psalmist, God is no longer far away. The psalmist is no longer
abandoned. God's face is no longer hidden. And there is nothing in the
psalm to indicate that the psalmist experienced death.[1] The cry of Jesus, on
the other hand, brought no relief, no personal intervention by the Father, no
army of angels to his rescue. He died with the cry of abandonment on his
lips, shouting out in agony to what he apparently experienced as a terrifying

---

[1]Robert Davidson, *The Vitality of Worship: A Commentary on the Book of the Psalms* (Grand Rapids:
Eerdmans, 1998), pp. 81-82.

emptiness. Seemingly feeling abandoned by God—thus Jesus died. Even so, I think, the Father-Son relationship, to which I have made frequent reference, even here must be maintained, albeit hidden in the mystery of the anguish of the dying Jesus. And in this he is one with most people today and throughout history who live lives of brutish horror, deepest suffering, appalling violence and dire hopelessness.

What was the Father doing when Jesus died this self-described God-abandoned death? That may sound like an impious question. But to take Matthew, Mark and Luke at their word, for each of them recorded it this way, Jesus died aware of the absence, even the withdrawal, of the Father from his side. The notion of abandonment or forsakenness entirely suggests some such rejection. On the face of it, Jesus died without God. So I ask again: What was the Father doing when Jesus died this God-abandoned death?

The question can begin to have an answer only when we ask, first of all, "Who died on the cross?" Certainly, Jesus died on the cross. He, the son of Mary, died a vicious death from capital punishment, approved by the Jewish temple authorities and carried out by the occupying forces of the Roman army. But, he, the son of Mary, was, as this one person, also the Son of God, Emmanuel, the Word of God as the man Jesus. There is no other Jesus, at his birth as at his death, who was not both son of Mary and Son of God in the deepest mystery and unity of his personal being. At his birth, as at his death, Jesus was wholly God and wholly human, yet one person. This is the heart of the mystery of faith. We cannot untie what was bound together at the incarnation—Jesus' humanity and divinity—in order now to make his death somehow more theologically palatable. Sometimes theologians have ripped apart the unity of his being as Jesus Christ and said that he died only in his human manhood, leaving his Godhood untouched by suffering and death. This is presumed to protect the immutability and impassibility of God. But that would be to sever at Jesus' death what was united at his birth. It would be to say that *God* has not been one with us at our places of deepest, darkest need; it would be to say that *God* has not entered hell and vanquished it; it would be to say that *God* has not walked through the valley of the shadow of death and made it his own. We cannot rip apart the miracle of Christmas when we come now to consider Jesus' Good Friday death. He died as who he was at his birth: Jesus Christ, God as this man.

This being so, the cross, as a Jesus event, has to be seen also as a God event. The man named "Jesus" is God, wholly God. He is not the whole Godhead, certainly, for he is not the Father or the Holy Spirit. But within the incomprehensible mystery of the Trinity, Jesus is understood still to be one in being with the Father and the Holy Spirit at his death as at his miraculous conception and birth. On his cross Jesus does not suddenly become who hitherto he never was, just a man, and not the God-man, one in being with the Father. He died as the God-man, in the unity of his person as son of Mary and Son of God.

We must now try and catch hold of something of what is going on here, aware that we are confronted with an utter mystery that is beyond explanation, and that our grasp will be loose and tentative. The death of Jesus, son of Mary and Son of God, in the unity of his one personhood, is a human event in history—no ambiguity there. He died as we will die; it is death as deadly as our death. But the death of Jesus, son of Mary and Son of God, in the unity of his one personhood, is also a God event—an event within the mystery of the Holy Trinity. In which case, we have to speak here of dying and death within God, for the Son of God died without ceasing to be God, though there must be no sense of divine death. Clearly and immediately we have hit a wall that we cannot get over; we are confronted by a mystery beyond understanding. We have to speak here of abandoning and abandonment within God, for the correspondence to the Son's feeling of abandonment is the Father's allowing the Son to die; and surely we say this with our hands clamped over our mouths, for this is a fearful thing of which we speak. We have to speak here of the Son's commitment of his spirit to the Father and of the Father's receipt of that spirit, for the union of love between the Father and the Son is not broken. We have to speak here not just of the terrible experience of the dying Jesus, but also of the terrible grief surely of the loving, sending, then waiting, Father. To speak otherwise would be to say that God, as the man Jesus, Son of the Father, is not dying on the cross, that God, as the man Jesus, Son of the Father, has not entered into our God-forsakenness, and that God, as the man Jesus, Son of the Father, has not descended into the hell of our sin-filled separation from God to reestablish us in communion with God. And to say these things would be to turn the gospel into what is not the gospel by refusing to see the cross of Jesus as a

God event. The cross is saving because it is an event within the relations between the Father and the Son in the unity of the Holy Spirit.

John McLeod Campbell warned us not to see the cross as the place where God punishes Jesus for our sins. The cross is not where God's justice is satisfied; it is where the Father's love is revealed. "The sufferings of Christ become to our minds *not the measure* of what God *can inflict*, but the *revelation* of what God can feel."[2] Jesus did not die in isolation from the Father or in symbolic opposition to the Father. Jesus was not God's pawn, to be sacrificed for a higher tactical goal. Even though the Son was in a far country, the Father-Son relationship surely was what it always was: a relationship of love and filial response within the perichoretic or relational co-inhering/co-indwelling unity of the Holy Trinity. It is this that reveals the mystery and the meaning of the cross. The gospel is a gospel of hope, therefore, for us who are godless, for us who feel abandoned by God and for us who will die, because *God*, as the man Jesus, has made his home among us at every point.

The deepest mystery and miracle of the gospel is that God, as the man Jesus, Son of the Father, has gone all the way—all the way down, we might say—taking upon himself not only our humanity, but also our death, not only our sense of hopelessness, but also our abandonment, not only our sin, but also our being judged guilty by God. God, as the man Jesus, Son of the Father, God-forsaken on Golgotha's cross, has penetrated into the deepest, darkest, most profoundly lost and derelict dimensions of our human being and has made these places God's places, these events God's events, these experiences God's experiences. In the cross of Jesus, Son of the Father, we are confronted with the entirely downwardly mobile God, as the logic of the incarnation runs its deadly course for us and for our salvation. And yet—and this cannot be overemphasized—all of this happens within the relation of the Son committing his spirit to the Father.

What is going on here was already anticipated by the psalmist: "Where can I go from your Spirit? Or where can I flee from your presence? If I ascend to heaven, you are there; if I make my bed in Sheol, you are there. If I take the wings of the morning and settle at the farthest limits of the sea, even there your hand shall lead me, and your right hand shall hold me fast" (Ps 139:7-10).

---

[2]John McLeod Campbell, *The Nature of the Atonement*, 2nd ed. (1867; repr., Eugene, OR: Wipf & Stock, 1999), p. 222. I am grateful to my wife, Catherine Purves, for pointing out this remark from McLeod Campbell.

What was the Father doing when Jesus died this God-abandoned death? As I have said, I believe that we are compelled to see the death of Jesus as a God event. Doing so, we see the death of Jesus as a trinitarian event, meaning by this (and here we must recognize that language is being stretched to breaking point) that the death of Jesus was an event within the life of God. In a mystery far beyond what our words can convey or our minds can understand, God—Father, Son and Holy Spirit—in, through and as the man Jesus (sent from the Father, conceived by the Holy Spirit) has utterly, wholly, entirely, taken on our lives and assumed us, everything we are, without remainder. Nothing is so dire, so terrible, so seemingly God-abandoned that already, for us, Jesus, son of Mary and Son of God, has not been there and made it his, that is, God's, own. And Jesus has done so, even in his cry of abandonment, as Son of the Father and from within the Father-Son relationship. And because he has been there, for us, already, our deepest sufferings, our deaths, our seeming God-forsakenness have henceforth and forever been enfolded into the inner life of God. For through the suffering, God-abandonment and death of Jesus the Son, the Father, in the unity of the Holy Spirit, has received all that we are and made it God's own. On this ground alone is there the future of a new life in God for us who know and experience the worst of the life we live here on earth.

Thus we must say: Golgotha in God; God-forsakenness in God; death in God. I am aware that there is much room for misunderstanding with this statement. Certainly I intend no patripassianism, the false doctrine of the death of the Father. And neither do I intend to say that somehow until Jesus' resurrection the Trinity is a Binity, reduced from three to two persons. Yet we are forced to say also that Jesus in the unity of his person as son of Mary and Son of God did die on the cross. To say otherwise would evacuate the cross of both its ontological meaning (leaving it to be seen only as a moral event of innocent suffering for one's values and cause) and saving power. And that is unacceptable. Only as a God event as the man Jesus is the cross a saving event for us; for only God can save, and God saves as this man on Golgotha's cross.

One final point in this reflection: none of what has been said here actually could be said without knowing what happened on the following Sunday. For both the writers of the New Testament and for us, the death of Jesus is entirely overlaid by the knowledge that Jesus is risen. As, by the Spirit, Christ assumed our humanity at his incarnation and lived it unto his death and carried it into his resurrection and ascension, so we are, by the Spirit, joined to Jesus at his resurrection and ascension, to live now in union with him through the gift of the pentecostal Spirit. He, son of Mary and Son of God, became what we are in incarnation, God-forsakenness and death, so that we will become as he is in resurrection and ascension. Christian tradition has called this "the magnificent exchange": he became what we are so that we might become what he is (2 Cor 8:9). This is the center of the good news of the gospel; this is the content of Christian hope. What happened to Jesus because he was one of us is, as a result, what will happen to us. He became as we are so that we will become as he is—alive and in communion with God. The magnificent exchange indeed!

On the day when we commemorate the execution of Jesus, we see his cross as the cross of the risen Jesus; and we see his God-forsakenness as the God-forsakenness of the beloved Son of the Father, who sits in glory and reigns in power in the unity of the Holy Spirit. As such, this Jesus, son of Mary and Son of God, is Lord, and as Lord he is our future beyond God-forsakenness and death. Jesus died. The Lord is risen. Jesus will come again. Only in the resurrection of the God-forsaken Lord is there hope for us in our abandonments and deaths. Thus it is so.

THE SETTING OF JOHN MCLEOD CAMPBELL'S
THE NATURE OF THE ATONEMENT

A brief historical and pastoral review is in order. McLeod Campbell's theology of the atonement arose out of his setting, life and ministry. Its roots lie in his pastoral experience and commitments. In order to establish this connection I will draw on his posthumously published, and incomplete, autobiographical retrospective of his brief ministry in the Church of Scotland, *Reminiscences and Reflections: Referring to His Early Parish Ministry in the Parish of Row, 1825-31*, edited, with an introduction, by his son Donald Campbell.[3] Written forty years after the painful events of his demission from the ministry by act of the General Assembly of the Church of Scotland in May

---

[3] John McLeod Campbell, *Reminiscences and Reflections: Referring to His Early Parish Ministry in the Parish of Row, 1825-31* (London: Macmillan, 1873).

of 1831, it provides an interpretive narrative by which his great book *The Nature of the Atonement* (1856) may be approached. Wistfully yet thankfully, his retrospective reflections allowed him to note, "The Christian ministry, as one form of the Christian life, is a progress in hope, not a surviving of hopes."[4]

John McLeod Campbell was ordained into the parish of Row (sometimes spelled after the Gaelic form, "Rhu") in Dumbartonshire in September of 1825. From the beginning of his ministry he was concerned to ground himself continually in his study of Scripture and to attend as best he could to the growth of what he called "personal religion" on the part of his parishioners. These were his primary questions: "How are we to conceive of the mind of God in relation to man?" and "What is the attitude of the mind of man towards God, to which the knowledge of the mind of God towards us calls us?" He comments, "Our thoughts in relation to these two questions lie at the roots of all our thinking . . . and the first and primary interest of the Gospel is in the personal answer to them which it gives."[5] The singular goal of ministry, he believed, was to answer the question as to God's will for himself and for those within his pastoral charge. His constant study of Scripture had the end of seeing himself and his people in relation to what God willed him and them to be. Thus he developed a theological apperception concerning what we are to believe with regard to God and what response this calls forth from us, a "faith that is the door of hope to us."[6] The expression of this faith came to full development twenty-five or so years later when he worked on and published *The Nature of the Atonement* in 1856.

Clearly, John McLeod Campbell entered ministry as an earnest young man. He understood the pastoral relationship to be a responsibility of solemn interest and hopeful promise. "I venture to say that I met my people under the over-canopying love of God. . . . Their very welcome of me coming to them as their minister, no less than my hope in accepting that relation to them, had root in some faith however vague in the hope that is in God for man."[7] He set forth on the belief that he and his people met on the common ground of his desire to help them to be what God wills them to be. His

---

4 Ibid., p. 76.
5 Ibid., p. 53.
6 Ibid., p. 58.
7 Ibid., p. 87.

ministry has that meaning or none at all. "I have never lost the feeling," he wrote, "of the impression made on me on the very first day of my Parochial visiting—at the close of that day's work—when the aged inmates of the last house to which I had been, came with me to the brow of the height on which their cottage stood; and the one solemnly said, 'Give us plain doctrine, for we are a sleeping people'; and the other solemnly quoted the words, 'Be thou faithful unto death, and I will give thee a crown of life.'"[8] To the end of the proper work of ministry, in his preaching as in his pastoral care, McLeod Campbell's focus was upon the realization of the will of God toward the people, and the elicitation of the personal expression of grateful faith from them. Only when this is clearly and habitually in mind, he believed, would he know what to speak and how to speak it. Citing Richard Baxter, the English Puritan pastor, he would speak "as a dying man to dying men" and preach the gospel of eternal life given us in God's Son. For McLeod Campbell, this, and this alone, is the true conception of the high calling of ministry.

No advocate for Federal Calvinism, McLeod Campbell nevertheless accepted the opening answers to the first two questions of the Westminster Shorter Catechism as warranted for teaching that the purpose of life was to glorify God and enjoy him, and that this teaching was the sum of the Scriptures. It is "man's end" and what he understood that to mean that drove McLeod Campbell forward and ineluctably led him to teach universal atonement and the corresponding response of personal holiness. Faith is a way of life, the life of sonship toward God quickened in those who respond to the gospel. This teaching is summed up in a central biblical verse for McLeod Campbell, Proverbs 23:26, "My son, give Me thine heart." "'My son,' this tells what I am to the heart of God; 'Give me thine heart,' this tells the will of God concerning me, what the Father of my spirit desires as to me His offspring, with what manner of blessedness the blessed God who has given me a being would make my existence blessed."[9]

Incarnation and atonement are to the end of our life of sonship, which is the gift of the Holy Spirit; sonship is no less than communion with the Father and the Son in the Spirit, being heirs of God and joint heirs with Christ. This was the ground on which McLeod Campbell met his people.

---

[8]Ibid., p. 90.
[9]Ibid., p. 110.

"Christianity is, to my mind, related to our relation to God as His offspring."[10]
A life of sonship is the purpose of God for people, and Scripture is for the
purpose of our knowledge of that purpose. Sonship, then, was McLeod
Campbell's deep spiritual and theological intuition, the fountain from which
his ministry flowed, and in time it became the ground for attack against him
and his subsequent demission from his pastoral charge.

McLeod Campbell believed in the divine will for himself and his people,
but not only as a conclusion to biblical exegesis. He recognized the divine
will as truth experienced as well as truth thought about. God, he believed,
spoke into his heart, not only into his mind. This clearly led him to work
with a scripture within the Scriptures.[11] That is, he was attracted to those
portions of Scripture that spoke to the conviction of assurance of faith. Or,
to put this in terms that he chose to frame his theology, we must decide, with
regard to the divine will for us, whether we have to do with law or gospel.
As law, the will of God reveals what is wrong but brings no deliverance, because we are unable to fulfill its demands; as gospel, the will of God has the
power, received by faith, to realize its end in us.[12] In his pastoral work he
found that the former, not the latter, was the case, for his parishioners were
a people rooted in law and fear rather than in gospel and hope. The gospel
was heard as demand, not as the hearing of the gospel secret as to how to be.
The people, he discovered, received the gospel as a condition proposed to
them, with assurance consequent upon compliance. "This something they
attempted to speak of as repentance, faith, or love, or 'being good enough,'
which last expression gave really the secret of their difficulty. Christ was to
be the reward of some goodness—not perfect goodness, but some goodness
that would sustain a personal hope of acceptance in drawing near to Him.
In this mind the Gospel was practically a law."[13]

In view of this, McLeod Campbell's labor was to fix people's attention on
the love of God revealed in Christ, and to teach the attitude of looking to
God to learn the divine will toward them vis-à-vis looking at themselves to
consider their feelings toward God. In doing so McLeod Campbell appealed

---

[10]Ibid., p. 112.
[11]Ibid., p. 126.
[12]Ibid., p. 131.
[13]Ibid., p. 133.

to a classical pastoral move, found already in Luther and Calvin. But it stood counter to much of the pastoral wisdom among McLeod Campbell's ministerial peers in Scotland in the later 1820s. At the heart of debate was the understanding of grace, which for McLeod Campbell is

> the apprehension of a love in God to us which is irrespective of what we are, and is sustained by the contemplation of what He both wills us to be and is able to make us. This apprehension attained, Christ is no longer thought of as intended to be the reward of anything in us individually, according to the vague thought that moves to blind efforts to appropriate Christ by some mental movement on our part. He is known as ours by the grace of God. . . . The subtlest form of self-righteousness is that which it presents when self-condemnation is made a reason for not venturing to trust in Christ with a rejoicing confidence.[14]

Calvinism in Scotland at this time was indeed a joyless, anxious expression of Christian faith. An inwardly directed piety led to loss of assurance and a religious expression reflected in earnest moral effort. These efforts were never quite successful at what they were intended to achieve. Assurance of faith was a chimera. Peace in Christ was a phantom, clutched at but always slipping out of reach. Rest in God, the welcome of our dependence upon him, and trust in his will for our lives, were replaced by the regular system of testing faith by its fruit.[15] McLeod Campbell asked how our own faith could be thus tested. "But to ask me to stand in suspense as to my trust in Christ—whether it is a right and saving trust—making this depend on the consciousness of fruits of holiness in myself,—this is really to suspend trust—that is, to suspend faith—until I am conscious of the effects of faith: a process which, if intelligently followed, obviously makes fruits of faith impossible."[16] This undoubtedly is a sad and dispiriting situation. Forgiveness becomes the more difficult to believe in proportion as the real need for it is felt. And holiness, truth and love are desired, not for their own sakes, but as evidences of saving faith. The grace of God, on this account, becomes personal only by some act of appropriation of our own. It is then a very short step to the inevitable conclusion that Christ died only for some people, not for all, making joy in the simple faith of Christ's dying love impossible.[17]

---

[14]Ibid., p. 134.
[15]Ibid., p. 138.
[16]Ibid., p. 139.
[17]Ibid., p. 151.

The issue, then, was about the nature of believing—whether the reference was toward ourselves, or believing what we are called to believe, which is trust in the free grace of God, with the reference toward God. True peace, according to McLeod Campbell's mind, was the fruit of a personal sense of God's redeeming love. But in order to be true peace and sure confidence in God's love, the atonement had to be understood as universal act on God's part and not an election limited only to some people.[18] "That Christ had tasted death for every man was to my mind the only clear and adequate foundation for that personal peace with God to which in preaching the Gospel I called men."[19]

McLeod Campbell used Luther at this point in support of his position insofar as Luther stressed repeatedly the need to look away from oneself and look exclusively at Jesus Christ. Indeed, faith is the opposite of self-trust or self-righteousness. But when faith took the form of the doctrine of the imputation of righteousness, according to which it was not the revelation of God in Christ that was the ground of peace but rather the assumed ascription creating an "as if," McLeod Campbell called this faith a legal fiction. This faith based on imputation became the sign that secures the peace that God should now will to see in us that which pleased God in Christ. Faith, McLeod Campbell concluded, that has its peace-giving power suspended on fruits arising from imputation is far from the faith for which Luther contended.

Thus McLeod Campbell believed that the proper center of ministry was found in declaring what God wills us to be *in connection with what God has done in Christ so that we might be it.*[20] To put that in different language: McLeod Campbell saw the imperatives of faith in the light of the prior actuality of the indicative of grace. "Ye are not your own, for ye are bought with a price; therefore glorify God in your body and in your spirit, which are God's" (1 Cor 6:19-20). The gospel is the divine provision in Christ for the full meeting of the divine claim upon our lives. McLeod Campbell's priority, then, was to help his people see themselves in these terms. The issue, of course, was the freeness of the grace of God that the gospel revealed, the

---

[18]Ibid., pp. 154-55.
[19]Ibid., p. 157.
[20]Ibid., pp. 171-72.

appreciation of which was inhibited by our seeming to be quicker in coming to know ourselves as sinners than in coming to know Christ as a savior.[21]

> I used to say, "If you knew the mind of God towards you as the Gospel reveals it,—if you knew about yourselves what in the light of the Gospel I know about you—knew as really your own unsearchable riches which you have in Christ,— you must needs rejoice in God through our Lord Jesus Christ. I only ask you to know what now is. I only labour to undeceive you in thinking that though it does not give you peace you know it already."[22]

McLeod Campbell contrasted his perspective with three alternative perspectives that ostensibly give the peace of assurance. First, he distinguished himself from "the extremest Calvinists," who argued that faith itself is the sign of the power given to believe in forgiveness of sins that is given only to the elect. Assurance now is its own foundation. Being able to believe is evidence that one so enabled is one to whom it is true. The emphasis here is placed on the consciousness of a direct faith in forgiveness that is possible only to the elect. Second, he distinguished himself from the Arminians, for whom peace with God has a personal history and rests on a personal transaction. Here trust is placed not in the mind of God toward us, but in personal experience. It appears that the issue here for McLeod Campbell is the highly individualized and subjective understanding of assurance of salvation. The emphasis is placed on a history of conversion, of mercy sought and granted. The third group (which he does not name) from which he separates himself, which appears similar to the second group, rests on consciousness of faith and a laying hold of the promise of forgiveness. Here the emphasis is placed on the consciousness of trusting a promise made to those who have faith in Christ. What is common to all is a confidence not grounded in a simple believing apprehension of grace revealed.[23]

The point of these distinctions is to say that the Church of Scotland at the time was prevailingly Arminian, but with a large minority of Calvinists. In McLeod Campbell's characterization, the former demanded a practical Christianity of conformity to Christ as our example, while with the latter the demand of faith was made in connection with the preaching of an atonement

---

[21]Ibid., p. 174.
[22]Ibid., p. 176.
[23]Ibid., p. 177.

limited to the elect. Put alongside these, McLeod Campbell's contention that the forgiveness of God is prior to our knowing of it (which, of course, was Calvin's teaching) leaves little wonder that it was only a matter of time before McLeod Campbell would fall foul of the church in general. In the light of the forgiveness revealed in Christ, the vanity of attempts to win or deserve it is clearly seen. With that perspective, McLeod Campbell sought to listen to God not for himself only, but also for his people.[24] "Our teaching assumes the existence of the relation we speak of to our people—of God as their Heavenly Father, of themselves as God's offspring."[25]

With this autobiographical theological retrospective overview before us, and with some sense now of his theological intuition, we now move to reflect on the theory of atonement in *The Nature of the Atonement*. There, over thirty years later, the burden of his teaching and preaching in the Row parish came to full systematic expression in what is surely one of the finest and enduring theological works penned upon Scotland's shores.

THE NATURE OF THE ATONEMENT

There is no more daunting task, as writer or reader, than the attempt to master in the compass of a few pages the complexity of John McLeod Campbell's atonement theory, and subsequently to offer a fruitful theological engagement with it. As previously noted, the style of the writing makes for demanding reading; the defense of his position is often rambling and arcane. Nevertheless, the core of his position is explicable, and to its exposition we now turn.

The center of the argument. I begin with a paragraph that summarizes the central point. Everything that we say of the atonement is determined by what we know of the love of the Father toward us and of his purpose for us as he is revealed by and in the Son. To that end, "the faith of the atonement presupposes the faith of the incarnation,"[26] for the incarnation is the revelation of God's purpose for us that is fulfilled or enacted through the atonement. The nature of the atonement is the working out of the meaning of the incarnation, which is that in Christ we know of and enjoy the love of God toward us. Thus, because the atoning life of Jesus is his perfect sonship toward God and perfect

---

[24]Ibid., p. 227.
[25]Ibid., p. 231.
[26]McLeod Campbell, *Nature of the Atonement*, p. 19.

"brotherhood" toward us, there is established a connection between the atonement and our participation in the life of Christ. The goal is to come to "the faith of God as the Father of our spirits,"[27] which means knowing our special place in God's heart as God's offspring. This is to live in personal relationship with God, accepting our "sonship" and welcoming our life in communion with God. The twofold purpose of the atonement, then, is in Christ to know God as the Father of our spirits and to live the life of faith in obedience and love to God in the spirit of sonship.[28] "It is as having a place in the kingdom of God that we understand the atonement; for it is our personal relation to God as the Father of our spirits that the atonement belongs; out of disorder in that relation has the need for it arisen; to bring that relation into harmony with its divine ideal is the end which it has contemplated."[29] The atonement addresses a broken relationship with God.

McLeod Campbell worked out the central tenets of his atonement theology in retrospective and prospective aspects, as we have already seen in the previous chapter. Briefly, retrospectively, Christ deals with people on the part of God *and* deals with God on behalf of humankind. This encompasses the "downward" movement of God in Christ toward us *and* the "upward" movement of God in Christ toward God with respect to our past sins and how they are dealt with. Prospectively, the Son honors the Father in the sight of humankind *and* the Son deals with the Father on our behalf with respect to our future life in God. Christ reveals the life of sonship in response to God's fatherhood as the "downward" movement of God toward us *and* Christ offers the true human response to the Father as the "upward" movement of God in Christ toward the Father, into which life we participate. Thus we have two parallel movements from and to God, looking backwards and forwards respectively. This, in a nutshell, is the central argument of *The Nature of the Atonement*. The remaining half of the book consists of a series of defenses of the argument. Having already outlined the argument in detail, I will turn now to its defense, in four parts, in order to understand it more deeply.

The defense of the argument (1). The first defense is characterized by the inward relations between the Father and the Son and what that means for

---

[27]Ibid., p. 24.
[28]Ibid., pp. 26, 28.
[29]Ibid., p. 34.

us. At its center the defense amounts to an extended theological meditation on John 14:6, wherein the character of salvation serves to determine the nature of the atonement. "That 'no man cometh to the Father but by the Son' is the great and all-including necessity that is revealed to us by the atonement. But, as combined with the gift of the Son to us as the living way to the Father, we rejoice to find ourselves shut up to 'so great a salvation.'"[30] For McLeod Campbell, the living way to the Father is the meaning of Hebrews 10:19-22, where reference is made to having boldness to enter into the holiest, which is now opened for us by the blood of Jesus. Worship is the gift and obligation of sonship. That is, the blood of Jesus cleans us for worship worthy of sonship. Citing 1 John 1:7, McLeod Campbell argues that our cleansing is from the pollution of sin, where the blood of Jesus is not to be understood in a legal sense as punishment but as cleansing having the effect of enabling fellowship with God. Christ is the propitiation for our sins as the way into communion, the living way for us to the Father.

Christ *is* the propitiation, the *hilasmos*, the atoning sacrifice (1 Jn 2:2). That is, propitiation is not a work of Christ understood in an instrumental manner, but rather is the living Christ himself,[31] who in the unity of his person brings God to us and us to God. To say it otherwise, Christ *is* reconciliation (*hilaskesthai*) (Heb 2:17); Christ is for us wisdom from God and righteousness and sanctification and redemption (1 Cor 1:30). McLeod Campbell acknowledges that he is making an unconventional point by arguing in this way (although it is not a unique point in the history of theology), but the force of the gospel derived from John 14:6, cited above, is allowed here to act as the hermeneutical lens through which he now examines the nature of the atonement. The salvation needed, in other words, is for us to have a way of drawing near to God. Christ has opened the way to the Father, for through him we "have access in one Spirit to the Father" (Eph 2:18). The atonement is not a punishment for sin but rather a spiritual and moral access to the Father through Christ's confessing of our sin and through union with Christ, having our adoption as "sons" of God. For McLeod Campbell, peace with God is none other than our participation in the life of Christ, both direct and immediate, having a moral and spiritual

---

[30]Ibid., p. 150.
[31]Ibid., p. 154.

meaning, by which, having access in one Spirit, we are free to draw near to God and have communion with the Father.

This is surely a remarkable argument to make. And McLeod Campbell does not shy away from the anticipated criticism. "Granting that our true well-being is to be ultimately found in peace and reconciliation in the spiritual sense of the words, have we not at first need of peace and reconciliation in a legal sense?"[32] His reply is, frankly, astonishingly audacious. "If an atonement be adequate morally and spiritually, it will of necessity be legally adequate. If it be sufficient in relation to our receiving the adoption of sons, it must be sufficient for our redemption as under the law."[33] If this were not the case, the argument continues, would we not subordinate the gospel to the law? Further, we are not under law, but under grace. McLeod Campbell cites Philip's words to Jesus in support, "Lord, show us the Father, and we will be satisfied" (Jn 14:8), emphasizing the sufficiency. And citing 1 John 5:11, "God gave us eternal life, and this life is in his Son," he asks rhetorically if this will be enough for us or will we need something else to save us from the wrath to come.[34] Were this to be the case, we would be seeing our relation to God as Father of our spirits in subordination to God as moral governor. "I have asked, 'Can the moral governor remain unsatisfied if the Father of spirits is satisfied?"[35] If our departure from the Father is the ultimate evil, our return is salvation. The issue, in other words, as McLeod Campbell sees it, is the fatherliness of the Father, sin as a broken relationship; and restoration to relationship, returning to the Father's house, is salvation. The nature of the atonement, then, is by the cleansing blood of Christ to have a way into the Father's heart. In this way, the argument continues, we are taken from under the law and placed under grace, to be alive to God. Developing his thoughts thus, McLeod Campbell has argued the opposite of imputation: life from the dead characterized by the cry, "Abba, Father."[36] To conclude this argument: salvation is participation in the love of the Father's heart; it is not the favorable sentence of a judge setting the mind at ease with reference to the demands of the law. The question remains to be asked whether McLeod Campbell, in giving the forensic approach no quarter, has gone too far in his negation.

---

[32]Ibid., pp. 159-60.
[33]Ibid., p. 160.
[34]Ibid.
[35]Ibid., p. 161.
[36]Ibid., p. 166.

If there is a familiar McLeod Campbell turn of phrase it may be the "Amen" of faith to the "Amen" of Christ.

> The Amen of the individual human spirit to the Amen of the Son to the mind of the Father in relation to man, is saving faith. . . . And the certainty that God has accepted that perfect and divine Amen as uttered by Christ in humanity is necessarily accompanied by the peaceful assurance that in uttering, in whatever feebleness, a true Amen to that high Amen, the individual who is yielding himself to the spirit of Christ to have it uttered in him is accepted of God.[37]

Our "Amen" is that which indicates "sonship." Thus the first defense amounts to our participation through Christ in the Father-Son relationship that reveals and enacts the Father's will concerning us.

The defense of the argument (2). The second defense is a consideration of the external and historical life of Christ, from the manger to the cross, the understanding of which should help our understanding of the inward life of Christ. What does it mean that the Son honored the Father in our sight? Or, more broadly, what is the actual history of our redemption? The sum of the answer to these questions is succinctly given: "He had to taste in all its bitterness that enmity to God to which He was exposing Himself in coming to men in His Father's name."[38] The pastor-theologian's eye is already cast in the direction of the cross rather than the manger, although his specific dealing with the cross he leaves to the third defense of the argument.

Coming to the fore now is the outworking of what we have previously noted, the importance for McLeod Campbell of Psalm 40:8, "Lo, I come to do thy will, O God." Christ's ministry was the outcome of his sonship, in which he served the will of the Father (Jn 5:30; 6:38). This is the great principle. Nothing is to be believed concerning the atonement which is not the working out of this principle, that here God is revealing himself to us and in Christ Jesus humankind is yielding to God.[39] "As to our Lord's personal ministry, its distinguishing character is to be seen in this, that that ministry was the *outcoming of the life of sonship*. . . . What He spake, as what He did,

---

[37]Ibid., p. 171.

[38]Ibid., p. 183.

[39]John McLeod Campbell, *Fragments of Truth: Being Expositions of Passages of Scripture Chiefly from the Teaching of John McLeod Campbell*, 4th ed. (1898; repr., Whitefish, MT: Kessinger Legacy Reprints), p. 241.

was a part of what He was."[40] Christ himself, in other words, was the gospel. Or, to say it differently, Christ's whole counsel and act was to keep the Father before us insofar as the gospel, Jesus Christ, is our filial relation to God and "brotherhood" toward one another.

It is time now to look directly at McLeod Campbell's defense of his atonement theory at the point of his understanding of Christ's suffering and death. It is here, perhaps, that his account might be most prone to foundering on the rocks of criticism.

With respect to Christ's suffering, McLeod Campbell programmatically states, "I entirely feel that our Lord's physical sufferings, viewed simply as physical sufferings and without relation to the mind that was in the sufferer, could not adequately explain the awful intensity of the feelings which accompanied His prayer in the garden of Gethsemane."[41] Citing Matthew's account of Jesus intimating that he could ask the Father for more than twelve legions of angels in his defense (Mt 26:53), McLeod Campbell argues that this suggests "not a wrath coming forth from the Father, but a power of evil which the Father permitted to have its course."[42] Thus, negatively, the core argument of the book reemerges: the Lord's sufferings are neither at the hand of God nor are they to be regarded as penal, in their aspect as sufferings merely. Christ suffers because of humankind's enmity toward and rejection of God, not because of God's anger toward him or punishment of him. Thus the positive argument is to contemplate Christ's suffering in its spiritual aspect as the response of love to enmity. For the life of Christ's sonship was precisely that of perfect love toward God as Father and perfect love toward his brothers and sisters. He came in his Father's name and was not accepted (Jn 5:43).

Deepening the analysis, McLeod Campbell brings back the bidirectional dual structure of the retrospective and prospective aspects of the atonement, considering the sufferings of Christ in his witnessing for God to humankind and to his dealing with God on behalf of humankind. I will take these two aspects in order.

First, the sufferings of Christ were the perfecting of the Son's witnessing for the Father, manifesting the perfect life of love as sonship toward God and

[40]McLeod Campbell, *Nature of the Atonement*, p. 184.
[41]Ibid., p. 190.
[42]Ibid.

brotherhood toward humankind.[43] That is, Christ had oneness of mind with the Father with respect to us. The Father's fatherliness was manifest as the fullness of Christ's love toward us. Thus the words "Father, forgive them" (Lk 23:34) testify to Jesus' living and dying within the Father's love as intercessor for us.[44]

McLeod Campbell now takes up the recitation of Psalm 22 to be interpreted as other than the convention of the Son's utterance of the sense of the Father's wrath endured under the imputation of our sins.[45] The psalm begins with "a cleaving appropriation on the part of the Sufferer of God as His God: My God, my God."[46] Jesus cries out in the intent of "Why, O God, are you far from helping me?" The cup of human enmity toward God is drunk fully, in Christ's utter weakness unto death. For McLeod Campbell, the recitation of Psalm 22 is the revelation of Christ's trust toward God while in utter weakness. This is trust that at the last the Father's favor has not been cut off; there is nothing here of the Father turning his face away from Jesus *as if* he were the enemy of God, *as if* God looked upon him with wrath, *as if* God regarded Jesus as a sinner.[47]

McLeod Campbell drives home his argument thus:

> While subjected to the hour and power of darkness, sustained by the simple faith of that original fatherliness of the Father's heart, which He had *come forth to reveal* and TO REVEAL BY TRUSTING IT . . . [he] now perfects His glorifying of the Father's Name, by being seen trusting in that Name alone when brought into the extremest need of a sure hold of God. . . . The Sinless One is seen trusting simply in that Name which he had come to reveal to sinners, that they also might trust in it and be saved; and thus the Father's response to that trust is preached as the gospel to the chief of sinners.[48]

McLeod Campbell develops the theme at the close of the citation just noted in a stunning and eloquent piece of pastoral theological writing. It is worth quoting in full. To the comment that one is not good enough or religious enough for salvation, he replies:

---

[43]Ibid., p. 200.
[44]Ibid.
[45]Ibid., pp. 200-201.
[46]Ibid., p. 201.
[47]Ibid., p. 203.
[48]Ibid., p. 206.

But you do not understand the secret of my peace. I am not trusting to my own merits. I am trusting simply and entirely to the free grace of God: the mercy of God revealed in Christ and which has just the same relation to you that it has to me is the source of all my peace. I indeed do seek to please God. Indeed I seek my life in His favour. But I do so altogether in the strength of that mind and heart of God toward me which the gospel reveals, and my doing so is only my welcoming of the salvation which is given me in the Son of God.[49]

The secret of the gospel is Jesus' trust in the fatherliness of the Father as the response of his sonship. We apprehend this by faith, which is the gift of our participation in Christ.

Second, the sufferings of Christ had an equally close relation to his dealing with the Father on our behalf. Here the focus is on the Son's confessing our sins and making intercession for us. Christ makes his response to the divine condemnation of our sin in a deep agony of spirit, casting himself entirely upon the depths of fatherliness in the Father.[50] Though not penal, Christ's experience is still of a moral and spiritual atonement for sin. There was a real and necessary proportion between our sins and Christ's suffering; of that McLeod Campbell is in no doubt. "The *peace-making* between God and man, which was perfected by our Lord on the cross, required to its reality the presence to the spirit of Christ of the *elements of the alienation* as well as the possession by Him of that eternal righteousness in which was the virtue to make peace."[51] The wrath of God against sin was not levied against Jesus, as if the Father saw him as a sinner, yet that judgment was present to and known in his spirit. This point seems to be the nub of the argument. "Yet must the love that was taking this form have suffered in itself, while interceding, all the pain proper to the heart of perfect sonship, in its sympathy with the feelings of perfect fatherhood against which His brethren had sinned."[52] Thus, to be "washed in the blood of Christ" means to have the moral and spiritual elements of Christ's sufferings revealed to our spirits and to earnestly enter into their depths such that we have an awareness of the terribleness of our sin and of Christ's bearing God's pain thus caused upon himself.

---

[49]Ibid.
[50]Ibid., p. 208.
[51]Ibid., p. 209.
[52]Ibid.

Mirroring an image from Calvin, McLeod Campbell draws his con-clusion: "In our life of sonship through the faith of the Son of God, in our feeble lisping of the Father's name, we have consciously the earnest of the eternal inheritance."[53] Christ has done the Father's will, perfectly declared his name, and borne the grief of God's judgment upon sin. It is in this way that McLeod Campbell sees the life of sonship as having accomplished the atonement, regarded entirely according to a nonpenal frame of under-standing, and as affecting us through our participation in Christ wherein we inherit his Father as our Father. In this way, whether satisfactorily or not, McLeod Campbell has reframed the older soteriological constructs of Christ bearing the cost, price and debt of sin for our salvation.

The defense of the argument (3). In taking up the consideration of the cross of Jesus specifically with respect to his understanding of the nature of the atonement, McLeod Campbell states that he has nothing to add to what has gone before. But the constant reference to the cross in Scripture and Christian tradition as suggestive of the whole means of redemption de-mands its treatment by him.[54] The text that controls the discussion is Luke 23:46: "Father, into your hands I commend my spirit." This commendation, in fact, is the secret of the life of Jesus, not only of the faith announced at his dying. It is the "perfect manifestation" and "consummation" of Christ's faith. Thus, not just the incarnation as such affected atonement, but the life of Christ as it progressed "under the Father's educating Him as the Captain of our salvation. . . . In substance, in spirit, He has all along said, 'Father, into thy hands I commend my spirit.' In actual death He now said so."[55] In his commendation of himself to the Father, Christ is tasting death while doing so. According to McLeod Campbell, this declaring of the Father's name is the primary act of faith, and it is done by Christ fully knowing the righteous mind of God toward sin and in perfect unity with that mind.

It was not just sin that here had to be dealt with, but God's law with its penalty of death. God had made death the wages of sin. Christ's death for us was no substitutionary punishment, however, but was, in the familiar

---

[53]Ibid., p. 212.
[54]Ibid., p. 213.
[55]Ibid., p. 215.

terms, a moral and spiritual sacrifice for sin.[56] "While death taking place simply as such, and the wages of sin, had been no atonement . . . death *filled with that moral and spiritual meaning in relation to God and His righteous law* which it had as tasted by Christ, and *passed through in the spirit of sonship,* was the *perfecting of the atonement*."[57] Thus Christ met his death not as a punishment, but rather on behalf of people in his righteous "Amen" to God's judgment on sin. That is, in his death Christ honored God's law; insofar as we broke it, Christ confessed our sin, and then he took the consequence, the wages, upon himself. In doing so Christ effected the atonement. In this way, God in Christ both condemns our sin and opens up the way of sonship to us.

In arguing thus, McLeod Campbell offers a profound and distinct framing of the theology of atoning propitiation. Understanding Christ's death as a propitiation for sin, tasted in the spirit of sonship and in unity with the Father in his condemnation of sin, means not that the Father accepted Christ's death as a vicarious punishment, but that the Father accepted Christ vicariously bearing the wages of sin: death. God's judgment is propitiated, not by punishment borne but by accepting that the wages have been paid on our behalf. Perhaps McLeod Campbell's positive point would be made clearer if we were to say that the Father accepts Christ's bearing the consequence of sin, which is death, on our behalf. And rather than faith being understood as the acceptance of the imputation of Christ's righteousness, in now familiar terms, faith is "'Amen' to that amen to the divine judgment in relation to sin which was in the death of Christ, and gave it its atoning virtue."[58] That sentence appears to be a summary of much of the whole argument.

Thus we note McLeod Campbell's intellectual relief when he comes to the end. He believes that he has discovered that the sense of the evil and guilt of sin that we receive when the sufferings and death of Christ come upon our minds should become not the measure of what God can inflict as punishment with respect to the imputation of our sin upon Christ, but rather the revelation of what God can feel.[59] Undoubtedly, this is a heavily psy-

---

[56]Ibid., p. 217.
[57]Ibid.
[58]Ibid., p. 221.
[59]Ibid., p. 222.

chologized account that has replaced a traditionally dominant legalized account. "I feel it *morally* and *spiritually* a relief not to be required to recognize legal fictions as having a place in this high region; in which the awful realities of sin and holiness, spiritual death and spiritual life, are the subjects of a transaction between the Father and the Son in the Eternal Spirit."[60] In offering an adequate repentance, Christ offers the only satisfaction to divine justice that could be called a moral and spiritual, as opposed to a legal, atonement or propitiation. With that, McLeod Campbell rests his case. The question is this: Has he made his case, and is it convincing?

The defense of the argument (4). Perhaps as an afterthought, McLeod Campbell seems to want one more round of defense arguments in setting forth his position over and against the penal theory of the atonement and in favor of his reframing of the satisfaction theory of the atonement. He offers it in four brief points with regard to light; unity and simplicity; natural relations with Christianity in other respects; and harmony with the divine righteousness.

First, we recall that the method of approach was to be the atonement seen in its own light. Psalm 40:8, "Lo, I come to do thy will, O God," is reintroduced as the key to the atonement, and "God is love" is reasserted as the law of the spirit of the life that was in Christ. These assertions are once again posited in opposition to the penal view of the atonement, "a horror of darkness, without one ray of light."[61]

Second, while having dealt with the atonement in regard to the bidirectional dual nature of Christ's life and ministry, McLeod Campbell trusts that the unity and simplicity of Christ's life have been clear all along. "It is all *grace reigning through righteousness unto eternal life*. All is in harmony with the purpose, 'Lo, I come to do thy will, O God.'"[62] This end is expressed as an unbroken testimony by the Father to the Son and an unbroken consciousness in the Son as hearing the voice of the Father, abiding in the Father's love, strong in living in the Father's favor, able to drink the cup given to him because it was received from the Father's hand, and commending himself at the end to the Father. The full array of Christ's life was doing the will of the Father in conscious oneness with him, to the Father's glory.

---

[60]Ibid.
[61]Ibid., p. 226.
[62]Ibid., p. 227.

Third, if the atonement is the form that the eternal life took in Christ, then the atonement is the development of the incarnation, though not reducible to the incarnation as such. This, as we have seen, was a key starting insight in McLeod Campbell's argument, and it is the ground for his insistence that there is a unity between the atonement as he has expounded it and Christianity. Lying back of this, as it were, is Christ's trust in the fatherly heart in God, which is the pulse and breath of our new life of sonship through union with Christ. Again this is posited over and against the penal view, in which there is a sharp break between Christ's death as a punishment in which we cannot share and that in Christ which we do share. Clearly, in McLeod Campbell's mind there is an unbridgeable chasm between being under the law and being under grace. Thus he comments, "No doubt Christ did fulfil the law—did fulfil all righteousness: not, however, in a *legal spirit*, but as *the Son* of God *following God as a dear child.*"[63]

Fourth, McLeod Campbell believes that his theory of the atonement is in harmony with divine righteousness. His argument is this: the highest honoring of God's law cannot be recognized as an atonement for sin apart from the results contemplated. The measure we take of eternal life must be the measure of the atonement. They must be congruent. Thus the life of salvation is the life of sonship, which is a higher righteousness than legal obedience.

These four points, briefly noted, and indeed the whole account, may be summed up as the relation in which the scheme of redemption stands to the fatherliness of God. "In that fatherliness has the atonement been now representing as originating."[64] The moral and spiritual expiation for sin that Christ has made has dealt with the justice of God when seen in terms of the gospel rather than in terms of law. Our relation to God as our righteous Lord is subordinate to our relation to God as the Father of our spirits, which is the original and root relation in terms of which everything else in Christianity is to be understood.[65] Sonship alone is the power to accomplish our reconciliation with God. Reconciliation with God, the life of sonship, is the sum of redemption, and its source is the fatherliness of God. "*Nothing extraneous to the nature of the divine will itself to which we are to be reconciled, can have a part in reconciling*

---

[63]Ibid., p. 230 (italics original).
[64]Ibid., p. 237.
[65]Ibid., p. 238.

us to that will."[66] Thus the fatherliness in God originates our salvation; the Son of God accomplishes it by the revelation of the Father. The life of sonship in us is quickened as the work of the Holy Spirit. In this way, the salvation given for us in Christ is duly contemplated and received. This is nothing less than the experience of orphans who have found their father.[67] Faith is the life of sonship toward the Father and the truth of "brotherhood" toward others. The Son draws us to the Father, the Father draws us to the Son. Thus, in a great summary sentence to the book: "Therefore Christ, as the Lord of our spirits and our life, *devotes us to God,* and *devotes us to men* in the *fellowship of His self-sacrifice.*"[68]

THEOLOGICAL ENGAGEMENT WITH THE ARGUMENT

It is now time to see what we can make of this amazing piece of theological reflection. We will look at some standard critical perspectives, and we must also make inquiry into what of McLeod Campbell's theory of the atonement is of enduring insight and value for an expression of the gospel of Christ's salvation today.

Satisfaction. The late Scottish theologian John McIntyre has noted helpfully that McLeod Campbell is to be interpreted as standing within the sphere of advancing a satisfaction theory of the atonement,[69] although McLeod Campbell did not designate his work as such. To his mind, the satisfaction theory denoted God's punishment and was represented in those theologians against whom he was writing, in particular John Owen or the federalist accounts.[70] Nevertheless, it is accurate to say that McLeod Campbell does offer a variation on the satisfaction model. Mention of two discussions should make the case.

This theory begins with Tertullian, and has full expression in Anselm's *Cur Deus Homo*, written between 1096 and 1098. In short, Anselm's theory states that God requires our obedience; in sin, however, we are incapable of offering that obedience. Making good that broken relationship with God requires

---

[66]Ibid., p. 239 (italics original).
[67]Ibid., p. 241.
[68]Ibid., p. 255 (italics original).
[69]John McIntyre, *The Shape of Soteriology: Studies in the Doctrine of the Death of Christ* (Edinburgh: T & T Clark, 1992), pp. 46-48.
[70]Leanne Van Dyk, *The Desire of Divine Love: John McLeod Campbell's Doctrine of the Atonement*, Studies in Church History 4 (New York: Peter Lang, 1995), pp. 146-47.

satisfaction involving full obedience to God's will and reparation for the dis-
honor caused to God by our disobedience. Out of the plenitude of his love,
and for the reordering of the beauty of the creation, God sent his Son, the
Deus-Homo, who made satisfaction by obeying God's will and offering the
reparation required. McIntyre observes that we had to wait nearly eight
hundred years for another satisfaction theory of the atonement, McLeod
Campbell's *The Nature of the Atonement*. What is different this time is that
Christ does not offer reparation to assuage the offense against divine honor,
but instead offers a perfect repentance by way of acknowledging the legitimacy of God's judgment against sin. This acknowledgment is a satisfaction
to God's righteousness. McLeod Campbell offers us a variant on the satisfaction theory that amounts to taking it in a new direction.

Leanne Van Dyk also offers an account of McLeod Campbell's atonement
theory as a satisfaction account, but now in conversation with Calvin, whom
McIntyre oddly left out.[71] Calvin understood the atonement as effected
through both the life and death of Christ, in which satisfaction is made to
God for human sin. Calvin, we must note, offered an atonement theory that
was more than a penal perspective on the death of Christ. Christ's obedient
life as well as his sacrificial death belongs in the account. For McLeod
Campbell, likewise, Christ's life and death are entailed in giving satisfaction
to the Father, though, as always, through a vicarious confession in which
Christ "absorbs" the wrath of God.

Thus the first critical point is this: stipulating that McLeod Campbell's
atonement theory is a variant on the satisfaction model, is satisfaction a
helpful theory of the atonement? As we have seen, characterized well by
Anselm (*aut poena aut satisfactio*, "either punishment or satisfaction"), a
distinction drawn more sharply than by Calvin, satisfaction is certainly
framed negatively by McLeod Campbell as rejection of punishment. But his
essential argument is positive. Satisfaction, for Anselm, became the way by
which God did not have to exact punishment. According to Anselm, there
is a substitution, but it is not a penal substitution.[72] Undoubtedly, there is

---

[71]Ibid., pp. 144-57.

[72]On this point, see Colin E. Gunton, *The Actuality of Atonement: A Study in Metaphor, Rationality, and the Christian Tradition* (Grand Rapids: Eerdmans, 1989), p. 90, citing favorably John
McIntyre, *St. Anselm and His Critics: A Re-interpretation of the Cur Deus Homo* (Edinburgh: Oli-
ver & Boyd, 1954), pp. 86-92.

something deeply problematic about the notion of an innocent person being punished in the stead of guilty persons and declaring such a transaction just. And nowhere does the New Testament say that God has to be reconciled to us by divine punishment induced by human sin. We, rather, are to be reconciled to God. McLeod Campbell turns the satisfaction theory in a distinctly positive direction, however, when he emphasizes that it arises out of the Father-Son relationship and is ethical and spiritual in nature. Satisfaction is humans being reconciled to God through Jesus Christ. For McLeod Campbell, the threat of punishment is not only avoided; it no longer lurks anywhere in the background. Satisfaction, then, is an appropriate scheme, but it seems that it is not dependent upon Anselm's "either/or." For McLeod Campbell, satisfaction has an entirely positive content.

It must be said that however we understand the atonement, sin must there be dealt with, for the sinner is called to repentance; and God's judgment with respect to sin must there be dealt with, for God's holiness will not be mocked. There is no way around this without massive soteriological reductionism, with respect either to the extent of sin or of God's holiness. McLeod Campbell's reconstruction of the satisfaction theory goes some way toward avoiding this reductionism *if vicarious repentance stands the test of examination.* Further, we will have to judge whether satisfaction goes far enough when we have the accounts of atonement by Mackintosh and Torrance before us. But for now, as an interim judgment, I find myself much moved by the theological intuition of the love and mercy of God and the setting of the atonement within the Father-Son relationship, while not casting aside the debt of sin and the righteousness of God's judgment against it that satisfaction theory demands. McLeod Campbell's move away from the notion of sin as a dishonoring of God, whether he had Anselm in mind or not, and toward confession of human sin with respect to God's righteousness is a step in the right direction, away from Anselm's limited notion of satisfaction.

McLeod Campbell was able to make his move away from satisfaction by means of punishment, and implicitly away from satisfaction by means of reparation, to satisfaction as confession because he saw that satisfaction had to be understood not in terms of legal requirements or divine justice and honor but that "in dealing with the Father, He dealt with a *living will and heart.*[73] That is to say, McLeod Campbell's categories by which he developed his doctrine of satisfaction were filial and relational, referring to moral and spiritual relations between the Father and the Son. As Torrance notes, "Christ's atoning sacrifice did not have to do with a penal infliction coming on Christ *from without*, but one which he received and endorsed in the depths of his vicarious life and divine humanity."[74] With this, McLeod Campbell set out a new direction for the satisfaction theory of the atonement precisely as Christ's satisfaction of the *Father's* love as God's Son.

Psychological. Once again noting McIntyre, the observation is made that McLeod Campbell's atonement theory amounts to an ethicizing of the divine attributes.[75] The process by which soteriological categories have been given personalized and ethical qualities had its likely beginning with McLeod Campbell's doctrine of Christ's filial faithfulness toward and revelation of the Father. Hitherto we have faced an antinomy: punishment or repentance. But let us put this otherwise: divine law and human disobedience, or divine love and a broken relationship with the God who loves us. Clearly, two different theological intuitions are in view. On the one hand, atonement is set in a legal context and is made by a suffering that mitigates the wrath of God against sin; on the other hand, atonement is set in terms of the filial relation and is made by Jesus Christ living out the ontological relation between incarnation and atonement as the Son of the Father, revealing God as our Father and dealing with God on our behalf. In the former case, the emphasis is on the work of Christ fulfilling a transactional requirement; in the latter case, the emphasis is on Christ's filial relation with and revelation of the Father. Brian Gerrish pronounced McLeod Campbell's atonement theology as "the protest of grace against the resurgence of legalistic piety in the church of the Reformation."[76]

With that given, it may be said rightly that McLeod Campbell advances a theology of Christian experience grounded in Jesus Christ's filial love toward the Father, and in Jesus Christ's filial love toward and in us. Leanne Van Dyk sums up McLeod Campbell's foundational motivating principle as

---

[73]McLeod Campbell, *Nature of the Atonement*, p. 186.

[74]Thomas F. Torrance, *Scottish Theology: From John Knox to John McLeod Campbell* (Edinburgh: T & T Clark, 1996), p. 309.

[75]McIntyre, *Shape of Soteriology*, pp. 23-24.

[76]B. A. Gerrish, *Tradition and the Modern World: Reformed Theology in the Nineteenth Century*, Zenos Lectures 1977 (Chicago: University of Chicago Press, 1978), p. 77.

the intention "to give an account of the experience of the Christian believer of having been dealt with graciously by God. Campbell's atonement theology is through and through an experiential theology."[77] Can the case be made that in making his argument McLeod Campbell has cast the atonement too much in psychological and anthropomorphic terms?

The critique made by James Goodloe amounts to this. Goodloe vigorously makes the argument that McLeod Campbell's understanding of Christian experience led to his theology of the atonement.[78] The consciousness of being a child of God is the base or primary Christian experience, and, argues Goodloe, the nature of the atonement is worked back, as it were, to meet the demands of that experience. The nature of the Christian experience requires the removal of legal and forensic categories and their replacement with personal and relational categories. Thus Goodloe argues that McLeod Campbell moved from consciousness of being a child of God through repentance, which requires assurance of faith, which requires universal pardon, which rests upon universal atonement, and which then reveals the true character of God as love.[79] Thus the nature of Christian experience ultimately prescribes the nature of the atonement. Goodloe is at pains to note that this turn toward interiority and the personal does not mean that there is no objective accomplishment of Christ in the atonement, or that McLeod Campbell has a low view of the authority of Scripture. But it is the understanding of Christian experience that informs his Christology and his selections from and interpretations of Scripture. Goodloe's analysis leads to this conclusion: "The entire significance of Campbell's understanding of the atonement in these personal categories, as a natural development of the incarnation, is that the atonement has a spiritual and moral power to transform us as persons. The entire purpose of the atonement is that it is to be reproduced in us. What Christ experienced, we are to experience."[80]

Does Goodloe turn McLeod Campbell into a Scottish, soteriologically oriented Schleiermacher who builds his theology from the consciousness of being a child of God? Goodloe's account is well-balanced, erudite and clearly written,

---

[77]Van Dyk, *Desire of Divine Love*, p. 63.
[78]James C. Goodloe IV, *John McLeod Campbell: The Extent and Nature of the Atonement*, Studies in Reformed Theology and History, New Series, no. 3 (Princeton, NJ: Princeton Theological Seminary, 1997), p. 1.
[79]Ibid., p. 33.
[80]Ibid., p. 57.

but I find his conclusions unconvincing for one overarching reason: McLeod Campbell's basic theological intuition concerning God. How God sees us, what God wills for us, and the act of God in Christ to draw us back into communion with God are through and through from the perspective of God's love. McLeod Campbell's pastoral heart longed for people to know this God and be at peace with this God. Undoubtedly, McLeod Campbell's metaphors and categories are relational and personal, well nigh exclusively so, and perhaps this gives his account a lack of balance, for there are other soteriological metaphors and categories in Scripture and Christian tradition for which a place should be found. But Goodloe claims too much with his insistence that McLeod Campbell cast the atonement in terms of the Christian experience of being a child of God.

To my mind, post–McLeod Campbell, no theory of the atonement can now be advanced that is devoid of filial, personal and relational categories, and indeed dominantly so. The theological intuition of the love of God as prior to and constraining the justice and law of God is an apperception that must rightly frame our interpretation of Scripture. While a place must be found for the latter in a fully orbed theology of the atonement, McLeod Campbell's ordering of the priority of the love of God seems rightly emphasized. And McLeod Campbell surely is correct in his insight that "the faith of atonement presupposes the faith of the incarnation."[81] That is to say, the atonement is to be seen in the light of the incarnation and the fulfillment of God's purpose for humankind that the incarnation intends. The meaning of the incarnation unfolds as the atonement insofar as we look at the atonement as the revealing of God's goal for humankind: standing in a filial relationship with God as a child of God. That statement compels assent, otherwise God acts as a mercantile actor in God's salvation. However, limiting atonement to McLeod Campbell's categories will not be adequate, but excluding them is not adequate or satisfying either. A fuller account of the atonement must yet be made, recognizing that McLeod Campbell's contribution remains before us.

Vicarious penitence. The most common complaint against John McLeod Campbell's *The Nature of the Atonement* is that there is no such thing as a coherent doctrine of vicarious penitence. Although McLeod Campbell nowhere uses that term, it has become the currency of critique. The first account

---

[81]McLeod Campbell, *Nature of the Atonement*, p. 19.

of this critique elicited a comment from McLeod Campbell, which he added as a note to chapter six, at the end of *The Nature of the Atonement*. A reviewer made his point by citing McLeod Campbell as saying that all the elements of a perfect repentance—a perfect sorrow and a perfect contrition—were found in Christ *excepting the personal consciousness of sin*. The reviewer then added, "This exception however contains just the essential element of the whole."[82] That is to say, has McLeod Campbell replaced a legal fiction with a moral or spiritual fiction?

McLeod Campbell's rebuttal is that he does not see Christ's confession of our sin before the Father as a substitute for our confession. That seems to imply that whatever it was that Christ did in confessing our sin to the Father, it does not take away from us the need to confess our own sin in due course. In other words, Christ's confession was not a vicarious confession in the sense that there would be no need for our confession, although it was a perfect repentance. McLeod Campbell judges that if he had said that Christ offered a substitute confession in our stead to save us from the necessity of repenting, then the reviewer would have made a fatal objection to his argument. We must still make our own confession, he insists, but we do so because Christ has showed the Father's heart and will toward us, and in doing so we come to find ourselves under a moral and spiritual persuasion, not a legal obligation, to honor the love of God and make our repentance. In McLeod Campbell's terms, this is to find ourselves in the position of sonship.

What was McLeod Campbell feeling after with regard to Christ's confession of sin and this moral and spiritual persuasion of which he speaks?[83] On the one hand, Christ revealed the Father to us, which revelation included the judgment of God against sin. In this context, Christ bears the burden as a man of sorrows because he looked on sinners with God's eyes and felt their burden with God's heart. In this way, Christ condemned sin and showed God's judgment upon it. Dealing with God on our behalf, Christ's oneness of mind with the Father took the form of a perfect confession of our sins. It was a perfect "Amen" from within humankind to the judgment of God. This is an acceptable satisfaction to God's righteous heart of love, and much more so than any punishment could ever be.

---

[82]Ibid., p. 273.
[83]For what follows, see H. R. Mackintosh, *Some Aspects of Christian Belief* (New York: George H. Doran, n.d. [preface, 1923]), chap. 5.

In his wonderful words, "There would be more atoning worth in one tear of the true and perfect sorrow which the memory of the past would awaken in this now holy spirit, than in endless ages of penal woe."[84] Thus Christ entered into the terrible mystery of the knowledge of sin's alienation and confessed the truth of God's holy judgment upon it. As Mackintosh sums up, "The feeling of God concerning sin has found its utterly satisfying response."[85] By faith, which is the gift of the spirit of sonship, we come to participate in Christ's "Amen" from within our humanity to God's judgment upon our sin, thus to enjoy the Father as our Father. This argument amounts to a redefinition of the mind, purpose and character of God vis-à-vis Federal Calvinism, for God is here understood entirely christologically and soteriologically.

Now let us look at Mackintosh's criticisms.[86] The first is that the doctrine of the vicarious penitence of Christ nowhere appears in the New Testament. But neither is vicarious penitence as it is presumed to be understood found within the pages of John McLeod Campbell, as we saw above. Second, Mackintosh makes the obvious point that vicarious penitence is not true to life, for penitence surely implies conscious guilt. If Christ was penitent, then he must have felt guilty in some manner; but if he was without sin, then feelings of guilt were not possible in him. Thus the logic of guilt and penitence forces the conclusion that Christ neither felt the former nor did the latter. Third, Mackintosh states that the atonement is something provided or done by God. Whatever constitutes the central aspects of the atonement must be predicable of God. But surely it makes no sense to say that penitence is predicable of God. In his defense, these words from the posthumously published *Fragments of Truth* find McLeod Campbell in entire agreement with Mackintosh: "The blood is human, but the person is divine; it is a man who dies, but it is God who has made the atonement."[87]

On a positive note, Mackintosh seems to advocate what in fact is McLeod Campbell's point. Christ's sufferings lay in his awareness and acceptance of the pain that sin caused God. Thus it was in Jesus' very being as God that he wrought out and discharged his vocation to be Savior in his life and death,

[84]McLeod Campbell, *Nature of the Atonement*, p. 124.
[85]Mackintosh, *Aspects of Christian Belief*, p. 83.
[86]Ibid., pp. 88-94.
[87]McLeod Campbell, *Fragments of Truth*, p. 218.

revealing the love of the Father and confessing the deadliness of sin unto his own death. Even if vicarious penitence as conventionally understood leads us astray, McLeod Campbell's point remains: Christ made a perfect acknowledgment of the righteous judgment of God. The cross, whatever else it means, means also that Christ acquiesces in God's judgment. Mackintosh judges, however, that McLeod Campbell has not yet said enough at the point of Christ's death. With his finger on the mark, he asks, "Why was a verbal acknowledgment not enough?"[88] Indeed!

Torrance suggests that what McLeod Campbell was feeling after may be made clearer by the terms *poena* (punishment) and *poenitentia* (repentance or penitence), found in patristic Latin.[89] The former can refer to the external infliction, while the latter can refer to the internal counterpart within a person. Christ endured both God's judgment and the acceptance of the legitimacy of that judgment. He took that judgment into himself. Thus Torrance concludes, Christ "wrought out in our human nature and in our human soul complete agreement with the Father in his righteous condemnation of our sin, his grief and sorrow over our rebellion and alienation. In vicarious penitence and sorrow for the sin of mankind, Christ met and responded to the judgment and vexation of the Father, absorbing it in his own being."[90] This hints at something that we must come to in due course, and that Torrance himself will lead us to: there remains the aspect of *poena* to be considered, expressed much more fully than the limited legal construct that so appalled McLeod Campbell. But what McLeod Campbell leaves with us at this point is a most profound theological intuition of *poenitentia*, without which *poena* must surely succumb to a solely legal interpretation as the imputation onto Christ of God's holy wrath.

But is there yet a case to be made for vicarious repentance other than as conventionally expressed in the common criticism of McLeod Campbell? In the citation from Torrance in the previous paragraph he used the term *vicarious penitence*. What might Torrance have meant, and has he entered more deeply into the thought of McLeod Campbell than most of his critics?

---

[88]Mackintosh, *Aspects of Christian Belief*, p. 97.

[89]Torrance, *Scottish Theology*, p. 305.

[90]Thomas F. Torrance, *Atonement: The Person and Work of Christ*, ed. Robert T. Walker (Downers Grove, IL: IVP Academic, 2009), p. 70.

A theme that runs through the thought of both theologians and is, of course, the central argument of this book is that Jesus Christ himself is the atonement, and God is hitherto understood christologically and soteriologically in terms of the filial relation between the Father and the Son. In which case, God as the man Jesus has stood in the gap and received the judgment of God upon us and acquiesced in that judgment so that as the person of Christ, Jesus the man acts in oneness with the Father and in oneness with all humankind. This is the ontological nature of the incarnation and atonement. In hypostatic union, Jesus is both judging God and judged human. To say otherwise would be to infer that Father and the Son are not one in being. Jesus, we can say, is judged vicariously. He is judged *for us*. As such, Jesus acquiesces in that judgment as he confesses our sin and bears upon the cross its consequence, for the wages of sin is death. This too makes any kind of sense only when Jesus' ministry to the Father on our behalf is understood vicariously. How would it be a saving ministry otherwise?

Christ's response to the Father in his confession of our sin on our behalf is the predicate of the ontological relation between the Father and the Son that is worked out savingly through the incarnation, the consequence of which is the atonement. It is saying too much that the atonement consists only of this vicarious confession. It would be saying too little of Christ's confession of our sin if it were not to be accepted as an aspect of the atonement that is faithful to Christ's ministry to the Father on our behalf.

The currency of criticism against John McLeod Campbell with respect to his supposed doctrine of vicarious penitence rests largely on the psychology of common sense with regard to guilt. That, arguably, was not the territory in which he labored, however. His approach was thoroughly theological, even if the desired end was the Christian's experience of forgiveness of sin and peace with God. He sought to bring the subtle and difficult theological intuition of the filial relation between the Son and the Father to expression at the point of Christ's saving mediation. By taking the incarnation so seriously, however, and by linking it so firmly to his understanding of the atonement, he also opened a door to another common complaint against him: universalism.

Universalism. Universalism is the doctrine that at the end everyone will be saved. Was John McLeod Campbell a universalist, and would it matter either way? Robert Letham finds a "strong universalist tendency" in McLeod

Campbell.[91] He then links McLeod Campbell with Barth and Torrance in advocating what he calls an "incarnational universalism." There is, says Letham, no satisfactory way around the conclusion that if Christ unites himself with all people in the incarnation, then he also dies for them on the cross. If the cross achieves what Christ intended, then all people are saved.[92]

James Goodloe, whose remarks on McLeod Campbell were discussed briefly above, is clear and helpful on this point in his presentation of McLeod Campbell's early preaching. Goodloe judges that he was not a universalist, though undoubtedly he stressed universal atonement, universal pardon and the love of God. In Christ we have the gift of making our own response to God, yet in some manner difficult to define it still remains within our power to reject the gospel.[93] Why, within McLeod Campbell's system, do some turn to God while others turn away? Why is the Christ-aided response to God not universally efficacious unto universal salvation? In an early sermon McLeod Campbell insists, "God gives you Christ, your brother, as your king, and holds you responsible for that gift."[94] Faith appears to be the means by which we accept our responsibility before God, but it is not to be seen as a precondition for salvation or as a work that merits salvation. That is, everything is cast upon Christ, but it is only in acknowledging Christ as the Lord who has won our salvation that we enter its joy and peace. Goodloe may be correct in his assessment that for McLeod Campbell, "the atonement, at first seen to be universal in extent, is now seen to be moral and spiritual in nature. This comes as a gift, yet as one for which we are responsible. We are expected to enter into and share the moral and spiritual change."[95] Salvation is understood in terms of our participation in Christ, by which, in the one Spirit, we share in his filial relationship with the Father.

Clearly, we are in difficult territory with this topic. Undoubtedly, the affirmation of an incarnation-centered approach to the atonement can lead in a universalist direction. Yet McLeod Campbell, Barth and Torrance all pull up short. I will have to come back to this issue later when I discuss Torrance on

---

[91]Robert Letham, *The Work of Christ*, Contours of Christian Theology (Downers Grove, IL: Inter-Varsity Press, 1993), p. 31.
[92]Ibid., p. 32.
[93]Goodloe, *John McLeod Campbell*, p. 16.
[94]Cited in ibid., p. 17.
[95]Ibid., p. 52.

the atonement, for he has his own way of dealing with what is a profound mystery that is not amenable to what he calls "logico-causal" explanations of the relation between the atoning death of Christ and the forgiveness of sins. At the end of the day, we are faced with a mystery that cannot be explained.[96]

Binitarian. McLeod Campbell's *The Nature of the Atonement* is so anchored in Father-Son relations that on the surface the Holy Spirit often seems absent from the discussion. Yet undoubtedly deeply embedded in McLeod Campbell's thought is that salvation is possible for us only through our sharing in the ascended life of Christ, to participate in his vicarious offering of himself to the Father. This gift of Christ to us to share in his self-presentation to the Father is by way of the gift of the Holy Spirit. As previously noted, Christ has opened the way to the Father, for through him we "have access in one Spirit to the Father" (Eph 2:18). The pneumatology of the atonement is implied in McLeod Campbell's cardinal conviction of the transformed life that marks Christian faith. Thus he says,

> My immediate object has been the urgent practical one of illustrating that spiritual constitution of things in which, in the grace of God, we have a place, and to which we must needs be conformed if we would partake in the great salvation. Such conformity, that amen of faith to the atonement which I have sought to illustrate, is that to which our Lord calls us when He says, "Seek ye first the kingdom of God and His righteousness,"—adding, in order that we may be altogether free to give heed to the call, the assurance "and all other things will be added unto you."[97]

McLeod Campbell did not fully or explicitly develop the pneumatology of the atonement. But, let me argue, it is present at every turn. It would be harsh and, I think, unwarranted to accuse him of binitarian heresy. A sympathetic reading surely will find his theology suffused through and through with the exaltation of the Holy Trinity—Father, Son and Holy Spirit.

---

[96]See Thomas F. Torrance, "The Atonement: The Singularity of Christ and the Finality of the Cross; The Atonement and the Moral Order," in *Universalism and the Doctrine of Hell*, ed. Nigel M. de S. Cameron, Scottish Bulletin of Evangelical Theology Special Study 5 (Grand Rapids: Baker Books, 1992), pp. 225-56.

[97]McLeod Campbell, *Nature of the Atonement*, p. 264.

5

ATONEMENT

Hugh Ross Mackintosh and the
Experience of Forgiveness

EUGEN ROSENSTOCK-HUESSY HAD AN INSIGHT that helpfully situates H. R. Mackintosh and his approach to the atonement: "As soon as the Gospels were written, speech without experience began to dabble with the new facts proposed by the existence of the church. . . . People tried to think the new life without being touched by it first in some form of call, listening, passion or change of heart."[1] Mackintosh will have nothing to do with speech without experience. He begins his book *The Christian Experience of Forgiveness* with these words:

> "The longer I live," said Rainy, "the more important and wonderful does the forgiveness of sins seem to me." In a series of works designed to present the great Christian doctrines afresh in their vital relations with experience, a treatment of Forgiveness may well find a place. It is a subject regarding which, except on the basis of experience, we should find it barely possible to say anything.[2]

The atonement, while necessarily directing us to the person and work of Jesus Christ for our salvation, must also direct us to the corollary, the experience of being forgiven. Thus the atonement is to be studied while giving forgiveness a central place in the account.

In regard to the atonement and experience, clearly Mackintosh follows in the draft of John McLeod Campbell. As we saw, McLeod Campbell was passionately convicted by the joy and peace of the discovery of "sonship"

---

[1]Eugen Rosenstock-Huessy, *The Fruit of Lips; Or, Why Four Gospels*, ed. Marion Davis Battles, Pittsburgh Theological Monographs 19 (Pittsburgh: Pickwick, 1978), p. 85.
[2]H. R. Mackintosh, *The Christian Experience of Forgiveness* (New York: Harper & Brothers 1927), p. xi.

with the Father, in union with Christ, by the gift of the Holy Spirit. For him, there could be no atonement without the experience of trust in God as one's Father and the life of hope opened up thereby. Mackintosh too wants to explore soteriology in terms of its intended consequences. God takes us sinners to his heart as a repentant child.[3] The consequence is that we are not just forgiven by God, but we live in the experience of being in a new relationship with God. Thus the focus now will be on forgiveness, understanding that this includes being forgiven.

Mackintosh is clear: "As a cardinal certainty we take *the felt presence of Jesus Christ with men.*"[4] Fellowship with Christ is not a metaphor or hyperbole in the heat of argument. Fellowship with Christ is an element of personal life. The communion is with an exalted and living Lord, present in power. In this regard Mackintosh, following in the tradition of John Calvin, is one with the move from a static, inertial notion of God. Christ is a felt presence who steps out of the pages of history as a tremendous and exacting reality.[5] Christ is someone we experience as an inexpugnable reality who stands on his own ground and does not need to be proved. This experienced Christ creates the impression of forgiveness, for we are confronted with our sin beaten, vanquished and powerless. We feel loved in the cross of Christ. Further, in all this we have the full revelation of God as our Father. "Through Christ the Saviour we see back into the Father's heart from which he came."[6] As we will see, Mackintosh gives us a theology of the atonement grounded in the internal relations between the Father and the incarnate Son. In union with Christ that atonement must take empirical form in lives transformed by our participation in the life of the ascended Lord.

THE WESTERN *ORDO SALUTIS*

This account of and engagement with Mackintosh on forgiveness, of its source, necessity and nature, may be put helpfully over against what he calls "a mechanically forensic idea of justification."[7] Doing so will place Mackin-

---

[3]Ibid., p. 3.
[4]H. R. Mackintosh, *The Person of Jesus Christ*, ed. T. F. Torrance (1912; repr., Edinburgh: T & T Clark, 2000), p. 30 (italics original).
[5]Ibid., p. 34.
[6]Ibid., p. 43.
[7]Mackintosh, *Christian Experience of Forgiveness*, p. 153.

tosh's treatment in sharp contrast with the Western *ordo salutis* (order of salvation). Its critique surely ripples throughout the theology of John McLeod Campbell. And our standing over and against it has been implied all along. Giving a very brief account here of the Western *ordo salutis* seems right, however, for two reasons. First, we are now well launched on a positive account of the relation between Christology and atonement, rather than presenting a reactionary response from the beginning. Second, Mackintosh is a writer and thinker of such clarity, over and against the periphrastic McLeod Campbell and the encyclopedic and multilayered theology of Torrance, that its insertion is timely and does not now overly complicate things.

Alan J. Torrance has already given a pointed and insightful account of the Western *ordo salutis*, and I will draw from that.[8] Torrance begins by noting the observation of the Scottish philosopher John Macmurray that there appears to be a threefold apperception underlying Western culture. First, there is the aesthetic/contemplative apperception, characteristic of Hellenic thought. Second, there is the pragmatic orientation associated with Latin and Roman thought and characterized by a legal cast of mind. Third, there is Hebrew consciousness, which shaped the Christian tradition and is notable in its relational and personal categories. Torrance wants to take from this Macmurray's awareness of the dangers of imposing in our questions an apperception that is foreign to our subject of inquiry. When this is done, says Torrance, our questions are "hermeneutically distortive."

Western theology has tended to interpret the gospel from a deontological perspective (*deon* = duty or obligation) on ethics and moral law. Behind this lies the assumption of a universally accessible law interpreted as setting the conditions of God's favor. Relationships, in this case, come to be mapped out in terms of legal requirements and conditions. Torrance suggests that this apperception has shaped the Western order of salvation in both its Roman and Protestant expressions.

The *ordo salutis* takes this form: law, written on the heart, is necessary for awareness of sin; this awareness is the impetus for repentance, the fruit of

---

[8] Alan J. Torrance, *Persons in Communion: An Essay on Trinitarian Description and Human Description, with Special Reference to Volume One of Karl Barth's Church Dogmatics* (Edinburgh: T & T Clark, 1996), pp. 59-64. See too the footnotes for bibliography, which allow readers to follow up with their own research.

which is God's grace and forgiveness and the joy of reconciliation. This law is perceived by natural reason through a universal moral sense that gives access to God's purposes. Epistemologically, this places the priority of law and nature over grace. While grace perfects the former, the die is cast. With scholastic Calvinism there developed the "federal" conditions of divine acceptance as a theological scheme. According to Torrance, this theological scheme in Britain and the United States, expressed especially in the Westminster tradition, operated with the notion of a twofold knowledge of God, the first mediated through nature revealing God's will and legal purposes, the second mediated through Christ revealing God's redemptive purposes. The tendency was to interpret revelation in terms of divine law and contractual obligations, with the concomitant notion of the propositional efficacy of ethical and legal truths. In sum, this trajectory of thought emphasized God's purposes for humankind in legal rather than filial terms, as contractual rather than covenantal, as *Lex* rather than *Torah*, as communication rather than communion. Let Alan Torrance have his own last word on this: "All this meant that revelation (together with redemption) was construed as an essentially extrinsic act of God rather than as a *creative* and *reconciling* event of divine communion with human persons on the part of God who has his Being in communion."[9]

There is much more that could be said of this, of course, but from this very brief review perhaps we have a better sense now of the vis-à-vis with which our Scottish theologians struggled to bring the gospel to an alternative expression. I think, now especially, we will see Mackintosh in sharper relief as we move to the account of his positive contribution to the human experience of forgiveness in Christ.

THE CHRISTIAN'S EXPERIENCE OF FORGIVENESS:
SALVATION IS PERSONAL AND EXPERIENCED

If in the Latin church the christological and soteriological categories have been too much formed by the procedure of the law court, Mackintosh, following Luther and Calvin, wishes to construe redemption in personal terms as a relation historically mediated between God and a person. Salvation is

---

[9]Ibid., p. 63.

fellowship with God. In Christ the divine life touches us; in Christ we are led to the Father.[10] The work of Christ is his person in movement, bringing God to us and us to God in the one work of salvation. In which case, it is a mistake in soteriology to abstract or separate the Christian from Christ, as if the work of Christ is some kind of act external to us—done outside of us, as it were—to which later we must be added.[11] Rather, for Mackintosh, soteriology is an interpretation of believing experience that arises, indeed is compelled by, our experienced union with Christ. There must be no attempt to put this experienced union in abeyance, for there can be no legitimate doctrine of the atonement otherwise. We stand within the experienced saving relationship with God; any attempt to put ourselves beyond it in order to construct a more "objective" construal is to force upon the atonement something other than its intended consequence. In this regard, Galatians 2:19-20 is the locus classicus: "I have been crucified with Christ; and it is no longer I who live, but it is Christ who lives in me."[12] The true spiritual union with Christ must not now be severed in a fictitious attempt at soteriological methodological neutrality. To this end, Mackintosh cites his beloved teacher from Marburg, Wilhelm Herrmann: "The forgiveness of God is not a demonstrable doctrine, still less a notion that can be appropriated by an act of will. It is a religious experience."[13]

To be saved is to be in communion with God as God's child, and with one another in a gathered communion of love. Thus immediately Mackintosh moves away from the notion that God's pardon is the end in view. It is rather the blessing that leads all other divine blessings by the hand. What, then, is forgiveness? Mackintosh will answer that question through a long discussion of nearly three hundred pages, but a brief sense of the journey's end will give us our direction.

It would appear that Mackintosh operates within a subtle dialectical tension. "Notoriously [forgiveness] has too often been identified, or confused, with remission of penalty."[14] In this external sense, forgiveness and remission of penalty have little in common, as even a sense of common

---

[10]H. R. Mackintosh, *The Doctrine of the Person of Jesus Christ*, 2nd ed. (Edinburgh: T & T Clark, 1913), p. 325.
[11]Ibid., p. 332.
[12]Ibid., p. 335.
[13]Mackintosh, *Christian Experience of Forgiveness*, p. 49.
[14]Ibid., p. 24.

grace can teach us. Certainly there need be no logical necessity in urging penalty as the price of forgiveness. On the other hand, this does not mitigate God's chastisement of sin in the act of God's forgiveness, for God is righteous and just. To posit a lack of divine judgment, indeed of loving wrath against sin, is simply a silly idea. Thus Mackintosh asserts that all sins are punished by God with a view to their being forgiven. Punishment is intrinsic to God's grace in this regard as it effects reconciliation at its own cost.[15] But such punishment is not the pagan idea of vindictive fury; rather, God's love is the ground of forgiveness.

If restoration to communion with God is the intended goal of the atonement, the forfeiture of this communion is the punishment of sin.[16] The punishment for sin is spiritual death, nothing less than the paralysis of the personal sense of oneself. Thus "Christianity conquered through its message that in Jesus there is personally present a God Who receives sinners."[17] As such, God's forgiveness in Jesus Christ is personalizing for sinners. We now turn to the explication and assessment of this perspective; I will follow the process of Mackintosh's presentation, commenting along the way.

GENERAL REMARKS: WHAT FORGIVENESS IS WITH RESPECT TO SIN

Forgiveness means God's communicated love for sinners through the creative act of God in Christ whereby the Father puts us right with himself. As noted, vengeance is excluded; chastisement is not. We are not smitten with the force of impersonal law; rather, we are confronted with grace that forgives and cleanses, and that is immeasurable in its infinitude and wonder.[18] The gospel is God's desire, at whatever cost, for our restoration to communion with God in view of the one barrier to such communion: our distrust and selfishness, which we call sin. Forgiveness is to discover that the Holy One is a heavenly Father who receives sinners. Reciprocally, we, who are confronted with such grace as eternity breaking into time, a divine love intervening beyond all measure as a unilateral and unconditional act of God,

---

[15]Ibid., p. 166.
[16]Ibid., p. 171.
[17]Ibid., p. 21.
[18]Ibid., pp. 28, 32.

receive it as an inexplicable gift.[19] "Of [God's] own movement He has altered our relation to Himself. . . . He, the Judge of men, brings the guilty sinner, as he is, into the enjoyment of His love, provided only that he chooses to be brought in and responds to the love willingly. . . . Gratitude, gladness, exhilaration is the only fit temper for all who have been thus blessed."[20] The end in view, as already with John McLeod Campbell, is filial communion with the Father as actual occurrence.

The concern that now comes immediately to Mackintosh is the understanding of sin, and he takes a chapter to make some general points. His discussion on points of exegesis, historical theology, dogmatics and pastoral care we will note in due course.

If we would understand what forgiveness is, we must have some sense of what it is over and against. Why do we need to be forgiven? At this point Mackintosh is uninterested in the reality and nature of the fall, of original sin, of the genesis of sin. These topics are, apparently, irrelevant to his purpose. Rather, he turns to what at first glance appears to be a phenomenology of sin, as he tries to stay true to the experiential method. We discover ourselves to be divided against ourselves, neighbor and God. We are morally unhinged. Thus Mackintosh turns to a brief analysis of conscience, a strangely dated move perhaps, post-Freud. Abruptly, however, he takes leave of this inquiry to discuss the will of the living God. "We now detect and measure sin by its unlikeness to the spirit of Jesus. . . . It is in the light of Christ that we see sin clearly and can in some real degree understand how it looks to God."[21] A truer knowledge of God is accompanied by a deeper insight into sin. This is altogether a more fruitful and appropriate move if our task is to do theology.

"Sin, essentially, is selfish failure to trust and obey God."[22] Sin is done against God. But as such it is more than misfortune, error or ignorance. Sin is knowing rebellion. It has the character not just of indifference toward God but also of blatant opposition to the will of God for our lives. In particular, sin is the refusal of faith and love and is manifestly relative to the character of God.[23] It is an intended move to live independently of God and to elevate

---

[19]Ibid., p. 37.
[20]Ibid., p. 36.
[21]Ibid., p. 54.
[22]Ibid., p. 55.
[23]Ibid., p. 61.

self or world into God's place. Yet more still is to be said, for sin is more than acts done evilly. More deeply, sin is a predicate of us. We are sinful. The reference is to something we are, and not just something we do: we are sinners. Ultimately it is persons who are sinners. Sin is godlessness, wherein we refuse God's relationship with us, and is as such a rebellion against and rejection of God. God has become our enemy, and it is our doing, and as such before our blinded eyes God's good will changes into what we believe to be ill will against us. The fact is that we are trapped. Sin's rectification is possible only if God takes the first steps to deal with it in such a manner that we become a new creation.

Sin, as such, is inexplicable. Why we turn away from personhood toward thinghood is unintelligible. There is no rational purpose to sin and no moral compass that guides us toward understanding. Mackintosh surely is correct in noting that sin is "a thoroughly irrational entity, impervious to light."[24] We sin unavoidably, while nevertheless it is a matter of personal choice. In this case, guilt is a corollary to sin, surely to be spoken of both objectively and subjectively. In reality sin is against God, and we live in dis-peace with ourselves. Before God we find ourselves impure and impotent, for which we are answerable. "The paradox confronts us: because we are answerable, there can be for us no excuse, yet because we *are* answerable, and sin has not merely happened to us as an infection might, it is possible for us to be forgiven. Only guilty sin can be pardoned."[25]

When we are confronted with Jesus Christ, if in him "we discover how awful goodness is and how great is the love we have violated, two kinds of changes occur in the consciousness of guilt we are considering: first, its gravity is painfully increased by the new perception of our sin as antagonism to utter goodness, but along with this comes a joyful and wondering knowledge that none the less His great love is receiving us, and that the estranging power of guilt has been abolished."[26] While God remembers our guilt no more, we retain the knowledge that we have sinned and done evil. We continue to remember our sin, and it remains oddly mysterious that in spite of so great a redemption we never quite forgive ourselves—*Simul justus et peccator.*

---

[24]Ibid., p. 63.
[25]Ibid., p. 67.
[26]Ibid., p. 75.

The Pardoning God

Our understanding of forgiveness must rest in the known character of God. What are the qualities in God that are revealed to those who experience the grace of God's forgiveness? Mackintosh makes three points in this regard.

First, God is personal.[27] Clearly Mackintosh, like Pascal, has in mind the God of Abraham, Isaac and Jacob rather than the God of the philosophers. "You can only ask for pardon if the Divine, ultimately, is a free, loving conscious spirit. It is as a Spirit, a personal Spirit, that God claims us, rebukes us, comforts us; above all, it is in that character that He forgives our sin. What has to be forgiven is relative to such a Being."[28] The point made is rather obvious, but it is well made nonetheless because it means that restoration to relationship is the heart of the matter. What is needed is a God who loves us, seeks us and restores us when we are weary with the burden of our sins. Thus we come to God believing that "Father" includes the idea that God is a personal being.

Second, God is a doer of miracles. In the biblical phrase, the God who pardons is the living God, a God who wills and acts, and in so doing produces a change in our relation to himself.[29] Forgiveness is a divine act to which our experience of being forgiven or being reconciled corresponds. Our attention is drawn here to what God initiates, for in forgiving our sin God acts toward us. God as Father opens the door of communion and places the sinner in the position of a reconciled child. In a wonderful turn of language Mackintosh suggests that it is the victorious love of God that deprives sins of their power to exclude us from God's fellowship.[30]

The simplicity of Mackintosh's observation stands over and against the longstanding view in theology that gave prominence to a conception of God as an unchanging substance, and necessarily impassible and immovable. So-called classical theism characterizes God as both living and true, yet without passions, immutable, immense, eternal, incomprehensible and so on. Much in the history of theology has involved the varied fortunes of these two interpretations of God. For Mackintosh, situating himself over and against the Western *ordo salutis*, God is characterized precisely by movability and

---

[27]Ibid., pp. 177-79.
[28]Ibid., p. 178.
[29]Ibid., pp. 179-87.
[30]Ibid., p. 181.

passion. God acts (can we say "God moves"?) supernaturally, intervening into our personal history. God cancels the sin and guilt that have barred us from communion with him; and God does so not by declaring that sin is not sinful, nor by forgetting sin, nor by simply not holding the sinner to account, "but by countervailing [sin's] power to estrange the Father and the child."[31] As noted earlier, by this act of God, we, who are headed toward "thinghood" (my word, not Mackintosh's), for we stand in a broken relationship with the ground of personhood, are forgiven into personhood in the fullest sense as persons in communion with God. Thus, by God's mercy, we do not reap what we have sown.

At this point Mackintosh makes a remarkable observation. Pondering how God forgives, Mackintosh pulls back from speculation by noting that we have no psychology of God.[32] In a different image, we have no access to the metaphysics of forgiveness, as we have no access to the metaphysics of creation, incarnation, resurrection and ascension. Biblically, what we have is "thus it is so." "On the one hand, we are assured in Jesus of a Divine mercy to which all—even the wonder of forgiveness—is possible; on the other, we have as believers the inward certainty that our sins *are* pardoned. But how the gap between the two is bridged, how God makes our forgiveness real, is hidden from us, and no enlargement of the human faculty is conceivable for which the mystery would be resolved."[33] God, so the gospel insists, has entered our personal lives in such fashion that we can give no account of how it was done. To what within the created nature could we appeal to explain that supernatural act of God's mercy by which we are forgiven? Yet, insists Mackintosh, we do experience such forgiveness. Thus it is so.

Third, Mackintosh gives us what amounts to a prolegomenon to the doctrine of the atonement. The person who experiences God's forgiveness knows that God's very nature is sacrificial love. This means that we cannot separate the question of God's forgiveness from the question of the atonement, which is God's act to reconcile the world to himself.[34] Atonement and forgiveness belong together in closest connection.

---

[31]Ibid., p. 182.
[32]Ibid., p. 185.
[33]Ibid.
[34]Ibid., pp. 187-93.

As I said, this is a prolegomenon to atonement. As such, Mackintosh offers an extended analogy between divine and human forgiveness on the ground that God and humankind are of one moral order, by means of which he thinks that he can establish the only conceivable medium for understanding forgiveness.[35] This is a risky endeavor, for who is like the Holy One of Israel? And is the sense of a shared moral order between God and humankind the proper basis for an analogy that will take us into the heart of the atonement? But to be fair to Mackintosh, his discussion is intended to be suggestive rather than definitive. He is probing, looking for correspondences between divine and human forgiveness that are heuristic, not absolute and eternal.

Thus Mackintosh presents us with a phenomenology of human forgiving, and his psychology at this point, to my mind at least, tends to suggest an autobiographical truth. One wonders whether he knows directly of what he writes. In any case, he knows that it is an exacting thing to pardon a great wrong.[36] An injured party, one to whom deep harm has been done and who feels deep hurt, reaches out in love beyond the wrong. In doing such the injured party acts out of costly suffering. There is surely consciousness of wrench and agony in proportion as one has been injured by another's evil.

> How true it is that in heart and mind the forgiver must set out on "voyages of anguish"! It is an experience of sacrificial pain, of vicarious suffering. . . . When he moves out to find and claim his friend again the other's evil, as never before, comes in upon him freshly in its indescribable repulsiveness and need of cleansing; yet he takes it on himself redemptively as by creative and substitutionary fellow-feeling, submerging it in love.[37]

In such a human endeavor forgiveness is mediated by costly suffering.

Analogically, the forgiveness of God may be construed as somewhat parallel: pain forming the vehicle of forgiveness. Switching now to a theological construal, Mackintosh asserts,

> The cross presents and represents God's anguish, an awful grief answering to the greatness of the remitted sin. . . . Thus at Gethsemane and Calvary most of all, faith discerns such an exhibition of Divine reconciling passion, such a

---

[35]Ibid., p. 192.
[36]Ibid., p. 190.
[37]Ibid., p. 191.

tragic tension in which God spares Himself nothing, as makes our hearts faint within us and stops every mouth before God. . . . Atonement is what it cost God to forgive the sins of the world.[38]

Thus the God who lives infinitely and immeasurably above and beyond us has in Christ Jesus entered decisively into the deepest human sin. And to see into the heart of this God we must gaze upon the man of sorrows upon the cross.

With this, Mackintosh has prepared his reader to step across the analogy that he has constructed to the doctrine of the atonement itself. To follow him there we will turn now to look briefly at his remarks on the life of Jesus.

God's Forgiveness Uniquely and Personally Present in the Life of Jesus

Forgiveness is present in Jesus, not just on the cross. Insofar as the Western *ordo salutis* has dominated thinking about the atonement with its central focus on the cross, little attention has been given to the soteriological aspect of the life of Jesus or, indeed, to the person of Jesus in this regard. According to Mackintosh, "We acquire [the] certainty of fatherly pardon, and in the full sense acquire it only, in the presence of Jesus Christ."[39] With echoes of the teaching of John McLeod Campbell, Mackintosh argues that in Jesus we discover that our relationship to God is of dear children to a Father. In encountering Jesus we have the consciousness that our sins are forgiven. His announcement is that to look at him is to know how God would have us think of God. In Christ we perceive the true nature and character of God. Mackintosh insists, "We have first to let Jesus show us what the Father is like, and that forgiveness . . . is His characteristic gift. As we contemplate Jesus presented in the Gospels, we discern not merely that God is love, but what *kind* of love this is."[40] The central question for us, then, is whether we have in Jesus—in his life, death and resurrection—a trustworthy presentation of God.

Mackintosh comments, "If older thought inclined to say that we can only believe in forgiveness because the Divine Son paid satisfaction to the Father, we preserve the same vital and solemn interest by proclaiming that forgiveness is credible, and is offered, in virtue of the fact that God is personally

---

[38]Ibid., pp. 192-93.
[39]Ibid., p. 77.
[40]Ibid., p. 84.

present in One who stood in with sinners to the last, and, refusing to abandon them, went for their sake to the Cross."[41] That is to say, Jesus' own words and practice show that the forgiveness of God was fully and, according to the New Testament, uniquely present in him.

Now Mackintosh, at least to contemporary eyes, draws an overly sharp contrast between the teaching of Jesus and the Judaism of Jesus' day as a religion interpreting relations with God in terms of law. However that may be, he is right to insist that Jesus intended people to understand that divine law was neither his own nor the Father's last word concerning their relation with God.[42] The gospel in this regard is that people, in their experience of Jesus' love for them, were receiving the forgiveness of God. Jesus was leading people into a new relationship with God, and this meant that God had forgiven them.

Mackintosh points to three incidents in which Jesus' mind about forgiveness is made clear. The first is at Mark 2:3-12, the account of the healing of the paralyzed man. Jesus' question to his interlocutors was this: "Which is easier, to say to the paralytic, 'Your sins are forgiven,' or to say, 'Stand up and take your mat and walk'?" (Mk 2:9) The onlookers had declared Jesus' declaration of forgiveness to be blasphemy. Jesus appears at once both to have declared forgiveness and guaranteed the declaration by being who he was, for only God can forgive sins. Both diseased limbs and a broken relationship with God were healed by Jesus' word. "Salvation—that comprehensive miracle— consisted for Him in admission to a Divine family in which men were children of a Father who both forgave all their iniquities and healed all their diseases."[43] Body and soul, as it were, are but the person in need of God, in an inseparable unity of experience in which God has acted to do what humans could not do. Further, Jesus' treatment of the paralyzed man was prior to his asking for help. The initiative was with God. Jesus spoke first.

Jesus' right to pronounce forgiveness to sinful people had been openly challenged. In the miracle Jesus appears to be making the case for his personal identity. In order for the declaration of pardon to be received as the situation now obtaining for the previously paralyzed man, something of Jesus' identity surely had to have been perceived. When Jesus proffers pardon, it is

---

[41]Ibid., p. 86.
[42]Ibid.
[43]Ibid., p. 90.

in virtue of himself.[44] Now, the danger here surely is that too easily we can move to impute psychological states to Jesus. How can we comment on his self-consciousness? Mackintosh, a man of his age, seems to drift in that direction when he argues that Jesus presented forgiveness in an absolute and personally authoritative way, and the explanation for this can lie only in his self-consciousness as the bearer of God's salvation.[45] My inclination is to exercise epistemological reserve at this point and avoid speculation. Even so, the point remains that the man found pardon at the words of Jesus.

One final word, not noted by Mackintosh: the paralyzed man was forgiven by Jesus *before* Jesus died on the cross. That, in short, appears to be the point that Mackintosh has tried to make without actually saying so. If that is correct, it is a startling point to make. More often than not we are given to locate the locus of divine pardon singularly on the cross. The cross is the focus of soteriological attention. As such, we are robustly en route to an instrumentalist soteriology in which the cross affects some kind of atoning exchange. Locating the locus of divine pardon in Jesus, however, and in Jesus before his death, opens us up to a larger soteriological vision.

The second incident that Mackintosh uses to illustrate the mind of Jesus about forgiveness is drawn from Luke 7:36-50. This is the account of the incident in the house of Simon the Pharisee, where a woman wept over Jesus' feet, dried them with her hair, and anointed them with ointment. Here the word of forgiveness is spoken by Jesus at the close of the story (Lk 7:48). Mackintosh is struck by the omission of any explicit condemnation, though her sins were many. Further, he notes the virtue of simple penitence. ("At the touch of penitence all doors fly open, and the child is at the Father's breast"[46]— a characteristic expression of Mackintosh's theology as piety.) Jesus represents God to the woman's aching heart and agitated spirit. Yet nowhere in the account is the name of God mentioned. The assumption, surely, is that in and as the person of Jesus, God is savingly present. Had he turned from her, undoubtedly she would have been lost without a trace. Jesus' attitude was to announce that God was on her side and was receiving her as a child.

Mackintosh makes a lovely closing point: it is inconceivable that in Jesus'

---

[44]Ibid., p. 92.
[45]Ibid., p. 93.
[46]Ibid., p. 94.

view a pardoned person should not begin to love. And where love is absent, there has been no reception of forgiveness.[47] This is brought out in the sharp contrast between the gratitude of the forgiven woman and the cold heart of the Pharisee. If Simon knew that he was the Father's child, how could his heart be so cold? "To know oneself forgiven is to have the spring of love unsealed."[48]

The third incident is taken from Luke 5:8-10, the story that marks the beginning of Peter's discipleship. We can be brief. Before the Lord, Peter makes his declaration, "Go away from me, Lord, for I am a sinful man!" (Lk 5:8). Jesus responds, "Do not be afraid; from now on you will be catching people" (Lk 5:10). In a manner similar to the call of Isaiah (Is 6:5), Peter, in the face of the divine call, is overwhelmed with his feeling of sinfulness. The presence and call of Jesus were to Peter a revelation not merely of unworthiness, but of sinfulness. In responding, Jesus bids Peter to have courage; then Jesus bids Peter to trust him with the service of God's salvation. Although pardon is not mentioned, Peter is not thrust away; rather, Jesus joins him to his mission. Further, Peter is made aware that he is now God's man. Peter surely knows with clarity that God has been gracious to him.

Mackintosh sees one outstanding feature in these three cross sections: "It is that Jesus meets the natural hesitation of sinners to believe in God's forgiveness, by His own attitude to them of loving friendliness and goodwill."[49] There is no word on sin's horror. Yet Jesus often sought out the company of sinners as if by virtue of his mission he could do no other. His ministry of mercy was in view of the end contemplated. And in doing so he pointed out surely that to act thus, to be in the company of sinners, is a reflection of the mind and character of God. None of this is to say that in doing what he did, and in announcing the word of pardon, Jesus was not struck to his core by the evil and sin to which he drew so near. Such love toward sinners did not mitigate the divine pain that is so central to the Christian understanding of redemption.

Mackintosh asserts that forgiveness in the New Testament is invariably presented as a free gift of the Father.[50] Pardon is not wrung from God by sacrifice that assuages the divine wrath or palliates the divine pain. But the

---

[47]Ibid., p. 96.
[48]Ibid.
[49]Ibid., p. 99.
[50]Ibid., p. 100.

question arises "whether Divine sacrifice, visible and implemented in Jesus, may not have none the less been present in the impartation of forgiveness, not as a precondition but as an element."[51] Pardon is costly. And Jesus could not convey the Father's forgiveness except that he gave himself utterly for sinners. Ultimately, the bearer of forgiveness, its agent, gave himself up to death.

In this section we have a prolegomenon to the full doctrine of the atonement, for Mackintosh has not yet considered the meaning of the cross or given a full account of Jesus' suffering. But even if prolegomenon, the intimation of the soteriological efficacy of the ministry of Jesus leads to the initial conclusion that atonement has everything to do with the person of Jesus, with who he is, rather than being limited to the instrumentality focused only on the cross as the place of penalty, the cost paid for broken law, associated with the Western *ordo salutis*.

THE ATONEMENT

It is undoubtedly impossible to think through the meaning of divine forgiveness without awareness of the great cost to God. The price that God pays, apart from which there could be no forgiveness, is the *prius*, the first, and evoking cause of the experience of pardon.[52] Our peace is the fruit of God's love and the suffering savingly endured for us that reached its terrible climax on the cross. We have seen already how Mackintosh has drawn an analogy between God's forgiveness and human forgiveness. And in general terms the conclusion has been suggested that atonement, on any level, is costly to the party who forgives. The sin that is forgiven must in a real sense be borne by the party who pardons. Now the argument must move from general considerations to a fully orbed reflection on the career of Jesus, for it is as Jesus that God has interposed into our sinfulness, and through Jesus that reconciliation has been accomplished.

Methodologically, the truth about atonement is arrived at a posteriori, discoverable only for those who know they have been set right before God. Doctrine is but the expression of the subject matter of faith of those who have been brought home to the Father. For Mackintosh, in other words, atonement theory is personal rather than final. Once again, he bids us to move in the field

---

[51] Ibid.
[52] Ibid., p. 194.

of Christian experience. We take up our task in soteriology as those who with penitent eyes look toward Jesus and his cross. Putting aside the actual Christ in search a priori of a theory leads in a hopeless direction. "How could we know that *Christ* is necessary, if we did not know by acquaintance the person called 'Christ'?"[53] But as such, we are confronted with inexpressible mystery for which we have no complete theory; atonement is a reality that we cannot manage. There are no masters of atonement (although, oddly, we appear to be unfazed by ostensible masters of divinity!). With the atonement we have before us the inexplicable enigma of the innocent suffering of Jesus, indeed of God, as the just man suffering for the unjust.

Mackintosh announces his central theme: "The death of Jesus has significance for reconciliation only when considered in the light, and as an expression, of His life."[54] This statement is congruent with what we have already seen in Mackintosh. But it means more than that we are not saved by an unknown divinity. Mackintosh intends that we are directed to the person of Jesus, to who he is as God with us and for us in the flesh of his humanity. Neither is atonement worked out in such a way that it is limited to reflection on Christ's death. Rather, as Jesus is presented to us in the New Testament, we see his deeper and deeper self-identification with sinful people throughout his life. Already in his baptism, for example, he made our sins his own as he insisted on being reckoned as one of us. Thus the cross is the culmination of what he lived. Nevertheless, the special significance of the cross cannot be avoided. To do so would be to betray the New Testament; to do so would be to betray the Lord's Supper: "This is my body given for you." The cross, though inseparable from the life of Jesus, has its own meaning and distinction, and that must figure in our reflections.

Prefiguring what we will find later with T. F. Torrance on the atonement, Mackintosh situates his reflections in the context of the Lord's Supper. What comes home to us when we eat the bread and drink the wine? In the posture of inestimable reception from Christ and of our self-abandonment to him, two predominant impressions register in our minds: in Jesus' death we behold God's absolute judgment and condemnation of sin; and in Jesus'

---

[53]Ibid., p. 197.
[54]Ibid., p. 198.

death we behold the absolute revelation of God's love toward sinful people.[55] We will now take time to see what Mackintosh has to say on these matters as he draws toward the center of his presentation.

God's judgment on and condemnation of sin. Mackintosh has three points under this head. First, Mackintosh notes that sin is condemned on the cross because there its true nature is exposed.[56] There it is seen for what it really is in its antagonism to perfect love. God gave us Jesus Christ, and we killed him. On the cross human evil is exposed once for all.

Second, sin is judged by Jesus. He loved with the purity of God. In doing so he utterly opposed sin, dying at the hands of sinners who vented their hate upon him, thus revealing and condemning sin as the contrary of love. Christ resisted sin unto the shedding of his own blood. "The cup He must drink was in part the knowledge that His love had evoked the sin of others to the full."[57] And because Jesus was in unbroken sonship with the Father, on the cross we are confronted with God's holy judgment upon sin. "The cross reveals in a final and for ever unmistakable way God's mind regarding sin and His active attitude towards it. . . . Forgiveness is possible only insofar as all concealments which hide the real nature of sin are torn away and men are convicted of utter and inexcusable unworthiness."[58] Thus forgiveness must always be associated with God's judgment on human sin.

Third, on the cross the connection between sin, divine judgment and suffering is made utterly clear. Now, there is a problem here. The death of Jesus was occasioned at the hands of people, not God. Sinners, not the Father, killed Jesus. How is it possible, in this case, to say that the cross represents *God's* judgment and manifests *God's* righteousness?[59] Mackintosh moves toward his answer by noting that sin is always followed by evil consequences. Jesus, by his total association with humankind, with sinners, by taking our nature, reveals that sin and condemning pain go together. Drawing from Isaiah 53 and the account of the Suffering Servant, Mackintosh shows that the "spiritual principle" emerges of the vicarious character of the suffering of the

---

[55]Ibid., pp. 200-217.
[56]Ibid., p. 200.
[57]Ibid., p. 203.
[58]Ibid.
[59]Ibid., p. 204.

Servant.[60] Suffering at the hands of the wicked, the Servant bears the consequence of their sins. But this could not as yet be fulfilled redemptively. It is
as if the Suffering Servant has gone as far as humanly possible with regard to
vicarious suffering, excepting incarnation. And surely there is little doubt that
Jesus himself had the Servant much in mind. "The Divine reaction against
the sin of man He perceived to be falling upon Him. . . . It was because He
thus in love made Himself one with the sinful that He bore their burden. . . .
His sufferings were the bitter fruit of sin vicariously borne."[61]

Another, longer, citation is worth noting:

> It was not that God stretched His hand from the sky, seized the mass of human
> iniquity, transferred it to Jesus by capricious fiat, then chastised Him for it.
> God does nothing in that way. But when Jesus entered into our life, took the
> responsibility of our evil upon Himself, identifying His life with ours to the
> uttermost and placing Himself where the sinful are by strong sympathy in a
> fashion so real that the pain and affliction due to us became unspeakable suf-
> fering with His soul—*that* was the act of God, that (if we take seriously Jesus'
> oneness of mind and will with the Father) was indeed the experience of God.[62]

Before we move on, let us note once again how Mackintosh will not stray
in any way into the theological territory marked out by the Western *ordo
salutis*. There is not even a hint here of the Father punishing the Son in wrath,
or of sin as broken law, or of forgiveness as imputed righteousness. The
setting is not that of the law court or of broken contracts precipitating
penalty, but rather it speaks of the broken heart of God and of a love that
stretches to the beams of the cross, vicariously bearing the consequence of
God's condemnation of sin and the suffering concomitant to it.

Jesus' death discloses the fullness of God's love toward sinners. The point
for Mackintosh here is that there is oneness of being between Jesus and the
Father such that in Jesus' suffering and death, and in the love toward us that
is therein represented, there is no distinction to be made between the grace
of the Lord Jesus Christ and the grace of God himself.[63] Interposed with
God's condemnation of sin, then, there is apprehended (but surely not com-

---

[60]Ibid., p. 206.
[61]Ibid., p. 207.
[62]Ibid., pp. 207-8.
[63]Ibid., p. 208.

prehended) in the cross of Christ love acting on an infinite scale. This love is present as enduring a vicarious burden caused by sin. Thus atonement and the divinity of Jesus must be held together in our minds. "The history of theology proves to the hilt that the great ideas of Atonement and Incarnation lose the life-blood of meaning when they drift apart from each other."[64] While the cross of Christ is set before the eyes of history for all to see, we must also speak rightly of the suffering of the Father, though different from the suffering of the Son, and thus of suffering within God.

There is nothing here in Mackintosh of God having to be induced to love us, and that it was Christ's death that provided that inducement. Like McLeod Campbell before him, Mackintosh sees the atonement as the result of the love of God, not the condition for it. That is not to question God's wrath against sin; to posit God's wrath is in no way to question God's eternal love toward us.[65] God's judgment against sin is the act of God's love. Too much, perhaps, in theology there has been the tendency to see a divided will within God, as if the satisfaction of divine wrath was necessary for divine love to be given to us.

Further, and this is a point of cardinal importance, through the reconciliation effected in the life and death of Jesus we see not only God's love toward us, but also the opening up of a new future between God and us. "If the cross be thus God's creative act, in relation to sin, it is impossible that it should leave things between Him and us as before. . . . All that went to the death of Christ, constituting it the definitive self-expression of God towards the sinful, not merely *reveals* God's antecedently forgiving love; it actually *conveys* forgiveness and renders it effective."[66] That is to say, pardon is not just announced, or even imputed; rather, a new relationship between God and sinners is established *that is the Christian experience of forgiveness.*

Mackintosh now raises an objection. How necessary was the cross for divine mercy to be given to us? Jesus, we recall, imparted God's forgiveness during his life, and not only through the cross. The answer, I think, is that Jesus himself is the medium of God's grace, and God's forgiveness is not to be limited to the instrumentality of the cross. Mackintosh seems to say that Jesus, in his life as in his death, entered into the human situation and took it upon

---

[64]Ibid., p. 211.
[65]Ibid., p. 212 (italics original).
[66]Ibid., p. 214.

himself. When this happened, forgiveness was given. Even so, clearly we encounter atonement as mystery. It most certainly has to do with Jesus. His suffering for and with the sinner is profoundly the nature of the case. And in Christ it is God who acts. All this is integral to Christian proclamation. That said, Mackintosh doubts that any complete answer can be given to the problem of how closely to tie together the cross and God's forgiveness in Jesus Christ.

Nevertheless, Mackintosh now circles back to his starting point in the Lord's Supper. "This is my body, which is given for you" (Lk 22:19); "This cup that is poured out for you is the new covenant in my blood" (Lk 22:20). These words indicate the spiritual actuality of the cross for our redemption. Mackintosh uses the phrase "spiritual necessity" of the cross.[67] It had to be, because God is holy and is love. With the words "spiritual necessity," I wonder, however, if Mackintosh has not inadvertently brought an instrumental perspective on the cross back into view. By using the alternative phrase "spiritual actuality," I am suggesting that the cross is so strongly indicative of atonement in Christian tradition that it cannot be downplayed, but I choose to operate with a degree of epistemological reserve in order to protect the essential mystery. This, though, is affirmed: it is Jesus who saves—in his life as in his death. Jesus saves by suffering love as he takes the burden of sin upon himself and bears its consequence, showing God's judgment upon it and God's love for sinners.

I can happily walk with Mackintosh on the next step he takes, when he considers the cross of Christ as a sacrifice in which we by faith participate.[68] Sacrifice is not to be understood as a device through which God is propitiated. It means that sin is covered from God's sight by the means that God provides. "If Jesus' death is a sacrifice, then the sacrifice originates with God. . . . In Jesus the self-giving of God to man and the self-giving of man to God meet and absorb each other."[69] (Recall that McLeod Campbell used the word "absorb" at this point; we will see that in a similar manner Torrance also uses it.) Jesus' sacrifice—his life as also his death—comes from God and is given to God. Its source is surely that he came to do the will of the one who sent him, as we see referenced repeatedly in John's Gospel, for example. He is the mission of God. His sacrifice is the obedient fulfillment of that

---

[67]Ibid., p. 219.
[68]Ibid., p. 222.
[69]Ibid., p. 223.

mission, both inwardly as in his oneness of will with the Father, and out-
wardly insofar as he lays down his life for sinners. Says Mackintosh, Jesus,
already at his baptism, coming to a head in his death, gave himself in utter
self-identification with the sinners he forgave.

> For us, with us, He there bowed under the Father's judgment on sin, con-
> fessing the sinfulness of wrong and its utter evil in God's sight. His bowing
> thus, in perfect love, *was* His sacrifice. . . . We take His confession as our own,
> pronouncing our Amen to His utter acceptance of the righteous will of God.
> . . . When He does so, he exhibits the mind and spirit of perfect sonship, which
> alone is satisfying to the Father's heart.[70]

The only wonder at this point is why Mackintosh did not note, in the almost
verbatim similarity with the theology of vicarious penitence identified with
John McLeod Campbell, his dependence upon his Scottish theological forebear.

Union with Christ. Thus in atonement Christ did not propitiate God or
move God to remit our sins. To make his point, Mackintosh insists once
again that the Father's love is the font of redemption, while the atonement is
the manner appropriate to that love in which God's pardon is given. Citing
John 16:27, where Jesus says, "The Father himself loves you, because you have
loved me," Mackintosh comments, "Christ takes us with Him, as it were, into
communion with God."[71] Thus nearing his conclusion, Mackintosh robustly
asserts that through union with Christ two great truths must be announced:
God in Christ for us; we in Christ for God. This, in effect, is the sum of Christianity. To be forgiven for Christ's sake means that we are one with him, and
God sees us as such and acknowledges us as such.

So far now has Mackintosh moved toward the organic reality of union
with Christ, and away from external perspectives on the atonement, that he
will have nothing to do with our guilt being externally imputed to Christ
and his righteousness externally imputed to us.[72] Rather, we are to understand ourselves as in such spiritual union with Jesus Christ that it is by no
fiction (again, McLeod Campbell is in the background) but by Christ's actual
will and spirit that we are now right with the Father. And so much is it that
we are in Christ, that Christ is now seen to be our substitute, doing for us

---

[70]Ibid., pp. 224-25.
[71]Ibid., p. 226.
[72]Ibid., p. 227.

what we could not have done for ourselves.[73] Thus is atonement seen ultimately in the light of union with Christ, and the sinner who knows Christ by faith now possesses the power of radical goodness. Forgiveness is not just an outward announcement; it is an inward reality. The spirit of Christ's sacrifice becomes our spirit, and thus we are "sons" of God.

In sum: "Reconciliation can consist in nothing but the actual effectuation of fellowship between men and God, through seeking, costly Divine love on the one hand and its penitent reception by man on the other. Hence reconciliation, due to Christ's great act of love at Calvary, is still proceeding."[74] But one last point to note before we move on: Mackintosh, while emphasizing most strongly that atonement is God's act of love, nevertheless insists that a personal response is solicited. We are not saved en masse, as it were. While God's grace is for everyone, each of us is called upon penitently to receive the new life freely and unconditionally given in Christ for us. As such, it is known and experienced indeed as an inward reality, as the Christian experience of forgiveness.

JUSTIFICATION IN PAUL AND LUTHER

As we have seen, Mackintosh's perspective on the atonement is devoid of forensic and penal categories, especially as developed by the scholasticism of post-Reformation orthodoxy. It is appropriate that brief account must now be given of his understanding of justification. Does his argument stand up against how justification is taught by Paul and Luther?

Mackintosh regards justification in Paul as a statement of the gospel drawn from the nature of the gospel itself.[75] The emerging theology of the apostles brought out new truths implied in Christ's salvation. Thus Paul's letters are his reading of the gospel. There is little verbal identity between Jesus and Paul, but identity of meaning is recognizable. The heart of Paul's teaching on justification reveals this: salvation begins from God's side; in Jesus Christ it expresses God's love and assures the sinner of God's forgiveness. To seek sinners is God's way. Paul's teaching in sum is that, in view of Jesus, sinners may by faith in him have

---

[73]Ibid., p. 228.
[74]Ibid., p. 229.
[75]Ibid., p. 106.

God for a savior and friend.[76] The righteousness after which Paul strove, he discovered, was bestowed once for all in Christ. Gone finally was any view that salvation comes as a result of moral or religious excellence. The gospel, Paul saw, was the justification of the sinful, in pure grace through Jesus Christ, received by faith, and establishing the sinner in a new relationship with God.

Thus Paul, according to Mackintosh, did not regard faith as a meritorious attainment. Following McLeod Campbell, neither did Mackintosh believe that the righteousness of Christ is imputed to the believer as a sort of legal fiction. Rather, the objects of God's grace are the ungodly who have faith. "He is telling us simply that the man who has faith is now in a right relationship to God; where enmity was, there is peace. . . . He means, and it is the glory of his message, that God rather is acknowledging an actually established new relationship, which has been produced through the instrumentality of the cross of Jesus."[77] (It is not clear what Mackintosh means here by the use of "instrumentality," a characterization that elsewhere he mostly seems to reject.) According to Mackintosh, in his doctrine of justification Paul, employing legal categories, nevertheless put legal categories out of court in view of a new relationship with God established in undeserved grace.

Now, how is faith understood here? According to Mackintosh, "It is in virtue of union with Christ, in an unspeakably intimate sense which faith denotes, that [sinners] are forgiven. . . . This union with Christ is the religious starting-point, which all [Paul's] doctrines seek to interpret. . . . God comes into touch with men in virtue of their relation to Christ."[78] Thus faith is neither orthodox assent nor laying hold of imputed righteousness; rather, faith is partaking of fellowship with Christ, thus putting sinners right with God.

There is no need here to draw out Mackintosh's presentation of the subsequent history of justification in the Latin tradition. Suffice it to say that it developed into a merit system. It was forgotten that God freely pardons. And operationally, faith arose by way of infused supernatural grace. That is to say, justification became a process concerned with how people get saved. Luther broke with this manner of thinking. He thought of grace in terms of the personal mercy of God, which we encounter in Christ, and which is

---

[76]Ibid., p. 111.
[77]Ibid., p. 120.
[78]Ibid., p. 123.

received by us primarily as forgiveness.[79] God gives what we cannot claim. Faith apprehends the grace proffered to sinners in Christ, receives assurance, and by the work of the Holy Spirit one finds a measure of personal change and renewal. Like Paul before him, Luther discovered that justification is a work of God. Luther finds himself like a forgiven child who is met with tenderness when punishment was expected and in glad wonder resolves never to be naughty again.[80] Justification is both declaratory and effective: being justified means being regenerated. Not only do we have a new status before God, but we also live a new life. Faith renews the heart, and a new obedience is indissolubly united to it.

According to Mackintosh,[81] then, in Paul and Luther justification is deliverance from guilt; it is forgiveness, and it is tied through and through to Jesus Christ. A person is taken in by God as a reconciled "son" through union with Christ. This forgiveness is regenerative. Justification is an act of God, but justification is also a personal experience that registers itself as assurance of God's love, peace, joy and so on. There is an experience of being justified. In this manner, sinners are ushered into a new and permanent relation to the Father that leads to a new way of life. There is nothing here in Mackintosh's account of forgiveness that is understood as an external acquittal at the bar of heaven. If forgiveness were a kind of divine judicial decision outside a person, it could not change the inner person. That would require a second divine act, as it were, if the justified were to be made good. And that, for Mackintosh, simply will not do.

Mackintosh's great work on forgiveness was published in 1927. It is all the more remarkable, in this case, that while he preceded the so-called New Perspective on Paul by many decades, there is something of a contemporary flavor in his perspective. This is not the place to go into this new perspective in any detail, and we should note in passing that this interpretation may be more accurately referred to as new perspectives. But a couple of observations will make the case that there are anticipations already in Mackintosh. Mackintosh and the new perspectives make the point that the major theme in Paul is God's promised covenant faithfulness in putting things right with respect

---

[79]Ibid., p. 126.
[80]Ibid., p. 150.
[81]Ibid., pp. 155-56.

to relations to God, and not just between people and God, but also between the creation and God. Undoubtedly, God's covenant faithfulness was expressed in the metaphor of the law court in Second Temple Judaism and in Paul, and Mackintosh all along has been reluctant to give it too much play. But the metaphor or a doctrine derived from the metaphor is not the center; the center of the gospel is the proclamation of Jesus as God's Messiah and the inauguration of God's reign in him. Now, the new perspectives arguably make more of God's restorative justice than Mackintosh does and are stronger on eschatology than he is, but the initial theological intuition seems similar. God in salvation, in Christ, is true to who God is. Further, God's faithfulness as found in the theology of Mackintosh and in the new perspectives is actual as the faithfulness of Jesus (Rom 3:22 and elsewhere: *pistis Iēsou Christou*). That is to say, Jesus and his sovereign lordship, and not a doctrine or system of thought, are at the heart of the gospel.[82] If this is correct, there appears to be no ground for concluding that Mackintosh's interpretation of the atonement founders on a Pauline doctrine of justification. On the contrary, in making his case, Mackintosh appears to exhibit a degree of congruence with the new perspectives on Paul that he anticipated.

FORGIVEN

Whenever there has been an opportunity to discuss Mackintosh on Christology or atonement, we have felt the power of his piety and the force of the immediacy of convicting experience. As we read him, his sense of being in relationship with God is ubiquitous and compelling. For him, there is indeed the experience of being forgiven by God. From this the attitude of thought that arises is twofold: repentance and faith. Repentance and faith "are living dispositions of the soul, to whose essence it belongs to move and grow, as by inherent quality."[83]

Repentance unfolds by way of three distinct and interrelated cognitions: recognition of sin, sorrow for sin, and abandonment of sin.[84] The primary emphasis is placed on the third cognition, where Mackintosh displays a degree

---

[82]For a helpful account, see N. T. Wright, *What Saint Paul Really Said: Was Paul of Tarsus the Real Founder of Christianity?* (Grand Rapids: Eerdmans, 1997), especially chap. 7; also, more recently, idem, *Justification: God's Plan and Paul's Vision* (Downers Grove, IL: IVP Academic, 2009).
[83]Mackintosh, *Christian Experience of Forgiveness*, p. 236.
[84]Ibid., pp. 237-43.

of moralism. Nevertheless, the resolve to stop sinning, even if not achieved in completeness, is an integral part of repentance. Without it, repentance dies out. Repentance without the practical action of amendment of life is of little use. To know that you are pardoned by God, to find yourself in a new relationship with God, and to trust God with your life *is* to seek to live as God's person. Such repentance is unto life, indeed to a new way of living.

What saves is not faith as such, but rather faith in God our Savior.[85] It is the condition of being in fellowship with God. The forgiving grace of God calls our worth into being so that fellowship with God is grounded not in human virtue but rather in God's will that we be in that fellowship. As one with Christ, we have become new persons.

The corollary to repentance and faith is assurance, the mark that faith is of the right kind. Assurance is characterized by Mackintosh as allowing "Jesus to make Himself so familiar that you know God's very self is touching you through His holy love. Thus we escape from subjectivity, as the New Testament invariably does, to the great fact of Christ and God's trustworthiness in Him."[86] The reality of communion with God in prayer will be the evidence of this presence, wherein we have access to the Father. And we awaken to the astonishing experience that God is permitting us to cooperate with him in doing good. God gives us a share in the tasks of God's kingdom.

Clearly, Mackintosh is moving quickly now onto the ground marked out by the theological notion of sanctification. "Forgiveness is the experience by which we pass from Christian truth to Christian duty."[87] Faith and trust in God's forgiveness have ennobling effects. And once and for all the painful and disabling solitude of moral conflict is abolished. The grasp of the past is loosed as the center of attention is transferred from us to God and our fellowship with God.[88] A new moral intention is generated thereby. Mackintosh, in an interesting phrase, calls it "the Law *in* the Gospel."[89] The moral claim upon us by grace is more demanding than law apart from gospel, but with the gospel the frame of the moral claim upon us has profoundly shifted. "The grateful surrender to God which forms a living element of faith in His

---

[85]Ibid., pp. 243-50.
[86]Ibid., p. 253.
[87]Ibid., p. 255.
[88]Ibid., p. 260.
[89]Ibid., p. 263 (italics original).

pardoning love creates goodness by the way."[90] To be clear, Mackintosh is not making an argument for adherence to moral ideals to be achieved; rather, deepening in our appreciation of fellowship with God by the gift of God's pardon, Christian character becomes increasingly our desire. "It is fellowship with the God of holy and sin-remitting love which forms the fertile secret of Christian goodness."[91] Knowing that sin is forgiven, we have the heart to fight and forsake it in a response of grateful love toward God and our neighbor. Fellowship with God entails fellowship with our neighbor.

In this way, then, Mackintosh argues that the moral life is the concomitant of communion with the Father. There is something blissful and lovely in his vision. And he surely is right to uphold the positive thrust of moral life. However, and this is said sadly, the reality of human experience, and Christian experience at that, may be more confusing and messy than Mackintosh allows for. The moral life, it seems to me, though undoubtedly aspired for and intended, and at times faithfully lived, can also be fleeting, out of reach and elusive. The past is not easily loosed, as psychotherapy surely teaches us. And the moral clarity sought is often dimmed both by the overwhelming complexity of life today and by our own deep neediness in its many expressions, conscious and unconscious. Christians continue to act evilly, and if that is too strongly put for some tastes, then "wrongly" and "hurtfully" point in the same direction. This is why forgiveness is daily received and repentance is daily offered. Sanctification, which we have in Christ, is also dialectically worked out inch by inch. Mackintosh offers some hint of this awareness, but he seems moved more by moral possibility than by its failure.

One final point: communion with God leads not just generically, as it were, to a moral response to the neighbor; it forms the communion of believing people, the church.[92] Divine pardon is announced and received through the medium of the church. It is the church that preaches Jesus Christ as Lord. It is the community of those who know that they are forgiven by God. People cannot encounter the pardon of God outside of encountering the church; otherwise conviction of forgiveness could be attained on the ground of our own desires and hopes and efforts. "The forgiveness of God is only believable

---

[90]Ibid., p. 265.
[91]Ibid., p. 266.
[92]Ibid., p. 275.

in a certain psychological atmosphere. For that atmosphere two ingredients are essential: first, the living witness of pardoned men to the truth in which they themselves have found life and power, and secondly, the Christian habit of *practising* forgiveness."[93] Mackintosh puts very strongly the relation between being pardoned by God and our pardoning others; he calls it an "absolutely binding precondition."[94] He cites Mark 11:25 and Matthew 6:15 in evidence: "Whenever you stand praying, forgive, if you have anything against anyone; so that your Father in heaven may also forgive your trespasses"; and "But if you do not forgive others, neither will your Father forgive your trespasses." How is the "precondition" understood? "Pardon is no longer a Divine injunction simply; it is a grace in which the Father enables us to co-operate with His own attitude to the sinful."[95] Ephesians 4:32 is now cited in evidence: "forgiving one another, as God in Christ has forgiven you."

Mackintosh surely is correct to put God's pardon and our pardoning a neighbor in very close relation, though it is not clear how "precondition" and "enabling grace" hold together. Perhaps, with Calvin, we must say that forgiveness is prior to but requires repentance (*Institutes* 3.3.20) and at the same time say that forgiving another is required of us, for otherwise the forgiveness that we have received is nullified in experience within us. And in the mind of the sinner unforgiven by us, all gospel credibility is lost. Perhaps something like that was intended by Mackintosh in his notion of the law in the gospel. To refuse forgiveness toward another is certainly to act outside the forgiveness that we have been given such as to suggest that we have rejected the Christian experience of forgiveness and turned our backs on God's forgiving love. When we reject the forgiving God, forgiveness has no hold on our lives, with no repentance, no faith, no assurance and no forgiving of others. The gospel, however, is surely that even so (and this is the character of God and the task of the church to proclaim), God will bear the cost of still forgiving us, and as such will again and again interpose himself through the efficacy of the cross of Jesus Christ—Mackintosh says "directly and supernaturally."[96] Again and again we find ourselves pardoned and received into his fellowship. "In every

[93]Ibid., p. 281 (italics original).
[94]Ibid., p. 282.
[95]Ibid.
[96]Ibid., p. 293.

age the guilty must be told of the remission of sins—it must be brought close to them by self-abnegating friendship—if their life is to be commensurate with the Divine thought of reconciliation. 'With the Lord there is mercy, and with Him is plenteous redemption'—this is the note of authentic Christianity."[97] With that, Mackintosh brings his discussion of the Christian experience of forgiveness to a close.

THEOLOGICAL ENGAGEMENT WITH THE ARGUMENT

What is faithful and pious in striking a gospel note in Mackintosh's treatment I have pointed out as we have moved through his account. The strengths speak for themselves: his sense of the centrality of the Father-Son relationship; his commitment to the character of God as a God of love and mercy who desires that we live in "sonship" in relation to him through union with Christ; his clarity about God's total opposition to sin; his conviction that atonement theory must be developed to include the life as well as the death of Jesus Christ while recognizing that the cross must be given special place; his emphasis on forgiveness as meaning a new relationship with God; and his attention to the responses of repentance, faith, moral renewal and the character of Christian responsibility as the church to be a forgiving community. With none of this do I disagree. These insights should be upheld as valuable, and a fully orbed theology of Christology and atonement must include them. In upholding Mackintosh's theological virtues, I note in passing that these are not always evident in soteriological theory.

The major concern is signaled by the way I framed Mackintosh's soteriology in the beginning vis-à-vis the Western *ordo salutis*. To be clear, I have no brief here for casting the atonement within forensic and penal categories, or at least for setting them up as the organizing and controlling categories. Too much has been learned from both John McLeod Campbell and H. R. Mackintosh to do so now. In fact, the whole journey thus far has steered away from the organizing centrality of God as lawgiver, of sin as broken law and atonement as Christ paying the penalty that in some manner ameliorates the judgment. But as with McLeod Campbell, so too with Mackintosh, a nagging question arises: Is the reaction to Latin soteriology so severely felt by them

---

[97]Ibid., p. 294.

that something important for atonement theology is missing here? Or to put that concern differently, is God's character as the Holy One to be taken yet more seriously, more robustly, than we find here with these Scottish theologians? And is sin not more dire, perhaps more deadly, than my Scottish theological forebears have thought? And is the cost to God in the death of Jesus even more sorely borne than we find in the proposals before us? While the reaction to the atonement in its legal and external instrumentality is rightly called forth and most helpfully developed, has the reaction become an overreaction to the extent that something valuable has been lost?

These questions suggest an implied critique. The task now becomes to see if these concerns can be incorporated into a theology of the atonement *without casting it in terms of the legalizing categories* of the Latin and Protestant scholastic traditions. In no manner do I wish now to leave behind McLeod Campbell's and Mackintosh's theological intuitions, analyses and conclusions. Too much is gained; but not enough is yet said. Thus to build on what we have, and to build higher and wider and deeper, we now turn to the theology of the atonement in Thomas F. Torrance, where a more complete soteriology may be found.

6

ATONEMENT

Thomas F. Torrance on the Atonement as Ransom, Priestly Atonement, Justification, Reconciliation and Redemption

Introductory Notes: The Doctrine of the Death of Christ

By any measure, Thomas F. Torrance's *Atonement: The Person and Work of Christ* is a daunting book to read. It is long, at times quite dense, and often conceptually difficult. But it is the one place where his teaching on the atonement, scattered throughout his published works, is gathered together. Already we have made note that atonement is not to be limited to consideration of the meaning of the death of Jesus Christ. In fact, Torrance insists that Christology and atonement are organic in the sense of one whole dynamic reality that cannot be separated into discrete parts without causing massive damage to our understanding of them. Neither are they to be causally connected or logically distinguished in some kind of mechanistic manner. While Christology and atonement can be distinguished, even in doing so Torrance would insist that they remain profoundly related and interconnected.

Further, Torrance is a vigorous advocate of the view that the person and life of Jesus are understood properly only when the soteriological implications are brought to light. In this way, Torrance follows the intent of Nicene theology, where the clauses of the Nicene Creed that refer to the incarnation are dominated by soteriological concerns.[1] That Jesus is Savior has been the content of Christology all along as we considered the meaning of the whole incarnate life of Jesus. God saves *as* the man Jesus. What is new now is the

---

[1]Thomas F. Torrance, *The Trinitarian Faith: The Evangelical Theology of the Ancient Catholic Church* (Edinburgh: T & T Clark, 1993), p. 146.

focus of our attention as we turn to consider Torrance's teaching on the meaning of the death of Jesus. And as Torrance explores the meaning of the death of Jesus, he is drawn to reflection on the resurrection and ascension of Jesus, for these must not be held apart. Christ's resurrection and ascension play an essential part in the explication of Christ's death, and they are included because they are integrally related to as full an understanding of Christology and atonement as is possible for us to have.

I have selected no single notion of the atonement to be the way into Torrance at this point. Certainly, understanding Christ as the atoning priest is the theological counterpart to Torrance's consideration of Christ as prophet, as Word made flesh, which was discussed at a number of places in the reflections on Christology. *Atoning priest* refers specifically to God the Son undertaking our reconciliation to communion with God, but Torrance's teaching on the atonement is not to be characterized only by such an image. No single word or theological construct quite does justice to the depth and complexity of Torrance's treatment, and certainly not justification, although he gives it major treatment. His teaching on the atonement is multilayered, or, in a different figure, multitextured.

Undoubtedly, Torrance built on what was before him from McLeod Campbell and Mackintosh, for with them he shared the concern to emphasize the *person* of Jesus in his saving mission. Their attempts to find a way into the atonement that avoided a mechanistic interpretation of the work of Christ construed according to a forensic framework were frequently noted and applauded insofar as they saw reconciliation with God to be something far deeper than an imputed new legal status before God. They were reacting against a narrowly developed theory of penal substitution, and this finds a strong echo in Torrance's work. "In Western Christianity the atonement tends to be interpreted almost exclusively in terms of external forensic relations as a judicial transaction in the transference of the penalty for sin from the sinner to the sin-bearer."[2] Instead, understanding of incarnation and atonement must be developed in terms of falling within the being and life of God as the man Jesus from cradle to grave. Noted too, however, was the subsequent seeming loss of an appropriate place for the expiatory and substitutionary aspects of the atonement en route to a complete account of

---

[2]Thomas F. Torrance, *The Mediation of Christ* (Grand Rapids: Eerdmans, 1983), p. 50.

Christ's saving mission. In the accounts given by McLeod Campbell and Mackintosh the cross, while undoubtedly seriously considered as something integral to the passion of Jesus, was placed somewhat off center. The fact of the matter is that we cannot avoid dealing with the shedding of Christ's blood on the cross, for it is an irreducible and central aspect of atonement in the New Testament. McLeod Campbell and Mackintosh made important gains toward a deeper understanding of the atonement, but there was loss as well. This loss, in my judgment, is corrected by Torrance in his theology of the death of Christ.

As noted previously when we considered Torrance on aspects of Christology, now also with soteriology, he is adamant that we are confronted with essential mystery. The inner mystery of the atonement is not available for public inspection.[3] The atonement is an event of divine intervention into the human situation. But as such, if we cannot think our way to it, we can think our way from it as we allow the cross itself to direct us. Even so, the atonement is not amenable to formal rational or neutral analysis. In order to grasp something of its essential mystery as God's act for us and our salvation, we must allow our minds to be conformed to its pattern. Yet in so being conformed, no formal, final theory of the atonement can be in view.

According to Torrance, Jesus revealed the mystery of his passion in two supreme "words" about his atoning death. The first is from Matthew 20:28 // Mark 10:45: "The Son of Man came not to be served but to serve, and to give his life as a ransom for many." The second is from the words at the center of the Lord's Supper, from Luke 22:19-20: "This is my body, which is given for you. . . . This cup that is poured out for you is the new covenant in my blood."[4] I will discuss these two "words" in the order of Torrance's presentation. I begin with the theology of the new covenant that is announced and enacted at the institution of the Lord's Supper. Discussion of atonement as ransom will follow. This takes us deeply into Torrance's theology of the priesthood of Christ and unfolds as the nature of the atoning event upon which the new covenant is based. After these reflections I will give accounts of Torrance on atonement as justification, as reconciliation and as redemption—accounts that, as it were, unfold the meaning and significance of Christ's life as the ransom for many.

---

[3]Thomas F. Torrance, *Atonement: The Person and Work of Christ*, ed. Robert T. Walker (Downers Grove, IL: IVP Academic, 2009), p. 2.
[4]Ibid., p. 7.

Two "Words" about the Atoning Death of Christ

The blood of the new covenant. For Torrance, there is the deepest connection between Jesus' words and acts at the Last Supper and God's covenant
with his people.[5] The essential pattern is this: "I will be your God, and you
will be my people." Jesus came to fulfill that covenant from two sides, as God
to us and from us to God. We have already had occasion to note this bidirectional Christology. But the bidirectional nature of Christology was already prefigured even at Sinai when God mercifully gave both his law and
a covenanted way of response in the cult. The ground of hope was established in God's faithfulness, even in judgment. Now in Jesus Christ both the
promises and the commands of the covenant are fulfilled. "This realisation
of the covenant will and faithfulness of God in Christ is *atonement*—
atonement in its fullest sense embracing the whole incarnate life and work
of Christ. It involves the self-giving of God to man and the assuming of man
into union with God, thus restoring the broken communion between man
and God."[6] Thus the whole work of atonement is fulfilled by Christ as mediator, acting at once from the side of God as God and from the side of
humankind as the man Jesus, all within the unity of his person. God's covenant with Israel is gathered up as the new covenant announced at the Last
Supper and fulfilled on the cross. How should this be understood?

Torrance gives three aspects that point toward understanding the fulfillment
of the new covenant in the blood of Christ. First, we note the God-given signs
that marked out and sealed the covenant: circumcision and Passover, the two
Old Testament sacraments. There the blood of the covenant sealed the covenant, cutting into the flesh and marking out Israel respectively. The meaning
of the Last Supper is deeply rooted in the theology of covenant blood that Jesus
would have accepted. At the Last Supper Jesus announced a new covenant tied
explicitly to himself, through the eating of his own body and blood. In Torrance's words, "God himself steps into the place of the sacrifice required in the
making of the covenant, and offers himself in Jesus Christ as the sacrificial
lamb."[7] The Old Testament lamb of atonement and the lamb of the Passover are
conflated into the image of Jesus in John's Gospel as "the lamb of God" (Jn 1:29).

---

[5]Ibid., p. 8.
[6]Ibid., p. 9.
[7]Ibid., p. 14.

Jesus offers himself as the paschal lamb bearing the sins of the world. He is thereby the way of the new covenant between God and humankind, ever remembered as such in the paschal mystery of the Lord's Supper.

The second aspect of the Old Testament covenant to be considered is the mighty act of God in the redemption of Israel out of Egypt and the establishment of Israel as God's covenant people upon the basis of the law and the cult.[8] The pledges of this were the Decalogue and the worship in the tabernacle. The once-for-all events of the exodus and Sinai were given cultic extension in two ways. The annual covenant sacrifice of the Day of Atonement was concerned with the founding or renewing of the covenant. The daily sacrifices of the cult were concerned with infringements of the law and were dependent upon the primary, annual covenant renewal. Sins of "a high hand," however—blasphemy, adultery, murder and the like—could not be covered by sacrifice, because those who committed such sins had put themselves outside the bounds of the covenant. A direct act of God was required for these sins to be forgiven.[9] When Jesus Christ came to fulfill the covenant sacrifice, it was to be the basis upon which all divine words of pardon would depend.

Third, we have seen that God appoints the sacrifices as a divinely given response to his word. The liturgical sacrifices have no efficacy in themselves but have efficacy only insofar as they are acts of obedience to the divine ordinances. That is to say, "It is God who forgives; liturgical sacrifice is only witness to God's forgiveness."[10] God is not the object of atonement; God is the subject who provides atonement and who performs the acts of forgiveness. The soteriologically oriented biblical words are not intended to mean the placation or propitiation of God. The cultic actions bear witness to God's forgiveness toward sinners. This third point is profoundly important and will shape almost everything that Torrance has to say on the matter. And even though he will develop cultic and sacrificial perspectives on atonement, and later introduce a forensic aspect, these are not to be interpreted as a relapse into the Western *ordo salutis*. They are to be interpreted as locating the atonement in God's mercy and love. The covenant between God and Israel was established out of sheer grace, a covenant between God and Israel pre-

---

[8]Ibid., p. 15.
[9]Ibid., p. 16.
[10]Ibid., p. 18.

cisely in its sinful, rebellious and estranged existence.[11]

Included in this third aspect is Torrance's account of the twofold priesthood in the Old Testament: the priesthood of the word, which is the priesthood of Moses, and the priesthood of liturgical witness, which is the priesthood of Aaron. The former, of course, is primary, yet the two priesthoods work together. The worship of Israel thus established, however, looks forward to the Day of the Lord, when a new covenant will be inscribed upon the hearts of the people. According to Torrance, this prospective orientation comes to its fullest expression in the doctrine of the Suffering Servant.

> Here the two aspects of priesthood are brought together into one, for the conceptions of Moses and Aaron are telescoped together in the vicarious life and mission of the Servant of the Lord in order to set forth at once the redeeming action of God for Israel and the sacrifice of obedience enacted in Israel, thus pointing ahead to the union of God and man in messianic redemption and breaking into the gospel.[12]

Jesus, then, is the fulfillment of the Old Testament priesthood in this dual regard who brings in the new covenant in his life and death. Thus it was that Jesus thought of himself at the Last Supper. He is the paschal lamb and, as it were, the Day of Atonement, as the lines converge. "In him the covenant word is translated into his obedient humanity, and in him the symbolic sacrifices are no longer symbolic witnesses to God's will to forgive, for *he is himself the sacrifice in which God's will for forgiveness and salvation is fully enacted and carried out.*"[13] The old covenant between God and Israel is fulfilled, becoming a new, but not a different, covenant in Jesus' embodied communion between God and humankind. Perhaps it can be expressed in this way: Jesus is at once the law/word of God and the cult, both the high priest and victim, in the hypostatic unity of his person. Jesus is God's covenant, fulfilling these roles/functions in the vicarious act of his death. As such, Jesus is our propitiation, for in and by him our personal healing is effected.

In this way, Torrance has outlined what he called the second "word" of redemption as it relates to the covenant will of God announced and enacted at the Last Supper. We will turn in a moment to the first "word," the actual

---

[11]Torrance, *Mediation of Christ*, p. 37.
[12]Torrance, *Atonement*, p. 21.
[13]Ibid. (italics original).

event of redemption in which Jesus gives himself as a ransom for many. But before we make that turn, two brief comments are appropriate. First, it was probably helpful, although the reason is not immediately obvious, for Torrance to begin with his discussion of the Old Testament background to the new covenant announced and enacted at the Last Supper. This is not an easy read; at times he is very, even overly, detailed, while again sometimes he draws quick conclusions without adequate presentation of detail. Detail and conclusion do not always match up. Nevertheless, the theology of the new covenant demanded some account of cultic atonement; otherwise Jesus' conception of his life as a ransom would have inadequate biblical anchor. We have that anchor, more or less, before us.

One other brief point may be noted. Torrance is a biblical theologian. At times, in fact, he reads like a "Kittel" biblical theologian, placing high value on biblical words and concepts. We will see this played out as we go on. He attempts at all points to allow the biblical words and accounts to control his thinking in a thoroughgoing way. The reason undoubtedly is that he regards his topic as an essential mystery; any other approach will lead him astray. There is nothing here, for example, of Mackintosh's analogy between the suffering in human and divine forgiveness. Neither has he set up in advance his disinclination toward a forensically centered account of the atonement, as we saw with McLeod Campbell. My sense is that he is trying to let the theology unfold as he moves along and in this way come en route to his criticisms of the Western *ordo salutis*.

Ransom for many: the Old Testament background.[14] Torrance is clear that a number of biblical passages were in the forefront of Jesus' mind, among them Psalm 49, Job 33, Exodus 12, Jeremiah 31 and Isaiah 53. Immediately Torrance alerts us to the central point: Jesus understood redemption in terms of the cost or ransom (*lytron* in Greek).[15] Behind this conception lie three Hebrew terms that carry tremendous weight: *padah*, *kipper* and *goel*.[16] Each of these offers a different aspect of the meaning of redemption.

---

[14]Torrance gives us a wealth of detail in his account that will not be recorded here. The intention here is to give an overview and identify the main points of the argument. For a briefer account of these Old Testament terms, see Torrance, *Trinitarian Faith*, pp. 170-72. On a personal note, I add that anyone who sat in Torrance's Edinburgh classroom will be very familiar with these words.

[15]Torrance, *Atonement*, p. 26.

[16]I am using Torrance's Hebrew transliterations. The term *padah* can also be transliterated as *pādâ*, and the term *goel* as *gōʾēl*.

The word *padah* refers to redemption with emphasis upon the cost and the nature of the redeeming act.[17] The primary reference is to the redemption of Israel out of Egypt, an act of God's mighty hand carried out with the substitutionary sacrifice of the Passover lamb. This redemption was seen as an act of God's grace and became in due course the ground for the prophetic speech of redemption out of Babylon, as well as for the anticipation of the messianic kingdom (Is 35:10; Jer 31:11-14; Lk 21:28, 31). Behind this lies the biblical meaning of redemption as redemption out of the judgment of God and out of a repressive power. Thus *padah* expresses the mighty hand of God that redeems Israel out of oppression and into a covenant bond with God through the blood of sacrifice. As such, it means also redemption *into* freedom.

According to Torrance, this background is important for understanding redemption in the New Testament.[18] In the Synoptic Gospels redemption understood as achieved by the mighty hand of God is related to the breaking in of the kingdom of God upon those bound by sin or disease or evil, for example. This understanding is evident also in Paul's notion of redemption from the bondage of the law. In these cases, God, as it were, claims back the people of his love. The New Testament makes it clear that Jesus met and overcame the powers of evil by his holiness and obedience to the will of the Father. "That, in the New Testament, is the unique sense of *apolutrōsis* as redemption which robs the authorities and powers of darkness and evil of their vaunted right, and by expiation before the holy will of God reveals that they have no inherent right, and no right to the price of ransom."[19] The emphasis appears to be on the far-reaching effect of atonement, looking to the full consequences. The Greek notion of *apolytrōsis* points to a state of redemption that is the result of God's mighty act, carrying finally an eschatological anticipation. Torrance often makes reference to the *padah* root of redemption as the dramatic aspect, for its emphasis on God's mighty act.

The word *kipper* refers to the cost or price of redemption. "Thus if the term *padah* has to do with redemption from the power of sin, the term *kipper* has to do rather with redemption as the actual wiping out of sin and guilt, and so

---

[17]Torrance, *Atonement*, p. 27.
[18]Ibid., p. 29.
[19]Ibid., p. 32.

of effecting propitiation between man and God."[20] The basic meaning is "to cover or blot out." It is used to speak of the covering over of sin before the face of God. God, then, is not the object of the atonement but rather the subject, for it is God himself who blots out sin, covers it, invalidates it or annuls it. *Kipper* involves both judgment upon the wrong—liturgically through the priest covering sin with the blood of the sacrifice, which is God's gift and appointment (Lev 17:11)—and subsequent reinstatement to favor before God.[21] We should note in passing that the word belongs more to the cult than civil law, although elements of both appear to inhere in the meaning of the word.

The means of atonement expressed through the actions of the cult do not have efficacy in themselves. Their efficacy lies within the covenant relationship between God and Israel by which they are the ways and means given by God, who regards people as covered with the blood of the covenant. The sacrifices, as we have seen before, are acts of liturgical witness to God's will to forgive. It is God who atones, and who does so on the ground of his judgment upon sin. Behind this redemption lies the covenant mercy of God, who provides the sacrifice. God, as it were, provides the lamb.[22] The provision of the ram that led to the life of Isaac instead of his death appears to be an instance of this understanding of God's redemptive provision (Gen 22:1-14). God pardons through his own provision of sacrifice. The sacrifice "stands in the gap." Torrance often characterized the *kipper* aspect as the cultic-forensic aspect of redemption. Looking back, Israel saw Moses standing in the gap; looking forward, the prophet sees the Suffering Servant standing in the gap. Who is the Servant?

This question brings us to the third word, *goel*. Behind this word lies one's redemption out of bankruptcy or bondage, undertaken by one's kin. The *goel* is the kinsman-redeemer. "While in the *padah* type of redemption the main emphasis is laid upon the nature of the act, and in the *kipper* type of redemption the main emphasis is laid upon the nature of the atoning expiation as sacrifice, here in the *gaal* type of redemption the emphasis is laid upon the nature of the *redeemer*, upon the person of the *goel*."[23] The *goel* redeems by claiming a person's cause as his own cause.

---

[20]Ibid., p. 33.
[21]Ibid., pp. 34-35.
[22]Ibid., p. 42.
[23]Ibid., p. 45.

What is remarkable here is that this concept is applied to God. One example will suffice, from Psalm 74:2: "Remember your congregation, which you acquired long ago, which you redeemed to be the tribe of your heritage. Remember Mount Zion, where you came to dwell." Torrance gives numerous instances of similar verses.[24] Ultimately, no human can stand in the gap. Only God is faithful and can step into the gap and redeem. As the faithful redeemer, God is faithful to the covenantal relation established with Israel. And when the prophet in the Isaiah tradition thinks of the Servant as bearing upon himself vicariously the sins of God's people, bearing God's judgment upon himself, it seems right, says Torrance, to identify the Servant with the divine *goel*.[25] That connection is not actually made, of course, but it presses to that eventual conclusion. It is this kind of thinking that lies behind aspects of the New Testament understanding of redemption, where Jesus is seen as the kinsman-redeemer, the advocate, the guarantor of our inheritance. Thus Torrance often refers to this aspect of redemption as the ontological aspect, with stress laid on the nature and identity of the redeemer in relationship to the redeemed.

To pull this discussion together: redemption by the mighty hand of God means redemption as an act of grace, redemption by expiatory sacrifice for sin means redemption through blood, and redemption by the kinsman-redeemer refers to the person of the redeemer. Now Torrance draws his own tentative conclusion: *padah* redemption in the New Testament is characterized by the term *redemption* itself; *kipper* redemption is described by atonement or reconciliation, where notions of expiation and substitutionary sacrifice are involved; *goel* redemption is described as reconciliation, meaning restoration to communion with God. These characterizations overlap, of course, and perhaps the term *salvation* covers them all.[26] The correlation of the three aspects may also be summarized in this way:

1. *Padah* redemption—kingly office of Christ—active obedience;

2. *Kipper* redemption—priestly office of Christ—passive obedience;

3. *Goel* redemption—prophetic office of Christ—incarnational.[27]

---

[24]Ibid., p. 46.

[25]Ibid., p. 48.

[26]Ibid., p. 52.

[27]Ibid., p. 60. This typology has the feel of being a bit forced; it is too neatly drawn. But it is suggestive

Torrance moves now to explore the many-sided teaching of the New Testament on what it means that Jesus gave himself as a ransom for many, moving from the teaching of Jesus himself to theological reflection on it. The explorations that follow are complex, and there is no tidy package at the end. What we have, perhaps, are probes into the essential mystery of the atonement that at times overlap and at other times point along trajectories of thought such that no one "theory" of the atonement stands alone or dominates the others. In his analysis Torrance will return often to his three aspects of redemption drawn from the Old Testament, which are highly suggestive of different pathways toward the understanding of the atonement within the one saving arc of God's redemption of humankind in Christ.

THE PRIESTHOOD OF CHRIST

The priesthood of Christ the incarnate Son. The *goel* aspect of redemption has been behind the consideration of the incarnate person and life of Jesus leading up to his passion.[28] The *padah* aspect of redemption is seen in God breaking the power of sin and death, and in Christ's resurrection and ascension, where he takes up his kingdom and reign through the gospel. The *kipper* aspect of redemption corresponds to the work of Christ as priest who is sacrificial victim, and judge who takes his place among the judged. It is this *kipper* aspect of redemption that is before us now, but we must not consider it in separation from the *goel* aspect, for as priest Christ *is* the kinsman-redeemer, or from the *padah* aspect, for as incarnate king Christ is the mighty act of God.

As noted, the priestly ministry of Aaron was subordinate to the prophetic ministry of Moses. According to Torrance, that proper relation was broken by the time of Jesus, when the law was liturgized and liturgy legalized. There was no room for the prophet.[29] Jesus steps into that situation, insisting again on the subordination of the priesthood to God's word and on the primacy of the word in forgiveness and worship. "While in word Jesus exercises his prophetic ministry, in his action he exercises his priestly ministry, and it is as suffering servant of the Lord that he combines both."[30]

---

of a manner in which the Old Testament terms might be applied to Christology and the atonement.

[28]Ibid., p. 61.

[29]Ibid., p. 65.

[30]Ibid., p. 67.

To set up his presentation of the priestly ministry of Jesus, Torrance offers a fairly extensive definition of propitiation that leads to a very important conclusion. It may be helpful to lay out this conclusion and then work back to the definition.

> Priestly atonement involves the notion of *propitiation* in which God turns away from his wrath to man in forgiveness and man is turned away from rebellion to draw near to God in love. But while in the Old Testament, it is the forensic aspect of this that is dominant, in the New Testament the whole concept of propitiation together with that of wrath, judgment and forgiveness is drawn into the personal Father-Son relationship. . . . The *goel* notion is pulled over the *kipper* notion of redemption.[31]

What Torrance means with this important statement is that the penal aspect of atonement is to be treated not in the forensic and detached categories of the Western *ordo salutis* but rather in terms of the intimacy of the Father-Son relationship. Here, certainly, the Son submits to the Father's judgment on sin. But this submission is not to punishment in our place. The New Testament nowhere uses *kolazō* (punish) of the relation between the Father and the Son.

We return now to Torrance's definition to open up more clearly what he intends by this conclusion. "Propitiation," from its Latin root, refers to the cultic or priestly act through which fellowship between God and humankind is restored. A relationship is repaired. "Propitiation" refers thus to personal healing and reconciliation. "The distinctive thing about the biblical notion of propitiation is that it is initiated and carried through by God, but by God both from the side of God towards humanity and from the side of humanity towards God. God *himself* draws near—*he* propitiates himself."[32] This propitiation is carried through in Jesus Christ. He is God who judges human sin but draws near to us in doing so; he is also the human for us who draws near to God and submits himself to God's judgment in a sacrificial offering. Remarkably, Jesus Christ does both within the unity of his incarnate person. Jesus *is* propitiation, his person in action, as it were, both toward humankind and toward God. We might say that Jesus is the at-one-ment between God

---

[31]Ibid., p. 72.
[32]Ibid., p. 68.

and humankind as he lives out who he is in person. In this way, propitiation is not to be understood as an external and judicial transaction; rather, it happens within the life of God in Jesus Christ, in which there is a oneness of mind between God and humankind. In vicarious penitence for human sin Christ accepted and responded to God's judgment, taking it into himself and bearing the consequence. To clarify: the penitence of Christ is to be understood as related to *poenitentia* (regret, repentance) rather than *poena* (penalty).[33] In taking our humanity Christ took our minds and wills in their estrangement from God, bending them back into agreement to God's will. This is the *palingenesia*, the new birth or regeneration of humanity before God.

The sacrificial work of Christ is reflected in Paul's teaching, in terms of expiation and justification before the word of God, and in Hebrews, which is concerned with atonement in terms of Christ's high priestly oblation.[34] These two approaches are seen as complementary, and a proper account of the atonement must entail both. We would be hard pressed to put the case for what Torrance is after more clearly than in his own words. "In both, the main stress is upon the person of Christ atoning and reconciling, not upon an act of atonement *in abstracto*. . . . We are not saved by the atoning death of Christ, far less by sacramental liturgical action, but by *Christ himself* who in his own person made atonement for us. *He is* the atonement."[35] The theology of the atonement is grounded upon the person of Christ. The focus of attention, thereby, is drawn to his work of mediation and intercession in his person as at once judging God and judged human, as loving God and obedient human.[36] That oneness in person between God and humankind in Christ, and the oneness in being between the Father and the incarnate Son, constitute the inner heart of the atonement. Thus the atonement is the atoning mediation of Christ as an act of God dealing with sinful humanity in judgment against sin *and* the atoning mediation of Christ as an act of humankind in confessing our sin and vicariously bearing it before God.

Clearly, then, Christ does not act as a man reconciling or appeasing God. Rather, Christ is God in the flesh of our humanity who brings himself into

---

[33]Ibid., p. 69n33.
[34]Ibid., p. 73.
[35]Ibid. (italics original).
[36]Ibid., p. 76.

reconciliation with humankind and brings humankind into reconciliation with himself.

Explaining this, Torrance notes that the doctrines of *anhypostasis* and *enhypostasis* are important as applied to the atonement for they mean that as a man in atoning action Christ is act of God, and as God in atoning action Christ is act of a man. These late patristic doctrines bear a little unpacking. The doctrine of the *anhypostasis* refers to the person of Christ as divine. The man Jesus is one in being with the Father, as Nicaea confessed. He is God. There is no existing human being whom Jesus takes over, as it were. This means that when Jesus acts and speaks, God acts and speaks. The doctrine of the *enhypostasis* refers to the human manhood of Jesus. This can be summed up with the words of the Nicene Creed, "born of the Virgin Mary." Jesus acts and speaks as a man within history, as a human being, who is truly a personalized man in his union with God. Thus the two doctrines, inevitably held in tension and irresolvable into a tidy synthesis, bear witness to the essential mystery of Jesus, who was fully and wholly God, and fully and wholly a man. As such, the atonement is understood as, in the person of Christ, the act of God and, in his human nature, the act of a man. To be clear: while Torrance is at pains to emphasize the objective act of God in Christ for us, he is also at pains to emphasize that atonement takes place within our humanity in such a manner that the human person is neither lost or displaced.

Thus Torrance has prepared us for detailed discussion on the atonement, first as we find it in the Epistle to the Hebrews, then successively as justification, reconciliation and redemption.

The Epistle to the Hebrews: reconciliation through sacrifice. Undoubtedly, Hebrews 3:1 was one of Torrance's favorite biblical verses. He cited it often: Jesus Christ is "the apostle and high priest of our confession." Christ is the faithful apostle. In him God has uttered himself. Christ is also the obedient man. As Jesus the human has heard and answered God.[37] In Hebrews the priesthood of Christ is exercised through his faithful sonship in the flesh of our humanity. It is the union of Christ's apostleship from God and priesthood toward God that makes his priesthood unique and eternal. Until Christ, the

---

[37]Ibid., p. 78.

liturgy of the Old Testament was unfulfilled. Until Christ, the way into the holiest of all was not yet manifested (Heb 9:8). Until Christ, full access to God was hindered, for a full and complete atonement had not yet been made. The temple veil protected the people from the fire of God's holiness. On the Day of Atonement, at the risk of his life, only the high priest, under the cloud of incense and bearing the blood of the covenant, entered the holiest to ask for pardon and renewal of God's covenant mercy. When the atonement in Christ was completed, the temple veil necessarily was torn aside (Mt 27:51; Mk 15:38; Lk 23:45), for now the access to God was blocked no longer.

According to Hebrews, atonement is through Christ's self-offering. In this way, he is priest and oblation. Christ, made like us in all things (Heb 2:14-18), on the ground of that solidarity with us by which he carries our estrangement from God, entered the presence of God, offering himself as the atoning sacrifice for us and consecrating himself on our behalf.[38] In his incarnate union with us *we* entered the holiest with him and are accepted by God in Christ's person as having suffered and died with him, as if we had made our own atonement.

> The whole teaching of Hebrews pivots upon the profound fact that Jesus Christ *actually* entered into our existence and *actually* shouldered our sin. . . . He so acted for us in his own person, that God regards us and accepts us in the person of Christ. Thus when Christ offered himself in sacrifice and consecrated himself, he so did that for us that we were offered to God and we were consecrated in him, for *in his act he who consecrated and we who are consecrated are for ever bound up in one consummated act.*[39]

The writer of Hebrews, in other words, has emphasized the priesthood of Christ, the *kipper* aspect of redemption, while the concepts of the *goel*, the kinsman-redeemer, and the *padah*, salvation through the mighty act of God, provided the frame.

It is almost a matter of fact in Hebrews that atonement is expiation through the shedding of blood by which sins are purged (Heb 9:22). Atonement by blood means substitution: a life for a life. Torrance comments that at this point,

---

[38]Ibid., p. 82.
[39]Ibid., p. 83 (italics original).

The atonement knows no *why,* no ultimate *why* except God himself. All rests on his ordinance of grace. That means that the ultimate mystery of the atonement recedes into the eternal being of God far beyond our human grasp, to "the lamb slain before the foundation of the world." Thus though the writer to the Hebrews appears to take it for granted that atonement is through the expiatory shedding of blood, he is intent on respecting its ultimate mystery.[40]

A careful reading of Torrance will note that this kind of conclusion is often found in his writing when he becomes aware that our forms of thought and speech break off in wonder, as he refuses to advance along the path laid out by logico-causal attempts at explanation. To cite Athanasius: "Thus far human knowledge goes. Here the cherubim spread the covering of their wings."[41] Torrance has pushed as far into the atonement as he could, so to speak, and understanding can go no farther. Before the mystery of God's salvation in Jesus Christ the theologian must now kneel in adoration.

According to Hebrews, access to God is now on the basis of what God has done through grace in Jesus Christ. Thus we come to think of Jesus as the mediator of the new covenant. By the spilling of Jesus' blood God has once for all founded a new covenant such that he will not—indeed, cannot—go back on what has happened in Christ.[42] The finality of this must be stressed, for it is God's testament.

Atonement through the mediation of Christ means, then, that Jesus Christ is at once the apostle of God, and by God's appointment and incarnate qualification our high priest, who makes his confession (*homologia*) as he enters within the veil of the holiest.[43] As apostle, Christ bears witness to God's holiness, God's judgment on sin, and God's mercy, grace and will to pardon. As high priest, Christ acknowledges that God is holy and judges sin, Christ says "Amen" to that judgment, and Christ intercedes for us and confesses us before God's face as his own flesh and blood. By his life and word Christ submits to God's truth and judgment on our behalf after the manner in which the identity of the person of the atoner and the deed of atonement are one. In other words, "*Jesus Christ IS the atonement.*"[44] The

---

[40]Ibid., p. 88.
[41]Torrance, *Trinitarian Faith,* p. 213, citing Athanasius, *Epistulae ad Serapionem* 1.17.
[42]Torrance, *Atonement,* p. 84.
[43]Ibid., pp. 88-89.
[44]Ibid., p. 94 (italics original).

biblical word that carries the weight of this atonement in Hebrews is *hilask-esthai* (expiation), which is the usual translation of *kipper*. The consequence is emancipation out of bondage, out of the thralldom of sin unto death, to receive a new freedom in relation to God that is *apolytrōsis* (redemption).

The conclusion that Torrance draws is that in this conception of the atonement Jesus Christ *has made a past*—for all time put aside the old Adam, the old aeon. The atonement created a past because it created a future, a "better hope" (Heb 7:19). Thus the consequence of what Christ has done by his redemption: he has

> opened up an eschatological vista for faith in which we are already planted in Christ, and with Christ already enter through the veil into God's presence. It is because Christ ever lives as our redeemer, our surety, our atonement, that our life is set on a wholly and eternally new basis. . . . Through Christ the forerunner, the great *podeh-goel*, or mighty kinsman-redeemer, the author and finisher of our faith, we enter already into redemption, tasting already the powers of the age to come, already in anticipation of the great *anapausis*, the final resting place that is the full and blessed enjoyment of the world to come.[45]

Torrance ends his reflection on the priestly ministry of Jesus on a note of extravagant doxology. His language and imagery are stretched to write of God's salvation with quivering excitement. Here are words of faith, not cool reason, of exultation rather than mastery of mystery, and of astonishment, not prosaic depiction. Torrance seems to be caught up with, or maybe into, the glory of Christ's redemption. This now is the theology not of the academy but of the cathedral as he joins his voice to choirs of angels in praise of God.

I make these observations because I believe that we have here, in theology that seemingly cannot help giving God the praise due for so great a redemption, a criterion of truth in theology. For the mathematician, there is truth in the beauty of the equation. For the physicist, there is truth in the coherence of the theory that allows a deeper penetration of mind into the meaning of the experimental data. For the theologian, there is truth in theology that leads to worship and the adoration of the trinitarian God. This is not the only criterion of truth in theology, of course; nevertheless, this is a criterion of truth appropriate to the subject of our inquiry.

---

[45]Ibid., p. 96.

I judge that Torrance has succeeded in laying the foundation for building a case for an understanding of substitutionary atonement through the blood of Christ without having to lay hold of forensic categories of thinking that might tend to dominate the discussion. By doing so he has given an important service by taking us more deeply into the complexity of the atonement than the Western *ordo salutis* usually allows for. His insistence on grounding the priestly ministry of Jesus within both the ontological relation between the Father and the incarnate Son, on the one hand, and the hypostatic union developed through a bidirectional Christology, on the other hand, has served as a remarkable hermeneutical strategy that both arises out of the Epistle to the Hebrews itself and serves as a heuristic pattern of thought that makes for an ever-deeper interpretation.

Torrance now turns to consideration of the atonement in the teaching of Paul, beginning with atonement as justification.

ATONEMENT AS JUSTIFICATION, RECONCILIATION, REDEMPTION

Atonement as justification. Paul gives the same doctrine given in Hebrews, but from a different perspective. With Paul, the positive teaching on the atonement is seen in terms of God's righteousness justifying the ungodly (Rom 3:24-26). The significant New Testament word is *dikaiosynē*, which refers to a life or conduct according to *dikē* (custom, justice). It may also indicate a judicial proceeding or the execution of a sentence or a judgment.[46] The Hebrew thought in the background relates to God's holy will for humankind and God's act of putting a person in the right. In the New Testament *dikaiosynē* is the Greek equivalent for the Hebraic understanding of positive acts of righteous mercy. According to Torrance's word study, "This means that we must take the meaning of *dikaiosunē* to be a positive act of divine deliverance in mercy and truth, as in the Old Testament expressions."[47] In its verbal form, *dikaioō*, there is a twofold meaning: "to do justice to someone" and "to deem right." The basic meaning, then, is "to be put in the right."

There are three key elements in justification. First, God's righteousness is God's supreme righteousness in which humans are given to participate. Second, and of high importance, God's act of righteousness is on God's part both rev-

---

[46]Ibid., p. 99.
[47]Ibid., p. 101.

elation and deed, and on the part of humankind both knowing and being. "These two sides are inseparable, and both of them, God's part and humanity's part, are fulfilled for us in Jesus Christ. *He is the righteousness of God and the righteousness of humanity.* . . . In his [Christ's] faith (*pistis*), God's righteousness actualises itself as truth."[48] And third, the righteousness of Christ is proclaimed as the gospel of grace, which is freely given to us in and through Christ. In view of these definitions and meanings, what is the meaning of atoning justification?

The first point that Torrance makes we have met before: in God's righteous act of grace, which is the atonement, God is the subject throughout. Atonement is an act of God, even when seen from the perspective of the humanity of Jesus Christ.[49] Whether referred to in terms of expiation or propitiation, the atonement is God's act flowing from the font of mercy and love. God mercifully bears his judgment upon sin in the passion of Christ. But note again: "That is not simply a legal transaction but a dynamic concrete reality, and therefore 'apart from the law' (*chōris nomou*) [Rom 3:21], an actualisation of righteousness in the flesh and blood, in the concrete reality of Christ Jesus. In him we are given a new humanity and a new human righteousness in the very righteousness of God."[50]

Justification is the revelation of righteousness. This revelation is the word that puts us in the truth; the corollary is that we are in untruth (Rom 3:4 surely is one of Torrance's favorite verses). Thus we cannot boast of our orthodoxy. God's word uncovers our untruth and judges it, and this is identical with God's word that tells us we are pardoned and forgiven. Torrance, however, must move further into the mystery of the atonement in Paul's thought, for justification is also an event of God's righteous intervention. Explaining the meaning of justification by faith, Torrance insists, "It is not that our faith justifies, for our faith is simply correlative to the justifying Christ, but as such faith involves radical self-denial, repentance (*metanoia*) in which we gladly place ourselves under God's judgment, in which we allow the act of justification to displace us, to dispossess us of our vaunted right and truth, in order that Christ Jesus himself alone may be our right and truth and our righteousness."[51]

---

[48]Ibid., p. 103.
[49]Ibid., p. 104.
[50]Ibid.
[51]Ibid., p. 108.

Now Torrance's argument is a little difficult to follow as he moves to unravel Paul's teaching on law and religion. According to Torrance, justification involves a double problem for God. How can God justify the ungodly? And how can God intensify sin? Sin is rebellion against God, and sin gains part of its identity from God's resistance to it. Yet God withheld his final resistance until the breach between God and humankind was "widened to an abysmal depth in the crucifixion."[52] For Torrance, the interim between the begetting of sin and its final judgment on the cross of Christ establishes the ethical order in which righteousness has valid authority and sinful humankind has relative immunity from final judgment.[53] Humankind lives under a moral order, which is divinely sanctioned yet itself is part of the separation between God and humankind. This is the context within which Old Testament faith is to be understood. But whether Jew or Gentile, all humankind stands under judgment because of unrighteousness. "The law of God which repudiates human sin at the same time holds the world together in law and order and gives it relative stability—but sin takes advantage of that and under cover of the law exerts itself more and more in independence of God. . . . The great problem here is that the law does not really deal with the root of sin, but on the contrary helps to maintain sin in being before the law."[54] In regard to this, religion becomes the highest expression of sin insofar as religion is the way of living in terms of truth and justice *that have become abstracted from their proper ground in a personal, covenantal relationship with God.*

Paul understands that the saving act of God in Christ confronts bondage to law and religion. God's saving intervention takes the form of the revelation of God's righteousness *apart* from law and religion. In Jesus Christ God steps out from behind the veil, coming among us directly, "cutting through all distance and abstraction, all law and religion, and sets men and women before him face to face. Here the Word of God is made flesh, in mercy and truth. That saving action Paul calls 'justification.'"[55] God's justification judges sin, cutting through all law and religion, as it were, to touch sinful humanity

---

[52]Ibid., p. 111.
[53]Ibid.
[54]Ibid., p. 113.
[55]Ibid., p. 115.

at the root of our willful rebellion against God. This is the legitimate forensic element in justification in which God will not be unfaithful to God's law, which, of course, must be referred back to God's covenant with Israel. But now the righteousness of God has been manifested *apart* from the law. How is this achieved? It is achieved by the faith/faithfulness *of* Jesus Christ (Rom 3:22: *dia pisteōs Iēsou Christou*). The law is suspended insofar as it works God's wrath and its strength is sin, suspended as the intermediary or mediator between God and humankind.[56] Torrance interprets Paul to mean that we must look past the law and religion in their legalistic form, refracted from living relations with God. Positively put, this means, I assume, to live in terms of covenant relations. In Christ God now confronts humankind directly, apart from law. God does that on the ground of atonement, which is the fulfillment of God's righteousness in Christ and on the cross so that the condemnation of the law is no longer in play (Rom 8:1).[57]

God thus now deals with us in Christ face to face, in grace, and no longer through the law. "With the actual coming of holy God in Christ to deal with our sin, the whole form of God's covenantal relation with humanity is changed. In place of the old covenant founded upon law, or rather administered through law, God has established a new covenant founded upon and ministered by his direct, utterly gracious, and personal dealing with sinners in which he freely grants forgiveness and life."[58] This intervention is the revelation of God's righteousness that could not otherwise be known, a righteousness that could not be inferred from law, ethics or religion. This means the breaking in of the reign of God. God has propitiated himself insofar as God has drawn near to sinners to draw sinners into fellowship with himself in an act of stupendous, miraculous grace. Of course, such an intervention by God is not explainable. It is an unfathomable mystery.

I am uncertain how strongly Torrance wants to make a case here for two covenants. Cannot a better case be made for a single narrative, and for God in Christ to be seen as the fulfillment of God's righteousness, the fulfillment of God's covenantal promises? God's faithfulness belonged to God's covenantal character all along. Or to ask the question differently: Is the new cov-

---

[56]Ibid., p. 117.
[57]Ibid.
[58]Ibid.

enant in the blood of Jesus another covenant vis-à-vis God's covenant with
Abraham? I trust that Torrance would answer that in Christ we now stand in
a right covenant relation with God, in a manner corresponding to Abraham
in his right standing within covenant relations with God (Rom 4:13).[59]

At this point the argument is not yet complete. Even so, we note consistent
themes emerging: God is the subject of atonement; the atonement is an act
of God's love, mercy and grace, which are understood in terms of God's covenantal faithfulness; the bidirectional Christology and the powerful place
given to the subjective genitive translation of the *dia pisteōs Iēsou Christou*;
Torrance's sense of wonder at the essential mystery of the atonement; and the
disregard for any human agency other than Christ's.

We turn finally under the topic of atonement as justification to the act of
atonement itself. To do so we turn to the theology of the death of Christ.
According to Torrance, the "death of Christ was an expiatory sacrifice in
which God judged sin and through which human guilt is completely taken
away."[60] From the side of humankind, the guilt was irredeemable because it
was irremovable. On God's part, guilt was judged, yet judged by God who
loves us and knows that we cannot survive the judgment. In Jesus Christ the
eternal, holy judge entered into the deepest depths of our estrangement
from and rebellion against God to reconcile us to God, bearing upon his
own body the totality of the divine judgment. Torrance sums up the atoning
exchange with these words: "God came in Christ to do from the side of
humanity what humanity could not do. . . . He died on our behalf and in that
death he offered the perfect submission of humanity to God in holy obedience, and brought to God humanity's perfect acquiescence in the divine
judgment. . . . Christ descended into the deepest depths of our guilt and
submitted to the complete judgment of God upon it."[61]

To expand upon this, Torrance, now moving away from his exposition of
Paul to a dogmatic reflection upon justification, insists upon what he calls
"enhypostatic atonement." Everything before us is to be seen as an act of God,
both from God's side and from the side of humankind, for God, to repeat, is

---

[59]N. T. Wright, *Justification: God's Plan and Paul's Vision* (Downers Grove, IL: IVP Academic, 2009),
p. 66.
[60]Torrance, *Atonement*, p. 120.
[61]Ibid., p. 121.

always the subject throughout the act of atonement. Atonement is not to be understood as humankind as the man Jesus propitiating God. In any case, humanity bearing God's judgment would only mean death without atonement. Yet God expiates sin and guilt, bears sin and guilt, and bears them away as the man Jesus, who is God for and with us. That is what enhypostatic atonement means. For justification is in Christ an act of humankind, the act of a man, while being an act of God. Here we are face to face with the soteriological meaning of incarnation, of the *homoousion*, and of the hypostatic union. On the one hand, we must hold up God's just condemnation of sin; on the other hand, we must hold up God's provision from the side of humankind of a righteousness that fulfills God's righteous judgment against sin.

> In that double deed of the God-man, of God and man in inconceivable union in Christ, atonement is wrought in the life and blood of Christ. It is at once substitutionary *sacrifice* in that life is given for life as Christ stands under the divine judgment obedient unto death, the death of the cross, and substitutionary *oblation* in that here obedience and holiness are offered to God in place of our disobedience and sin. . . . It is not merely the death of Christ, his suffering, his blood, his bearing of judgment, that atones or expiates guilt, but along with that and within it all the offering of perfect holiness to God from the side of humanity.[62]

Justification must be seen from two sides: from the side of God's faithfulness and from the side by which God's faithfulness is answered vicariously by human faithfulness as the man Jesus. This must be done trying to grasp atonement as the act of God who is indivisible and in Christ in his hypostatic union. In Christ, in the unity of his person, he was both the judge and the judged, and this in his whole life and not just in his death. For the death of Jesus was the working out of the whole movement of incarnation, and that which was joined at his conception as hypostatic union—God and humankind as one person—must not now be separated at his death; otherwise *God* has not entered into the terrible depths of our estrangement and rebellion. In which case, surely—and here we should turn away our eyes lest we look upon things too terrible to contemplate—there would be no atonement, and we are dead under the truth of God's judgment upon sin. Speaking in this way of God

---

[62]Ibid., p. 123.

as the man Jesus effecting the atonement, we grasp something of the complexity and mystery of that which we here discuss. At best, what is said bears witness but does not explain, attests but does not comprehend.

Approaching the end of his discussion, Torrance asks the question of how one person can die for another and do it justly. The question has a speculative edge, and, in Torrance's language, we might dismiss it as an unscientific question. In theology we have to deal with what we have before us rather than determine a priori what must be the case. Are incarnation and atonement beholden to some system of ethics? Of course not! But however we might understand the atonement, that understanding has to present a doctrine of substitution: "For our sake he made him to be sin who knew no sin, so that in him we might become the righteousness of God" (2 Cor 5:21). How did Christ take our guilt, the just for the unjust, and do that justly?

Torrance gives his answer by noting that humankind was created by the Word of God, and it is in and from that Word that we have true being and true humanity. "Because that Word made flesh is the creative source and true secret of our humanity, because in him our humanity is lodged, because all mankind consists in him, he is the only one who can really represent all men and women from the innermost centre and depth of human being."[63] That is, all humankind consists in Christ. As such, he can take our sin upon himself, not as an external transaction considered in forensic terms, which certainly raises the ethical question of the one for the many, but rather as coming to his own who belong to him. Christ does not just wear our flesh; in the incarnation he becomes as we are, entering into human nature from within and plunging thereby to the depths of our rebellion against and estrangement from God while living in perfect obedience to God. The gap of alienation between God and humankind is bridged. Now, in saying that all humankind consists in the Word of God, incarnation means that Christ has taken the human nature of all humankind, and that, therefore, the judgment of God upon all human nature is borne by Christ. Justification is a corporate and inclusive act. "As the creator and head of the race in whom all mankind consist, Christ died for all men and women, and the justification involved is total, for all."[64] Christ died for every sinner: "one has died for all; therefore all have died" (2 Cor 5:14).

---

[63]Ibid., p. 126.
[64]Ibid., p. 128.

Whether from Paul or Torrance, this is a remarkable conclusion. Of course, the question concerning the salvation of all—universalism—is raised immediately. To be very clear: according to Torrance, universalism is not a legitimate conclusion. There is a difference between Christ bearing all human nature in its estrangement from God and healing that estrangement, and Christ bearing all human persons in a manner that leaves us with atonement as so objectified that any agency on our part is downright abolished at the point of faith and obedience. At this point he is reflecting on universal atonement vis-à-vis limited atonement with respect to our human nature. God in Christ has acted for us, and nothing can change or undo that act. That act is not negated if we refuse Christ. We might go so far as to say that this is the ontological aspect of the atonement. However—and this is a terrible freedom!—we consign ourselves to hell when we refuse the divine reconciliation, leaving ourselves open now to the divine judgment. I will pick up this thread again a little later. The point for now is to emphasize the wholeness of substitutionary atonement, and to do so with awareness of the huge role that a doctrine of limited atonement has played in Western Protestantism.

Moving now to a conclusion, Torrance sees that justification in the act of atonement means rectification, the restoring of God's right over humankind and the restoration to humans of their right as children of God.[65] The sin and guilt of the past are utterly undone and done away by Christ's descent into hell. In Christ we are now given to participate in the new creation that is yet to be revealed. That is, as justified, we are given to share in the righteousness and glory of the Son of God. He who has put himself in our place now gives us to be put in his place; this is the magnificent exchange, to which I have already made reference. Justification is a past work but it has a future fulfillment, as we will manifestly share in the life of Christ.

Oddly, to my mind, Torrance ends his discussion on justification with a paragraph on imputation. He does so to emphasize the continuing forensic element. While complete, justification is yet to be fully disclosed at the parousia, the second advent of Christ. Yet as complete, justification is forensic insofar as it is grounded in the once-for-all judgment of God. But I say "oddly" because Torrance seems to bring the emphasis on imputation as a

---

[65] Ibid., p. 129.

deus ex machina. I do not see what he has achieved by doing so when he has gone to considerable effort to locate the meaning of the atoning death of Jesus within Father-Son relations. The discussion has trended toward atonement considered within an ontological-relational framework rather than a legal-instrumental framework, while not excluding a forensic aspect, of course. As noted already, he argued disapprovingly, "In Western Christianity the atonement tends to be interpreted almost exclusively in terms of external forensic relations as a judicial transaction in the transference of the penalty for sin from the sinner to the sin-bearer."[66] Are transference of the penalty on to Christ and imputation of the righteousness of Christ corollaries? If they are corollaries, Torrance appears to end on an uneven judicial note, having rejected the former. If they are not corollaries, it is hard to see how imputation works when Torrance has already stated that justification is participation in the righteousness of Christ, the new man.[67] It is a long stretch to assume that imputation or reckoning (*logizesthe*, as at Rom 6:11) means the same as participation.

However, the presentation of Paul's atonement theology is only partially complete, as Torrance moves on now to consider atonement as reconciliation. Insofar as he does not allow the atonement to come to expression *only* as justification, our understanding of the atonement must move now beyond the categories of justification and directly and explicitly toward the filial relation in which we are reconciled to God. Not only is guilt canceled, but also we are established in a new relationship with God. Indeed, through the Son we are established in a new relationship with the Father. Thus the turn is made toward the exploration of the bond of union between God and humankind, a bond that is ontological and, now emphasized, personal. In this framework atonement means at-one-ment. Justification is one trajectory of thought that explores the mystery of redemption. The Western inclination in atonement theory aside, it is not the only line of thought, even in Paul.

Atonement as reconciliation. Following his pattern, Torrance begins with a discussion of the New Testament word for reconciliation between God and humankind: *katallassō*. The verb refers to reconciliation through a substitutionary exchange, the result of which is expiation, the effecting of reconcili-

---

[66]Torrance, *Mediation of Christ*, p. 50.
[67]Torrance, *Atonement*, p. 133.

ation. The noun form, *katallagē*, refers to the atoning exchange brought about by substitution.[68] To complicate matters, however, we do not have an Old Testament equivalent to the actual terms. The Old Testament aspect of atonement as expiation, *kipper*, can be rendered by *hilaskesthai*, though the word is not much favored by the writers of the Septuagint or the New Testament. This term certainly means "to be merciful, to forgive, to atone." Why does Paul not use the word? The reason appears to be that in profane Greek it carried the notion of reconciling God, where God is the object rather than the subject—the opposite of the gospel. It is set aside in favor of *katallassō*. Thus behind Paul's use of *katallassō* lies the Old Testament doctrine of reconciliation through expiation or reconciliation, even though another word is substituted in New Testament Greek for the equivalent rendering.

Torrance cites four texts to unpack the meaning of *katallassō*. The first is Romans 5:8-11, where the verb is used twice at verse 10 and the noun once at verse 11. God is the subject throughout. The reconciliation effected concerns the personal relationship between God and humankind. "It is God himself who forms anew the relations between himself and humanity—the human part is to accept this reinstatement, this reconciliation, and so Paul in Romans speaks of 'receiving atonement or reconciliation' (*katallagēn*)."[69] The text also invites us to note the parallel between justification and reconciliation. "Reconciliation is just as objective as justification, but in reconciliation the personal relation is in view, envisaging a changed relationship. Reconciliation expresses more the positive side of justification."[70]

The second text is 2 Corinthians 5:14-21, where Paul writes, "In Christ God was reconciling the world to himself" (2 Cor 5:19). Again, the reconciling act is God's act. Through it everything becomes new. *Katallagē* refers to effected salvation that God has brought about by an exchange when God took atonement upon himself freely in love, and brought a new relationship with humankind to bear, a relationship of peace.

The third and fourth texts are Ephesians 2:13-16 and Colossians 1:19-22, where the word *apokatallassō* is used. The prefix intensifies the meaning. "Thus in the action described by *apokatallassō* there is the closest relation be-

---

[68]Ibid., p. 138.
[69]Ibid., p. 142.
[70]Ibid.

tween redemption and creation on the one hand, and the reaching out of reconciliation to all things, *ta panta*, on the other, to the eschatological *plērōma* or fullness. The whole universe comes under reconciliation, angels and all."[71] Here we must think of the complete unity of all things in Christ in a vast cosmic peace. The sweep of the meaning now is staggering in magnitude.

The brief word study done, Torrance turns to theological reflection on reconciliation under seven headings. First, while justification was the establishment of humankind in relation to the holy will of God, with reconciliation the emphasis is placed on the compassion of God in which he turned toward humankind in love and took our humanity unto himself in Christ in order to assume us into fellowship with himself.[72] The tone now is of free and unconditional grace. With humankind not even ready to repent of our sin, God nevertheless comes to us with a will to forgive, to give himself to the sinner and for the sinner. God gives *himself.* Torrance cites Calvin: "God loved us even when he hated us."[73] God prevents (i.e., goes before, as in prevenient grace) and anticipates our reconciliation. It is important to notice the ordering of thought here. We were not reconciled to God that God might love us; rather, we were loved by God even when we were enemies of God (Rom 5:8 is very much in mind here). God gives himself to humankind, the God who is opposed to human sin, and thereby to the bondage with which we are bound, thus overcoming the barrier between God and us. That is to say, God no longer tolerates the human "No" to God, and in doing so God says "Yes" to humankind, a yes that of course includes God's "No" to sin. "God," says Torrance, "ranges himself on the side of the sinner in opposition to their sin that he may deliver them from their bondage to sin and make them free for fellowship with God. God's love is his unconditional assertion that he is *for* man, on man's side."[74] Reconciliation, in sum, is the positive outpouring of God's love.

The second point is to insist that this reconciliation is achieved in the person of the incarnate Son, Jesus Christ. In a typical Torrance idiom: "Jesus Christ is in himself the hypostatic union of the judge and the judged."[75] In

---

[71]Ibid., p. 144.
[72]Ibid., p. 145.
[73]Ibid., p. 146, citing Calvin, *Institutes* 2.16.4.
[74]Ibid., p. 147.
[75]Ibid., p. 148.

justification Jesus is at once God the judge and the sin-bearer. Similarly, with regard to reconciliation, Jesus Christ is the God of the covenant that has been broken, but in his incarnation he has taken the humanity of the covenant-breakers and is thus both the turning of God toward humanity and the turning of humanity toward God. Jesus Christ, then, is our reconciliation, our propitiation in whom God has turned toward us and we are reconciled to God. Christ is the *hilastērion* (Rom 3:25: "a sacrifice of atonement") or the *hilasmos* (1 Jn 2:2: "the atoning sacrifice"). Here we encounter God being reconciled to humanity (although this is a disturbing notion, it is to be taken to mean God acting in such a way that human sin no longer determines the relation between God and humankind) and humanity being reconciled to God. This reconciliation is worked out within the incarnate person of Jesus Christ. This is the essential mystery at the center of the atonement.

The reference above to reconciliation being worked out within the hypostatic union means that reconciliation begins with the conception and birth of Jesus, when the real union between God and humankind is established via the Son's assumption of our human nature. In this way, the whole life of Jesus, including his death, constitutes reconciliation. "The hypostatic union is inserted into the abysmal chasm of divine judgment upon humanity, and in the heart of that divine judgment the union of God with humanity and humanity with God is established and maintained."[76] Even so, the *assumptio carnis* reaches into the deepest point of division between God and humankind to effect reconciliation where the Son assumes our damnation and judgment: "Eli, Eli, lema sabachthani?" (Mt 27:46). Jesus died on the cross under judgment. The assumption of the flesh is maintained in Christ's death and in his descent into hell. And it achieves its end on the third day with the resurrection of humankind in Christ out of hell, and the exaltation of humankind in Christ to begin his ascended reign.[77] This means no less than reconciliation that means restored communion with God to be partakers of the divine nature, as humankind may now live eternally within the overflow of the life and love of the Father.

The third point that Torrance makes is to comment upon reconciliation taking place through the magnificent exchange (a notion that keeps popping

---

[76]Ibid., p. 149.
[77]Ibid., p. 150.

up). Christ took our place that we might have Christ's place. This is also what reconciliation means: an act of reconciliation effected on the basis of an exchange.[78] Christ took our place, unto death, and freely gives us his place of holiness, glory and life. Through his poverty, we might become rich. Through his being made sin, we might be reconciled to God. In this way, Christ stands in the gap between God's holy judgment upon human sin and human guilt. "He was very God, descending into the depth of our wickedness and laying hold of us in sheer love, and he was very man, receiving and laying hold of God by submitting to the divine judgment and receiving all the self-giving of God in his love which we could not receive and live."[79] That is to say, Christ was God in such a manner that what he did, God did; and Christ was human, one with us, so that what he did, he did in our place, on our behalf, as our representative. There is no other God than the God who has stood in our place and acted on our behalf. And there is no humanity who has not died and risen with Christ, and in Christ's name been presented before the Father. This is the heart of reconciliation.

The fourth point in the development of the doctrine of reconciliation is to note the consequence: the establishment of peace with God. Reconciliation means that the enmity between God and humankind is removed, and with this removal humankind is reinstated to personal relations with God characterized by love and peace. This is the meaning of Colossians 1:20: "Through [Christ] God was pleased to reconcile to himself all things, whether on earth or in heaven, by making peace through the blood of his cross." This peace may be understood in two ways: as peace *with* God, where the reference is objective, and as the peace *of* God, where the reference is subjective.[80]

The fifth point is the consideration of reconciliation as peacemaking in its objective and subjective aspects. Objectively, peace between God and humankind is the result of the removal of the wrath of God against sin. God as the man Jesus has stood in the gap and taken the consequences of sin upon himself, and thereby he provides an expiation in himself in the sacrifice of his blood. Actively, Christ stepped into our place; passively, Christ accepted God's judgment. As such, therefore, God has no more to say to us

---

[78]Ibid., p. 151.
[79]Ibid., p. 152.
[80]Ibid., p. 153.

with respect to our sin and guilt. In an image found already in John McLeod Campbell, Torrance writes, "When in reconciliation God actually takes upon himself the sentence of rejection and bears it instead of mankind, then God takes all his own righteous enmity against sin and absorbs it in himself."[81] Absorption, indeed, is an odd notion, and Torrance does not explain its use. On the face of it, however, it means that God takes our sin into himself in Christ and transmutes it, creating a new relationship between God and humankind. Thus on the cross we have the ultimate human rejection of God and God's final rejection of the sin of humankind. There is only now God's acceptance of humankind.

However—and again we must return briefly to the issue of universalism—Torrance says that

> if a sinner is reprobated, if a sinner goes to hell, it is not because God rejected them, for God has only chosen to love them, and has only accepted them in Christ who died for them and on the cross consummated the divine act of love in accepting them and in taking their rejection upon himself. If anyone goes to hell they go to hell, only because, inconceivably, they refuse the positive act of the divine acceptance of them, and refuse to acknowledge that God has taken their rejection of him upon himself, so acknowledging that they deserved to be rejected.[82]

The reprobation is for the person who refuses the election of grace. Thus Torrance, following Calvin, sees the gospel as the gospel of salvation and not of destruction. And condemnation only arises out of the refusal of the reconciliation already established, and of the peace already prepared. To be clear: there is no prior decision of God to reject anyone. Torrance insists that he is no universalist, though he remains at the same time an advocate for atonement for all.

Subjectively, the atonement must be worked into the human heart and mind to the point where we accept God's judgment upon us and are restored in our deepest inner being to communion with God, loving God fully and knowing God rightly and serving God faithfully. Reconciliation, therefore, breaks down the personal rebellion against God within the human being

---

[81]Ibid., p. 155.
[82]Ibid., p. 157.

and wins the human heart and mind to God.[83] As McLeod Campbell would state the matter, it is not yet redemption that our sins are forgiven; we must yet be restored to a new relationship with God. The issues with which we are concerned are, in other words, personal. We must be reconciled with God in our inner depths. For Torrance, this means especially the renewal of our minds with respect to God. This is a persistent theme in Torrance's theology. Thus the reconciliation effected through the incarnation entails an onto-logical union—indeed, a Logos-union—between humankind and God, the result of which is thinking of God rightly. Christ "exegetes" the Father (Jn 1:18), and we, in Christ and reconciled to God, know the Father rightly. At this point Torrance refers again to the enhypostatic aspect of reconciliation, meaning the personal reality of Jesus in the person of the eternal Son, and therefore through our union with Christ our participation in his knowledge of and love for the Father. Reconciliation involves, therefore, both an ontic and a noetic aspect, the latter following from the former.[84]

This noetic aspect is twofold. The divine Logos united himself with our human nature, revealing himself within our humanity, but also within our humanity enabled us to receive his revelation personally in love and faith and understanding. In this way, we are delivered from untruth and made free for the truth of God. Reconciliation restored humankind to union with God in knowing as well as being.[85]

> The movement of divine love in assuming humanity into oneness with God is thus met and creatively integrated with a corresponding movement of humanity in yielding to the divine love and accepting the divine grace, in full agreement and obedience to the divine truth. In that *double movement in Christ*, objective and subjective reconciliation is completed and inserted as a finished reality into the midst of our human existence, and man is restored to the image and likeness of God, in perfect communion with him.[86]

In this way, then, we must speak of reconciliation characterized by at-one-ment in mind and being with the truth and reality of God, accomplished in the human nature of Christ to be shared with us by the Holy Spirit.

---

[83]Ibid., p. 159.
[84]Ibid., p. 162.
[85]Ibid., p. 164.
[86]Ibid., pp. 164-65 (italics added).

A comment: Torrance's presentation of this fifth point is a typical piece of Torrance theology. We see here two recurring themes sharply emphasized: the bidirectional Christology, and the relation between ontic and noetic aspects of reconciliation, with the renewed mind especially highlighted.

The sixth point is a return to the fourth, peace with God; but under the rubric of reconciliation this means "Immanuel," God with us. Already we have seen that the fact that we are sinners is, remarkably, the title and right to reconciliation by God's will and grace. God for us, however, entails also God with us in Christ in such a manner that God has bound himself up with us in the same bundle of life, so that we may share in his divine life.[87] This is the great *palingenesia*, the rebirth and renewal of all things by which God has bound himself to us in reconciliation that is unbreakable and irreversible. But that is not all that must be said. God with us and God for us means also us with God. We are already taken into the life of God, and we are, in a sense beyond explanation, already on the other side of judgment and death. We live in Christ on the side of resurrection and ascension. We live in the fellowship of God's kingdom.

Torrance concludes his discussion on this point cryptically, citing Calvin to declare that he cannot explain how anyone can fall out of the realm of divine love. On the one hand, we have the confidence of the children of God because the eternal Son took our flesh and became a man; what has happened to Jesus is now, for us in him, our hope. On the other hand (of course), there remains the terrible and incomprehensible reality that the ungodly break off and dissolve that relationship established by Christ on taking our human nature, and by doing so they render themselves strangers to him by their own fault.[88] Torrance names the terrible mystery of human rejection of so great a salvation, but rightly he does not bring his theological imagination to bear, for there is too little here given us to penetrate the darkness.

Finally, and briefly, bringing his theological reflections on reconciliation to a close, Torrance ponders the cosmic sweep of the effects of the hypostatic union, anticipating the discussion of redemption.

---

[87]Ibid., p. 167.
[88]Ibid., pp. 168-69.

> Because God has become man in Christ, has for ever bound himself up in existence and life with his creation, the whole of creation is involved in reconciliation. . . . The New Testament thus envisages a *cosmic peace* as the effect of the reconciliation. . . . Literally all things, visible and invisible, things animate and things inanimate, the whole creation, heaven and earth, are involved in this reconciliation.[89]

As such, reconciliation is identical with the person of Christ, for Christ is reconciliation in himself as the Son of God. Here Torrance anticipates the doctrines of the Holy Spirit and the church. Reconciliation in Christ is opened out, hinge-like, into all history and into all future. Reconciliation in Christ is the deepest and ultimate secret of all that happens in history, and in the cross especially, for there all things are made to cohere and work together for God's purpose.

Appropriately, Torrance ends with an ascription of glory: *Laus Deo* (thanks to God).

Before moving on to Torrance's view of atonement as redemption, I will pause here to make a brief provisional assessment. Surely there is little doubt that we have before us a theologian who is writing on a huge page. Painting analogies work better, however. Torrance is painting his theology of the atonement on a huge canvas. Mostly the detail is precise, but the sweep is enormous: covenant, the priesthood of Christ, justification, and now reconciliation. All will soon be gathered together as redemption as he applies the finishing strokes that will pull everything together into a coherent perspective. We see how he has layered his construction, allowing us to see depths of insight. While coming back again and again to the use of familiar brush strokes (bidirectional Christology, Father-Son relations, hypostatic union and so on), he has held a vision before us of the love, grace and mercy of the living God. We have not been blinded, for the light has been fixed constantly upon Jesus Christ. At times his depictions have been dense, certainly repetitive, but flashed through with vivid and arresting strokes of color that highlight the divine drama here portrayed. It remains now to finish things off as we move from grace to glory with the rendering of the Christian doctrine of redemption.

---

[89]Ibid., p. 169.

Atonement as redemption. We begin with a quotation in which Torrance defines the meaning of redemption in the New Testament.

> Redemption is used in the New Testament in a general comprehensive sense to speak of the great act of our salvation through justification, expiation and reconciliation in Christ. . . . But redemption has also a more particular sense in the New Testament, one in which it speaks of God's saving act in Christ as reaching out from grace, *charis*, to glory, *doxa*. That is, here in redemption it is the eschatological and teleological perspective of atonement that is prominent. . . . It is the term which expresses the act of God in bringing justification and reconciliation to their final end. . . . By redemption the New Testament tells us that *glorification* is an essential part of our salvation.[90]

Torrance suggests how the meaning of redemption may be developed in three sections: the mighty act of redemption, the range of redemption, and the eschatological aspect of redemption.

First, redemption is a mighty act of God delivering us from the power of darkness into freedom as God's children. This, we recall, is the *padah* aspect of redemption in the Old Testament. The stress now must fall on the new life of freedom in the Spirit into which we are redeemed. Reflecting on Matthew 12:28-29, where Jesus states that it is by the Spirit of God that he casts out demons, Torrance sees that the incarnate life of Christ leading up to the cross itself is the invasion of the Son into the domain of evil in order to break its bonds.[91] The other side of the cross is resurrection, ascension and Pentecost, where redemption is expressed as new life. "What we have in Pentecost is *ta eschata*, the end or final events of redemption, overtaking the church and filling the church with the Holy Spirit, with the Spirit of Christ."[92] The outpouring of the Spirit is then part of redemption; Pentecost is part of the atonement as the actualization of the new redeemed life that we have in Christ. Pentecost connects redemption through the blood of Christ with redemption through the Spirit of Christ. In this way, we see that we are redeemed from guilt and redeemed into the life of God. Through the communion of the Holy Spirit we, the church, participate in the atonement wrought in and by Jesus Christ. And to speak of this we must speak now in

---

[90]Ibid., p. 171.
[91]Ibid., p. 177.
[92]Ibid., p. 178.

the present tense, for this redemption is a present possession.

Yet as we speak of redemption with this strong, integral pneumatic aspect, we must remember that the Spirit is poured out upon all flesh (Joel 2:28-32; Acts 2:17-21). Redemption includes the redemption of the body, which means nothing less than the resurrection of the body. Because the redemption of the body is inseparable from the redemption of all creation, the whole creation "waits with eager longing for the revealing of the children of God. . . . We know that the whole creation has been groaning in labor pains until now; and not only the creation, but we ourselves, who have the first fruits of the Spirit, groan inwardly while we wait for adoption, the redemption of our bodies" (Rom 8:19, 22-23). Thus even more so we move from hope for the redemption of the body to hope for redemption in the body, which is to be conformed to the body of Christ's glory (Phil 3:21).

Second, Torrance reflects on the range of redemption. Who did Christ die for? For some time this question, the question of limited atonement, has been in the back of our minds. Torrance identifies three concerns. In the first place, he asks who Christ represented in his incarnation and death. Because incarnation and atonement cannot be separated, Christ represents in his death all whom he represented in his incarnation.[93] For all people, without exception, Jesus Christ has stood in as substitute in his life and death. To be precise, all human nature coheres in him; all human nature is assumed by him. In arguing thus, Torrance repudiates the notion that the humanity of Christ was merely the instrument of salvation, and that the atonement on the cross was only a forensic transaction by which Christ fulfilled the obligations of a legal contract. Rather, incarnation and atonement should be seen as the fulfilling of the one covenant of grace made by God with creation, and as such fulfilled for all.

Torrance insists on the universal assumption of all human nature by Jesus Christ. As such, we cannot speak of an election or predestination "behind the back" of Jesus Christ, thereby to divide God's salvation in two, into election and into the work of Christ on the cross.[94] Christ *is* God's election incarnate. God's eternal decree *is* God's eternal Word, and Christ *is* that decree made flesh. Christ *is* election in action. Election and covenant belong

---

[93]Ibid., p. 182.
[94]Ibid., p. 183.

together; election, in this case, is corporate; and this covenant-election is fulfilled in Christ.

In the second place, Torrance inquires of the relation between the death of Jesus on the cross and the Father in heaven.[95] Everything that we have surveyed before demands the observation that the hypostatic union must not be divided, even on the cross, and that the Father-Son relationship cannot be divided. That is to say, even on the cross Christ remains wholly human and wholly divine.

> If Christ acted only in his human nature on the cross and God remained utterly apart and utterly transcendent, except that he agreed in will with Christ whom he sent to die, then all that Christ does is not necessarily what God does or accepts. . . . We must hold the view that it is indeed *God himself* who bears our sins . . . so that we cannot divorce the action of Christ on the cross from the action of God. The concept of a limited atonement divides Christ's divinity from his humanity and thus rests upon a basic Nestorian heresy.[96]

To say anything else means that outside of Christ there is still a God of wrath who will judge humankind apart from the cross. In which case, a terrible wedge is inserted between God and Christ, and the Christian doctrine of salvation unravels into incoherence.

In the third place, Torrance asks if the death of Jesus is to be seen as sufficient for all humankind but as efficacious only for the elect, a distinction made by scholastic Calvinism. What sense does it make to say that Christ died for all humankind sufficiently, but not for all efficaciously? Torrance suggests that behind this distinction there lies a philosophical or metaphysical conception of divine causality and therefore of irresistible grace.[97] The "logic" that drives the issue is that divine causal efficacy for all humankind demands the salvation of all humankind, which conclusion is not acceptable. Does this "logic" not diminish the freedom and transcendence of God? Does it not lead irresistibly to universal salvation? The alternative view of Arminianism suggests that God provided the possibility of salvation on the cross, and that each person has to take up that general possibility into

---

[95]Ibid., p. 184.
[96]Ibid., p. 185.
[97]Ibid., p. 186.

actuality. On this view, says Torrance, in effect everyone is his or her own savior, in which case how can anyone be assured of salvation?[98]

Torrance once again appeals to essential mystery to make his case. Human reason, with at best only partial insight into the death of Jesus, should not be given free rein to push through to seemingly logical conclusions.

By way of a positive statement, Torrance reaffirms that Christ died for all humankind by taking our common human nature upon himself. This is a finished work, not a possibility. God has taken the soteriological decision on our behalf. God has given himself to all humankind whether anyone wills it or not. No human being can undo or escape this act of God who loves them. "Therefore when they do the inconceivable thing in the face of that divine love, namely refuse it, defy it, turn away from it, that unavoidable self-giving of God is their very judgment. It opposes their refusal of God."[99] The atonement is sufficient and efficacious for all humankind, but nevertheless it is on this rock of offense that the sinner who refuses the divine love is shattered unto damnation.

Further, as we have seen, Pentecost is to be considered as a part of the atonement. It is atonement actualizing itself within people's lives, within their decisions and actions, and upholding them in their real relationship with God.[100] The baptism of the Spirit effects our union with Christ, as Calvin had already noted. The church, then, is the community of Christ not only on the ground of Christ incorporating himself into humankind, but also on the ground that believers are incorporated into him. The church is the community of those who have accepted the decision that God has already made on their behalf in Christ's life and death. This community is identified by baptism, the sacrament of what Christ has done on our behalf. It is the sacrament of the fact that Christ has bound himself to us and bound us to himself. In this way, Torrance follows Calvin, who used to speak of a threefold ingrafting into Christ: to all, to the covenant community and to the individual believer in the decision of faith.

Before leaving this presentation on the range of redemption, I must briefly take up again Torrance's avoidance of universalism. Does his rejection of the

---

[98]Ibid., p. 187.
[99]Ibid., p. 189.
[100]Ibid.

"logic" of rationalism and appeal to essential mystery succeed? Whatever else we must say, his conclusion is messy. For him, it appears, mystery involves tension insofar as we do not have the satisfaction of pushing through to conclusions. As the church readily speaks of the incomprehensibility of God, so too we must speak of the incomprehensibility of atonement and redemption. We cannot flatten it out to unravel its mystery. At the end of the day, faith itself cannot be explained, but only lived. There remains a terrible awfulness in salvation rejected. It is a terrible freedom in Christ to turn away from him. Positively expressed, on the other hand, it is an amazing grace to accept the love of God in Christ—to believe, and in doing so yet to insist that everything is God's doing.

The third major point that Torrance makes in his discussion on redemption is to develop the initial statement on the eschatological perspective, though he has little to say that is new. Redemption reaches out to the new creation at the parousia of Christ. Christians live between the redemption of the time of Pentecost and the redemption of the time of the resurrection of the body. Redemption is at once completed and yet to be fully manifested. For now, in God's mercy, the actualization of redemption in all creation is held in check, for the gospel must be preached to all nations and all people must have time to repent and believe.[101]

The meaning of Christ's death is vast indeed, for all things in heaven and earth are affected. Redemption sets us and all creation within a universal context.

THEOLOGICAL ENGAGEMENT WITH THE ARGUMENT

As previously noted, Torrance's treatment of the atonement is comprehensive. No single New Testament perspective is given precedence. With his *Atonement: The Person and Work of Christ*, we have the benefit of having his teaching gathered in one place. The positive impact is stronger for this. Justification, given its continuing place in Western Protestant theology, is not downgraded as such, but rather is kept in its place alongside the treatment of Christ as high priest and also discussions on reconciliation and redemption. At times the presentations appeared disjointed, indeed as lectures edited for publication. Connections, sometimes, were not seamlessly made,

---

[101]Ibid., p. 195.

and occasional points remained opaque. Nevertheless, all the great themes that I identified in the Christology chapters when I discussed Torrance's work have their place in his work on the atonement: Father-Son relations, bidirectional Christology, the magnificent exchange, the hypostatic union, and God as the subject of the atonement. For Torrance, we can say without fear of contradiction, Christology and atonement, the person and work of Christ, are but the two aspects of the one subject that remains indivisible.

Torrance's soteriology is not readily put into a convenient category. We may view it as a ransom soteriology, but only in some regards, for it is also most assuredly a covenant soteriology. We may view it as a soteriology of satisfaction, but only in some regards, for it is also most assuredly a soteriology of the agency of God's love and mercy. In fact, there is little of an Anselmian feel to it. We can say, I think with great confidence, that Torrance's soteriology is not a moral influence theory of the atonement, as it is also not a presentation dominated by forensic categories. We may view it as a type of *Christus victor* approach to the atonement, though much more down-to-earth and less tidy than, say, the modern treatment by Gustaf Aulén. In calling it a type of *Christus victor* approach I want to emphasize the robust Christology rather than a particular model of the atonement. In the end, perhaps, it would be wrong to suggest that Torrance has any theory of the atonement at all, for a theory was not what he was after. His is a soteriology a posteriori, a confessional rather than an explanatory soteriology. I might be pushing this too far, but at times it reads as if it were a worship-full soteriology. It is theology as bearing witness to the essential mystery and miracle of God in Christ for us. As said previously, it is theology written to be read in a cathedral; but while it is written primarily for the church, it is written also for the academy.

Unlike the treatments of atonement by McLeod Campbell and Mackintosh, Torrance's account appears to be less reactive, and he spends little time telling his readers what he is against (apart from occasional observations). What Torrance has taken from his Scottish predecessors of a positive nature are (1) the location (as it were) of the atonement in Father-Son relations; and (2) the emphasis on the atoning nature of the person of Jesus in his life, and not only in his death. With these moves the atoning act of God in Christ is seen to be personally intrinsic to God. In them a larger doctrine of God emerges, for God's saving economy must now be construed beyond forensic categories. The divine relation with humankind is set within covenantal and filial rather than legal relations. More so than his predecessors, Torrance makes robust connections with Old Testament precedents, not only with covenantal traditions, but also with his unique identification of the *padah, kipper* and *goel* traditions in the Old Testament. Although he demonstrated these words in their (inexact) correspondences in New Testament soteriology, they were very useful heuristic devices that helped to open out the discussion of the atonement.

Setting Torrance in the trajectory that includes McLeod Campbell and Mackintosh indicates, I hope helpfully, that Torrance is properly viewed as much more than the student of Karl Barth. I said many pages ago that I do not see the three theologians as a Scottish school of theology in a tight sense, but nevertheless we have observed family influences and correspondences, as well as differences. From all three, but especially here with regard to Torrance, I have tried to bring out the breadth of reflection on the atonement, but also its essential mystery.

Over and against some interpreters of Torrance who see him in an overly objectivistic way, I have tried to emphasize the place of our human response to the gospel. While our human nature is totally assumed in and by Jesus Christ, our personhood is not swallowed up into Christ, as it were. Torrance will have nothing of such mythical ontology. Or to put that differently, Torrance certainly puts the emphasis on the human agency of Christ (in the unity of his divine personhood) for our redemption, as also for our faith and worship and ministry, for all things are in Christ. And the doctrine of our union with Christ through the Holy Spirit is most strongly emphasized. But we are not thereby voided of human personhood. On the contrary, in the freedom of sins forgiven and communion with God restored, and most certainly with the mystery of the Holy Spirit within, among and upon us, Torrance insists that we have now a terrible personal freedom to reject who we are in Christ, even if, at the end of the day, that cannot be satisfactorily explained. We also have freedom in union with Christ for faith, worship and ministry. Thus at no point will he allow that we are cast back upon the efficacy of our own agency; we rely solely upon Christ's agency. I noted already that Torrance did not fully develop a theology of sanctification, and that omission leaves his account of atonement a bit less fully formed than it might be. But I see every reason to believe from what he has left us, that he would encourage movement in that direction and that a theology of human agency in Christ is properly anticipated.

CHRISTOLOGY AND
ATONEMENT

Faith and Ministry

JUST AS EXEGESIS IS FOR PROCLAMATION, Christology and atonement are in service of the practices of faith and the ministries of the church. The point of exegesis is to the end of the faithfulness of the sermon and the sound teaching of the faith. Likewise, the doctrines of the person and work of Jesus Christ are not complete without some exploration of the implications arising for the understanding and practices of faith, worship and ministry. This is not, however, the application chapter, following the previous theoretical chapters. For while we rightly speak of theories of Christology and theories of the atonement, that to which they refer, Jesus Christ himself, is not a theory. While we cannot encircle Jesus with our minds, with our theologies and arguments by which we try in some manner to understand him, nevertheless we are compelled to say something about Jesus, and to do so more rather than less faithfully as best we can. The one of whom we speak is in and as himself the active agent in all proclamation and worship, faith and ministry. Our task, then, is to indicate something of the shape and content of faith and ministry in view of the understanding of Jesus Christ in the light of the discussion thus far, *given that he is an active, living and reigning Lord.*

To repeat: what follows is not the application of various theories on Christology and the atonement. Every chapter thus far has already been a practical chapter. How is that the case? All along I have tried to say something concerning the *ministry* of God in, through and as the man Jesus under the instruction of John McLeod Campbell, Hugh Ross Mackintosh and Thomas F. Torrance. It is not for us now to make God practical! The attempts to write

Christology and soteriology are but our efforts at the obedience of faith (Rom 1:5; 16:26). Our theology bears witness to the God who acts. The aim now is to see, however dimly that may be, the life of Jesus in the faith, worship and ministries of the church as our study of Christology and the atonement brings that life into focus at these points of connection.

It feels somewhat like a truism to say, but if Christology and the atonement are not thought through in the manner briefly suggested, what is the point? A theory concerning Jesus has no redemptive impact. It is Jesus who saves. And insofar as he has grasp upon our minds, we may say with the apostle Peter, relying upon the apostolic testimony and the present agency of the Holy Spirit, "We did not follow cleverly devised myths when we made known to you the power and coming of our Lord Jesus Christ, but we had been eyewitnesses of his divine majesty" (2 Pet 1:16).

In the first part of this chapter I present from the work of our three companions what they see of the living Jesus in the faith, worship and ministry of the church when they look through the lens of the Christology and soteriology that they have constructed. In the second part I offer some brief closing reflections on Christology, atonement and pastoral care.

THE RELATION OF CHRISTOLOGY AND SOTERIOLOGY TO FAITH AND MINISTRY IN MCLEOD CAMPBELL, MACKINTOSH AND TORRANCE

John McLeod Campbell. In 1851 the third church building of the Row parish in Dumbartonshire was built not far from the site of the building where John McLeod Campbell had preached his "heresy" sermons. One of two striking stained-glass windows in the building is the McLeod Campbell Memorial Window in the nave beside the baptismal font. Dedicated to the glory of God and in loving memory of John McLeod Campbell, minister of the parish, it carries an inscription from Psalm 126:6: "He that goeth forth and weepeth bearing precious seed, shall doubtless come again with rejoicing bringing his sheaves with him." Beneath the symbol of the burning bush, representing the Church of Scotland, the top two panels show the sower spreading his seed and the fruit of the harvest. The two lower panels depict Jesus carrying a representation of his cross and the procession of the saints up the steps of light.

McLeod Campbell sought to sow the seed of the gospel of Jesus Christ by way of helping people to see themselves in the light of God's love for them.

Speaking of his ministry in Row, he recalled, "I used to say, 'If you knew the mind of God towards you as the Gospel reveals it,—if you only knew about yourselves what in the light of the Gospel I know about you—knew as really your own the unsearchable riches which you have in Christ,—you must needs rejoice in God through our Lord Jesus Christ. I only ask you to know what now is.'"[1] The end to which his preaching and teaching were directed was that his people might know of this desire of the divine love toward them and rest in the peace that is its fruit. His message was of God as our heavenly Father, and of us as his offspring. The theme of his ministry was "Give me thine heart" (Prov 23:26), by which he meant that God's will was that we should rest in the security of "sonship," by trusting in the atonement wrought out in Jesus Christ. All pastoral work was to that end for his people, that they could give their hearts to God with utter assurance that God's will for them was "welcome home."

In a sermon preached in the parish of Row between 1829 and 1831, and entitled by the compiler "The Teaching of God in the Cross of Christ," McLeod Campbell anticipates the larger argument of *The Nature of the Atonement*. The heart of the sermon is his answer to this question: Why did God rejoice over Christ's sacrifice for sin? Condemning an approach focused on the pain of Christ as a punishment for sin vicariously borne, the sermon argues that in the cross God's love toward sinners and God's hatred of sin was expressed, and thus God was manifest. The cross shows the Father's love, the Father's yearning for us, the Father's holiness, and the Father's grief over our separation from God. "In that sacrifice God's eternal law of love was magnified and made honourable, because sin was thus condemned in our flesh; because in it God's love to sinners, God's hatred of sin was expressed; because the Eternal Word declared the Eternal Father, in that he became flesh and gave Himself to death for the life of the world. . . . On this foundation all rests."[2] This conclusion is no sermonic flourish; it is the truth of the gospel as McLeod Campbell saw it.

The response called for is repentance for love shown and forgiveness

---

[1]John McLeod Campbell, *Reminiscences and Reflections: Referring to His Early Parish Ministry in the Parish of Row, 1825-31* (London: Macmillan, 1873), p. 176.

[2]John McLeod Campbell, *Responsibility for the Gift of Eternal Life: Compiled by Permission of the Late Rev. John McLeod Campbell, D.D., from Sermons Preached Chiefly at Row, in the Years 1829-31* (London: Macmillan, 1873), p. 103.

given. "I am shut up into this one thing, to look unto Jesus and be healed; to look and be saved; to see my sins, and to see them forgiven: to know that the longing I feel to be like my God is no vain longing, but a thing within my reach; because though I cannot, yet Christ in me can glorify the Father."[3] This is, simply stated, the pastoral theology of Galatians 2:20: I, yet not I, but Christ. Or again, and note the appeal to personal faith: "I beseech you to know that you have to do, not primarily with laws and doctrines, but with the living God: that you have to do not with rules or precepts or opinions, but with a real Person, a living God, One who does at this moment as truly see you and as truly think of you individually, as if you saw Him in this room. *He is here.* He is saying, O that my people would trust me! O that my people would meet my love!"[4] The cross of Christ unveils the Father's heart in its reaching out to humankind seeking the answering love of his people. McLeod Campbell asks rhetorically how then we can dare to question God's love toward us. Lean not upon your self-assessment, or the knowledge of your sin, but upon the Lord your God.

For John McLeod Campbell, there must be no separation between Christology, soteriology and pastoral ministry. "Now in order to understand how Christ condemned sin in the flesh, remember that Christ is God. Let not this for a moment be out of your mind."[5] That admonition applies no less to the pastor than the parishioner, and it must be the directing force of all ministry. The heart of pastoral work lies not in the motivations, affection and acts of a pastor, but rather in who God is for us in Jesus Christ and what God thereby wills that we should be in Christ. This redirection away from the pastor to the person and work of Christ is entirely in keeping with the magisterial pastor-theologians of the Reformation: Luther, Calvin and Bucer. There is surely now no room for doubt that the dogmatics of the soteriology of McLeod Campbell is rightly understood as pastoral dogmatics. And even were we to part company with him on his understanding of Christ's atonement at some points, the point remains that pastoral ministry, whether as preaching, pastoral care or Christian instruction, has Christology and the atonement as its primary

---

[3]Ibid., p. 105.
[4]Ibid., p. 107.
[5]Ibid., p. 97.

content and purpose wherein the faith which is the life of "sonship" is quickened among the people.[6]

Hugh Ross Mackintosh. One abiding characteristic of the theology of Hugh Ross Mackintosh is his insistence that theology has experiential and ethical aspects that are integral to faithfulness to the gospel. A quirky illustration of this is found in a newspaper report from the *Glasgow Herald* of May 25, 1938, where there is an account of a dinner of the New College Union at which tribute was paid to Mackintosh following his death. Principal Martin said that when Mackintosh joined the teaching staff, he changed the somewhat scholastic and arid heritage of the systematic theology department. "He made it for long the centre of intellectual, almost religious, interest." Indeed, theology without religion is scholastic and arid and is unfaithful to its purpose. Thus Mackintosh could say, "When men are converted, it is not because they have been overwhelmed by irrefutable argument, but because they have been subjected to an irresistible impression; and in the great majority of instances the impression has been made specifically on the conscience."[7] Good doctrine touches equally the hearts and minds of people; this is the case because God has come personally to us and in Jesus Christ brought us into communion with himself. If divine omnipotence must be spoken of, it is of holy love and the omnipotence of grace that we must speak.[8] Or again: "What dawns gradually on us as we read the Gospels is that God is such a Father as evokes from Jesus a constant, reverential loving trust; He is *a Father worthy even of the perfect trust of Jesus. . . .* The Fatherhood of God is reflected in, and corresponds to, the Sonship of Jesus."[9] It is not now a big step, given this understanding of theology, to see that Mackintosh was trying to write theology that would preach. It is theology for ministry. And maybe even more so, his is a theology of Christian experience

Robert Redman has helpfully gathered some information regarding Mackintosh as preacher, minister and church leader.[10] Suffice it to note here

---

[6]McLeod Campbell, *Reminiscences and Reflections*, p. 110.

[7]H. R. Mackintosh, *The Christian Apprehension of God* (1929; repr., Eugene, OR: Wipf & Stock, 2008), p. 56.

[8]Ibid., p. 208.

[9]Ibid., p. 111.

[10]Robert R. Redman Jr., *Reformulating Reformed Theology: Jesus Christ in the Theology of Hugh Ross Mackintosh* (Lanham, MD: University Press of America, 1997), pp. 12-16.

that he was minister in two congregations prior to his appointment to the chair of systematic theology at New College in 1904. Of interest especially is the second ministerial call, to the Beechgrove parish in Aberdeen, where later T. F. Torrance would serve prior to his New College academic appointment in 1951. Mackintosh preached regularly during the years of his academic service, with volumes of his sermons periodically published. And he regularly gave courses on homiletics to divinity students. Redman cites a source noting that Mackintosh's preaching revolved around the biblical themes of sin and alienation from God, the cost of divine forgiveness in Jesus Christ, and the personal experience of that forgiveness.[11] In 1932 the Church of Scotland chose Mackintosh to be moderator of the General Assembly, during which year he traveled widely in Europe. It is also notable that Mackintosh was deeply involved in support of missionary work and especially held a keen interest in lay missions in the Highlands.

The relation between theology and the Christian's life of faith was beautifully captured by Mackintosh in a chapter entitled "The Christ of Experience," from his book *The Person of Jesus Christ*, first published in 1912.[12] Torrance called these chapters the inner evangelical heart of Mackintosh's great work, *The Doctrine of the Person of Jesus Christ*.[13] Setting out from the notion that redemption by Jesus Christ is an inexpugnable reality before it is ever analyzed, the experience that Jesus redeems, Mackintosh discusses three well-marked lines of response to Christ and of benefits received from him. First, the felt presence of Jesus Christ means that we are encountered by a living Lord. The felt sense of fellowship with him, in living and dying, is not metaphorical. It is the simple reporting of real elements in personal experience. "The Christ with whom believing men hold communion is not merely the Jesus who walked in Palestine; he is the exalted Lord, present with his people in the sovereign power of his resurrection and as inhabiting a higher order than that of time or space."[14]

Mackintosh scorns attempts that keep Jesus, prisoner-like, firmly in the first century.

---

[11]Ibid., pp. 12-13.

[12]H. R. Mackintosh, *The Person of Jesus Christ*, ed. T. F. Torrance (1912; repr., Edinburgh: T & T Clark, 2000).

[13]T. F. Torrance, foreword to Mackintosh, *Person of Jesus Christ*, p. vii.

[14]Mackintosh, *Person of Jesus Christ*, p. 31.

So long as we bring into play our intellect merely, or the reconstructive fancy of the historian, [Christ] is still far off; we need not even hold him at arm's length; he is not close to us at all. The change comes when we take up the moral issue. If we turn to him as men keen to gain the righteous, overcoming life, but conscious so far of failure, instantly he steps forward out of the page of history, a tremendous and exacting reality.[15]

The watershed is crossed between a merely past and a present Christ when we ask ourselves not only what we think of him, but also, more audaciously, what he thinks of us. The ground for the conviction of faith is not only one's experience of a present Christ, but also a trust in his promise, "Lo, I am with you always, even unto the end" (Mt 28:20 KJV). Christ promised his enduring presence and power to those who put their trust in him.

Mackintosh will not for now address the difficult problems regarding the meaning of the sense of the nearness of the Lord. He insists that he is merely registering the experience of Christian people. Of course we must ask, "Who is he?" "Whence has he come?" "How is it that death did not silence him?" Our minds seek answers. And in the pages of this book some attention has been given to questions like these. For now, Mackintosh would have us return and attend to a childlike intuition of a living Lord present with us and be satisfied to rest in that assurance.

Second, Mackintosh turns to the conquest of sin attained through Christ. Once again his eye is cast in the direction of Christian experience. This is not the place for yet another discussion on a theory of the atonement. Rather, he bids us reflect on our experience of knowing that the back of sin is broken and thus we gain an assurance of God's love that enables our Christian faith and the life that follows. We receive this impression of forgiveness in the presence of Jesus Christ and most especially in the presence of his cross.[16] There we encounter the mind of God toward both sinners and sin. Before the cross we discover sin to be beaten and powerless; it is paralyzed, vanquished, dethroned, stripped of every covering, and cast out in utter degradation.[17] With this discovery comes the awareness of the love of God in the cross, the love that has stooped down to suffer on our behalf.

---

[15]Ibid., pp. 33-34.
[16]Ibid., p. 38.
[17]Ibid., p. 39.

But more: we discover that the character of sin as tyranny over us is overcome. We are not only forgiven; we also have power to change and thus both to be saved into freedom to stop sinning, and saved into the pursuit of goodness.[18]

> For those who cast themselves on [Christ], in faith's great venture, accepting honourably the conditions under which alone spiritual truth can be verified, the truth becomes luminous and certain. They discover that to be Christians is not to repeat a creed, or to narrow life into a groove; but to have a strong, patient, divine Leader, whom they can trust perfectly and love supremely, who is always drawing out in them their true nature and making them resolve to be true to it through the future; who looks into their eyes when they betray him, making them ashamed, who imparts the forgiveness of sins and gives power to live in fellowship with God. Apart from this, his call would only mean a new despair. But his strength is made perfect in weakness.[19]

Third, Mackintosh affirms that in Christ we have a perfect revelation of God the Father. Here is a great theme found also in McLeod Campbell and Torrance: through Christ, knowing him as Savior, we see into the Father's heart, from which he came. Of course, there is some knowledge of God available elsewhere than in Christ. But "it *was* reserved for him to manifest God in the character of loving and holy Fatherhood, *a Fatherhood which embraces all the world.*"[20] Mackintosh inserts what may be his favorite verse from the New Testament, Matthew 11:27, adding also John 14:6: "Neither doth any know *the Father*, save the Son"; "No man cometh unto *the Father but by Me.*" For Mackintosh, these august words are confirmed by the facts of life, by men and women who know that God is like Jesus—holy, loving and full of saving, transforming power. As such, the person of Jesus shows us the personal God, for the Father is known only in the Son.[21] "He that hath seen me hath seen the Father" (Jn 14:9 KJV).

Mackintosh asks: who can reveal God other than he who is what he reveals? Apart from oneness in identity or unity between revealer and revealed, must there not be a discrepancy in the revelation, a refraction of truth? The core message of the gospel is that Jesus is one in identity with (consub-

---

[18]Ibid., p. 41.
[19]Ibid., pp. 42-43.
[20]Ibid., p. 44.
[21]Ibid., p. 46.

stantial, of the same being: our words can but bear witness to an essential mystery; this is no attempt at explanation) the Lord God Almighty. Christ saves; but only God can save.[22] For Mackintosh, the divinity of Christ is a transcript of experience—not only, of course, but none the less the case.

> To believe in Christ, always, is to believe in God. To do Christ's will is to do God's will. And secretly, in the hour of meditation, when we try to look into God's face, still it is the face of Christ that comes up before us. . . . Is he the passing creature of time, or has he not rather come forth out of the uncreated life of the Eternal? Eternity or time—do we have to choose between them? What if Christ belongs to both at once! What if he is as old as the saving love of God, yet emerging into history at a definite spot in the long past![23]

With Mackintosh, the line—if there is one—between theology and piety is comfortably and necessarily porous. The reason is that he writes only of the living God, who encounters us as the man Jesus. Arguments abound when he reflects on this, and his erudition with respect to theological and philosophical discourse is notable at every turn. But his ultimate criterion of truth is his inner conviction of faith, of Jesus Christ his Savior, who has met him and whom he knows person to person. Here is theology that lends itself to preaching for conversion and conviction. Here is theology that informs pastoral care to minister in terms of God who draws near in saving love to heal, bless and comfort. Mackintosh has left us a pastor's theology in a double sense: he writes as one who had a pastor's heart; and he writes a theology for pastors. In this way, his reflections on Christology and atonement are rightly given for us as pastoral theology not only for his day but also for our day as well.

Thomas F. Torrance. Torrance's published corpus is vast and mostly technical. No doubt many reviewers of his work would be unlikely to see him as a pastoral or practical theologian. But that would be to do him a grave injustice. Torrance was always a theologian of and for the church. The ministry of the word and sacraments was held by him in the very highest regard, but that not to the diminishment of lay ministry.[24] The vast majority of his

---

[22]Ibid., p. 47.

[23]Ibid., p. 48.

[24]See the reference to John Welch, a member of Torrance's parish in Alyth, in Thomas F. Torrance, *Gospel, Church and Ministry*, ed. Jock Stein, Thomas F. Torrance Collected Studies 1 (Eugene, OR: Pickwick, 2012), p. 51.

students were preparing for ministry, pastoral or academic. Central to the whole scheme of his work, and embedded within his theology at every turn, is the understanding of the ministry of the saving love of God in Jesus Christ. It is fashionable today to use the words *missio Dei* to speak of this; but Torrance was long persuaded that the starting point in theology is with the covenanting God who encounters us, and in particular with the actual God of the Bible who lays hold of our lives in the person of the man Jesus Christ. Torrance, following Calvin, sought to know God in the way God actually made himself known in revelation and reconciliation. As such, theology is knowledge of the God who acts, and in particular who acts in person in, through and as the man Jesus.

If the definition of "practical theology" is something like "a theology concerned with action," then the theology of T. F. Torrance is most assuredly, as theology of the God who acts, practical theology. The locus of practice is, of course, God. The practices of the church and ministry are derivative, best understood as our participation in God's ministry through union with Christ by the gift of the Holy Spirit.[25] We are practical in a godly way insofar as we share in God's practice, and only God's practice is redemptive. Says Torrance, "The order of the Church's ministry is the ordering of its life and work through participation in the obedience of Christ."[26] Thus the ministry of the church is inherently a theological event with Christology and atonement at the heart of it all, and even in its myriad expressions ministry is not an imitation of Christ, but rather a fulfilling of God's will through our participation in Christ's obedience through the power of the Holy Spirit. All of this is summed up according to the pattern given in the Lord's Supper: "For I received from the Lord what I also handed on to you" (1 Cor 11:23). The ministry is not ours but Christ's, and only as Christ's is it redemptive.

Clearly for Torrance, therefore, "the Church can never justify itself, therefore, by claiming historical succession or doctrinal faithfulness, by reference to its own place and time on earth and in history, but must cast itself upon the justification of Christ's grace alone, and rely upon His covenant-mercies who

---

[25]For a systematic account of this, see Andrew Purves, *Reconstructing Pastoral Theology: A Christological Foundation* (Louisville: Westminster John Knox, 2004).

[26]T. F. Torrance, *Conflict and Agreement in the Church*, vol. 2, *The Ministry and the Sacraments of the Gospel* (London: Lutterworth, 1960), p. 13.

promised that the gates of hell would not prevail against His Church, and that He would be in its midst until the end of the world."[27] Justification by grace alone refers back to the eternal purpose of God in Christ (*prosthesis*), to the setting forth of this purpose in the incarnation and atonement, and this continues to be set forth in the midst of the church in its *koinōnia*, which is participation in the relation of the Father and the Son through the Spirit.[28]

A long quotation from *The Mediation of Christ* provides an illustration of Torrance's understanding of faith and ministry in view of Christology and atonement.

> How, then, is the Gospel to be preached in a genuinely evangelical way? Surely in such a way that full and central place is given to the *vicarious humanity of Jesus* as the all-sufficient human response to the saving love of God. . . . We preach and teach the Gospel evangelically, then, in such a way as this: God loves you so utterly and completely that he has given himself for you in Jesus Christ his beloved Son, and has thereby pledged his very Being as God for your salvation. In Jesus Christ God has actualised his unconditional love for you in your human nature in such a once for all way, that he cannot go back upon it without undoing the Incarnation and the Cross and thereby denying himself. Jesus Christ died for you precisely because you are sinful and utterly unworthy of him, and has thereby already made you his own before and apart from you ever believing in him. He has bound you to himself by his love in a way that he will never let you go, for even if you refuse him and damn yourself in hell his love will never cease. Therefore, repent and believe in Jesus Christ as your Lord and Saviour. . . . He has acted in your place in the whole range of your human life and activity. . . . He acknowledges you before God as one who has already responded to God in him, who has already believed in God through him, and whose personal decision is already implicated in Christ's self-offering to the Father, in all of which he has been fully and completely accepted by the Father, so that in Jesus Christ you are already accepted by him. Therefore, renounce yourself, take up your cross and follow Jesus as your Lord and Saviour. . . . For in faith it is not upon my faith, my believing or my personal commitment that I rely, but solely upon what Jesus Christ has done for me, in my place and on my behalf.[29]

---

[27]Ibid., p. 29.

[28]Ibid., pp. 88-90.

[29]Thomas F. Torrance, *The Mediation of Christ* (Grand Rapids: Eerdmans, 1983), pp. 103-4. I am grateful to my student Matthew Williams for pointing out this passage to me.

This is a remarkable statement of the indicative of God's grace controlling and giving content to the imperative of the human response, of the full weight of the vicarious humanity of Christ in which he stands in for us at every point, and of the fundamentally practical (for the want of a better word) implication of the Father-Son relationship for salvation, faith and ministry. It is no less than a summary of justification by grace.

A recent and posthumous publication of essays includes a previously unpublished memoir of Torrance's parish ministry in Alyth, between 1940 and 1947, a ministry interrupted by war service. The account is given there of an event of which he spoke often concerning ministry in terms of justification by grace. Torrance was asked to preach a sermon series on Romans. At the end of the third sermon in the series, as he came out of the vestry following the close of the service, he found a number of people gathered around the person of Jim Ferguson, a fine, godly elder, but who was clearly agitated. Upon inquiry, Torrance learned that the parishioner was upset over the sermon, which had been devoted to the significance of justification by grace alone, and the implications for faith and life. The issue was the argument that no amount of faithfulness and service counted in any way toward salvation. The parishioner felt that the truth of justification by grace alone cut too deeply into his soul; the fact that godliness as a loyal member of the church counted for naught toward salvation was too costly to bear. The parishioner became ill, deteriorated, and died—although there was no medical reason. Torrance notes, "That incident taught me as never before what Luther used to say, that people could react to justification like a cow staring at a new gate—something I recalled in my farming parish. Luther also used to say about justification by grace alone that it roused bitter opposition and causes tumult."[30]

Thus Torrance could write,

> Again and again when I was lecturing about some aspect of the gospel or evangelical truth in Edinburgh, I recalled pastoral visits in Alyth where its deep significance had become clear to me, and I realized its spiritual power. As I could not separate my preaching in Alyth from my house to house visitation of the congregation, so I was never able to separate lecturing in my

---

[30]Torrance, *Gospel, Church and Ministry*, p. 41.

Christian Dogmatics class in New College from showing something of the personal and pastoral thrust and power of the truths of the gospel."[31]

Or again: "It was that combination of theological study with what I learned from people's hearts face to face with Christ in their homes that taught me a great deal which I was to recall and use when the time came for me to teach Christian Dogmatics in Edinburgh."[32] Jock Stein, who edited the volume from which these citations are taken, very rightly notes that Torrance regarded systematic theology as inherently practical.[33] For Torrance, the kind of boundaries that conventionally exist in academic theology between systematic and practical theology did not exist. For the gospel tells us we are dealing with the living God, who lays hold upon us in personal and intimate ways and calls us to participate in God's continuing ministry from the Father, through the Son, in the power of the Spirit, for the sake of the world, to the glory of God.

According to Torrance, "The Church is, in fact, the Community of the Voice of God."[34] The message is that God, as such, in, through and as Jesus Christ, has shared the life of God with us, telling us that God is unreservedly on our side in order that God might reconcile us to himself, and bringing us into union with himself. As the voice of Christ is loosed upon the world through the ministry of the church, through the vertical Word from above and through the horizontal ministry of others, Christ meets us personally and directly and redemptively. The truth with which we are encountered is a person, and as we hear his Word spoken to us we hear and recognize the voice of God.

CHRISTOLOGY AND ATONEMENT: CONCLUDING THOUGHTS

Some one hundred thousand words ago, this study began with this thesis: this book offers an account of the relations between Jesus Christ, who is the incarnate Son, and the Father, the result of which is the atonement, for in the incarnate Son the relation between God and humankind is savingly es-

---

[31]Ibid., p. 35.
[32]Ibid., pp. 41-42.
[33]Jock Stein, introduction to Torrance, *Gospel, Church and Ministry*, p. 14.
[34]Thomas F. Torrance, *When Christ Comes and Comes Again* (1957; repr., Eugene, OR: Wipf & Stock, 1996), p. 27.

tablished. As I have engaged the teaching of John McLeod Campbell, Hugh Ross Mackintosh and Thomas F. Torrance on Christology and atonement, and with that thesis statement as my lodestar, I have known all along where I would end up. Theology is to the end of the deeper faithfulness of the church in faith, worship and ministry. Whatever else theology must do, it must bring us back again and again to what the gospel has at its center: the person and work of Jesus Christ. As we face up squarely to Jesus Christ, to who he is and what he does, we are compelled to attend to his claims upon our minds, our hearts and our lives. It is clear to me that I cannot do the work of Christology and atonement without having to struggle with what I must know, whom I must love, and how I must live. To do theology is to expect the conversion of the theologian!

In 2004 I published *Reconstructing Pastoral Theology: A Christological Foundation*. There I was concerned to identify what it is that makes pastoral work Christian. I see this present work as complementary insofar as I have engaged more directly some of the principal sources. Writing on pastoral theology, I was forced to do Christology. Writing on Christology and atonement as I have been instructed by McLeod Campbell, Mackintosh and Torrance, I am struck most forcibly by the demand of the gospel that it is to be preached, taught and ministered unto those for whom Jesus lived, died, rose and ascended to the Father. Christology and atonement as they were preached, taught and ministered by the Scottish theologians with whom I have engaged are not primarily locus points on the academic theological curriculum, although that has its place. Their concern above all else, indeed their passion, was for the purpose of God in Jesus Christ to be known, and known in such a way that lives were transformed, relationships healed, sins forgiven, hope established, worship rightly centered, vocation faithfully accepted and God truly loved. *Ho logos sarx egeneto*—the Word became flesh—changed everything. McLeod Campbell, the theologian of the love of God, Mackintosh, the theologian of the experience of forgiveness in Jesus Christ, Torrance, the theologian of the grace of God in Jesus Christ—all searched for the same end by their various routes. They longed for people to know, and know in their inner beings, that "for freedom Christ has set us free" (Gal 5:1).

Christology and atonement compel us to do the work of evangelism, proclamation, instruction and the comfort of pastoral care. To know Christ and to know his benefits commits us to the ministry of reconciliation (2 Cor 5:11-21). And in union with Christ, the Pentecostal gift, we are given to share in the communion of love that is the essential mystery of God himself—one being, three persons.

AUTHOR INDEX

Finding the Textbook You Need

The IVP Academic Textbook Selector
is an online tool for instantly finding the IVP books
suitable for over 250 courses across 24 disciplines.

ivpacademic.com